DALLAS
WORLD-CLASS TEXAS

URBAN
TAPESTRY
SERIES

TOWERY
PUBLISHING, INC.

▲ DONOVAN REESE

By Annette Strauss and Carolyn Brown

Profiles in Excellence by Buzz McClain

Captions by Jim Donovan

Art Direction by Jil Foutch

LIBRARY OF CONGRESS CATALOGING-IN-PUBLICATION DATA

Strauss, Annette, date.
    Dallas : world-class Texas / Annette Strauss and Carolyn Brown ; profiles in excellence by Buzz McClain ; captions by Jim Donovan ; art direction by Jil Foutch.
        p.   cm. — (Urban tapestry series)
    Includes index.
    ISBN 1-881096-44-0 (alk. paper)
    1. Dallas (Tex.)—Civilization.   2. Dallas (Tex.)—Pictorial works.   3. Dallas (Tex.)—Economic conditions.   4. Business enterprises—Texas—Dallas.   I. Brown, Carolyn, date   .
II. McClain, Buzz, date   .   III. Series.
F394.D215S77 1997
976.4'2811—dc21   97-19944
                                                                            CIP

TOWERY PUBLISHING, INC., 1835 UNION AVENUE, MEMPHIS, TN 38104

PUBLISHER: J. Robert Towery
EXECUTIVE PUBLISHER: Jenny McDowell
NATIONAL SALES MANAGER: Stephen Hung
REGIONAL SALES MANAGER: Michelle Sylvestro
MARKETING DIRECTOR: Carol Culpepper
PROJECT DIRECTORS: Marc Black, Chad Kauffman, Tana Luedecke, Robert Philips, Brett Sechrest

EXECUTIVE EDITOR: David B. Dawson
MANAGING EDITOR: Michael C. James
SENIOR EDITORS: Lynn Conlee, Carlisle Hacker
EDITOR/PROFILES MANAGER: Mary Jane Adams
EDITORS: Lori Bond, Jana Files
ASSISTANT EDITOR: Jennifer C. Pyron

CREATIVE DIRECTOR: Brian Groppe
PROFILE DESIGNERS: Jennifer Baugher, Laurie Lewis, Ann Ward
TECHNICAL DIRECTOR: William H. Towery
DIGITAL COLOR SUPERVISOR: Brenda Pattat
PRODUCTION ASSISTANTS: Jeff McDonald, Robin McGehee
PRINT COORDINATOR: Beverly Thompson

CONTENTS

THANKS TO A HOST OF MEDIA ICONS, PEOPLE AROUND the world think they know Dallas. The blue stars on the silver helmets of the Dallas Cowboys are a well-known symbol, as are the fringed vests and white boots of the Cowboys cheerleaders. And, assuming almost mythical proportions, there is yet another media symbol that consumed the nation in the 1980s: J.R. Ewing, the lovable villain in *Dallas*, the prime-time soap opera about big oil, big money, and big passions.

Such symbols serve a purpose, to be sure. The Cowboys are "America's Team," and J.R. is the kind of character only American television could produce. But they are by no means the sum of what Dallas is all about. Not by a long shot.

During my years as mayor of the city, I was well aware of such images. I was proud to play off of them, to show people that Dallas is one of the world's best places to live and to make a living. Dallas is a great city: a city where commerce, education, medicine, recreation, and the arts flourish. It is a place that was built on the dreams and aspirations and ingenuity of its citizens. It is constantly evolving, improving, building on its successes, and learning from its failures.

Yes, we love the Cowboys. And thanks to the wide syndication of *Dallas*, we still love to hiss at J.R. But we also love to tell the world what a fine place our city really is, and how proud we are to live here.

BY ANNETTE STRAUSS

O UNDERSTAND JUST HOW GREAT DALLAS IS—AND WHAT AN INTER-
national center of commerce and culture it has become—you need
to go all the way back to the vision of a buckskinned Tennessee
lawyer, farmer, and trader named John Neely Bryan, the city's
founder. In 1839, when Bryan first came to the spot that would be
Dallas, he saw nothing more than the location where an east-west
Caddo Indian trail crossed the Trinity River. Vowing to return, he came
back two years later to find a tiny settlement of Frenchmen who were planning to carve a
north-south road through the area to handle the hordes of settlers streaming into what
was, at the time, the Republic of Texas. Recognizing the potential of the area, Bryan established a trading post and began operating a ferry. And from that point on, the modest
establishment grew from a regional (and literal) crossroads into an international one, handling transportation, trade, tourism, and technology. Fittingly, a replica of Bryan's cabin
stands at its center.

Just after Bryan set up shop, Charity Morris Gilbert entered the picture via a raft on the
Trinity River, becoming probably the only Dallasite to ever "sail" into town. Legend says
that Gilbert won a contest (sponsored by Bryan), choosing to name the city after Commo-
dore Alexander James Dallas, commander of the U.S. Navy's Gulf of Mexico squadron.

Along with rearing their families, Gilbert and the other remarkable women of early
Dallas brought education, culture, and a social conscience into the little town. It is said
that the men built the city, while the women furnished it with heart and art. This outstanding combination still works today, and the role of the Dallas woman—always important
and respected—has become even more prominent as the city has grown.

Over the years, a succession of events served to solidify Dallas' place as an international
player. It started in the 1870s, when the railroads came to town and the city of 7,000 residents was transformed into a bustling transportation hub and regional trading center. The
cotton that had found a fertile home in the rich soil of East Texas also helped fuel the
city's rapid expansion. Soon after the Dallas Cotton Exchange was established, the city
became the world's trading center for the "white rose of commerce." Bankers, hotel owners, retailers, and other entrepreneurs came in droves to set up shop in the downtown business district. When that first railroad whistle blew, it was like a signal to the world: Dallas
was destined to become something great.

As if to affirm the city's status as a major commercial center and the
most prosperous of all Texas cities, the *Dallas Morning News* printed
its first edition in 1885. In the years to come, the paper would survive
publishing rivals and would evolve into Texas' unofficial statewide
newspaper. Today, with a daily circulation of more than 500,000, the
News is one of the most widely read papers in the nation.

By the turn of the century, White Rock Lake, Dallas' first reservoir,
brought a new level of stability to the city of 42,000, and the young metropolis was bolstered even further in 1914, when it was chosen as a site
for a Federal Reserve Bank. Then, in 1917, the U.S. Army Air Service
established Love Field as a pilot training center. Purchased by city leaders 10 years later, the airport has helped establish Dallas as a kind of
inland port, where all manner of cargo and goods are traded. Providing
a close-in landing spot for Southwest Airlines and private corporate jets,
the centrally located airport today serves more than 7 million passengers annually.

I N A TWO-BLOCK AREA DOWN-
TOWN, VISITORS TO DALLAS CAN
RECEIVE A VERITABLE HISTORY LESSON.
A REPLICA OF JOHN NEELY BRYAN'S
CABIN STANDS IN CONTRAST TO THE
FORMER DALLAS COUNTY COURT-
HOUSE, BUILT IN THE EARLY 1890S
(BELOW). ORIGINALLY CONSTRUCTED
WITH A FOUR-FACED CLOCK TOWER
AND A THREE-TON BELL, WHICH WERE
LATER REMOVED FOR SAFETY REASONS,
THE RED SANDSTONE, ROMANESQUE
STRUCTURE IS LISTED ON THE NATION-
AL REGISTER OF HISTORIC PLACES.
NEARBY, THE 30-FOOT-HIGH, PHILIP
JOHNSON-DESIGNED JOHN F. KENNEDY
MEMORIAL, A GIFT FROM THE CITI-
ZENS OF DALLAS, COMMEMORATES
THE POPULAR PRESIDENT WHO WAS
ASSASSINATED HERE (OPPOSITE).

▼ CAROLYN BROWN

And, as if all that weren't enough to ensure Dallas' position as a leading city, along came oil. All over East Texas, wells were dug, fortunes were made, and booming metropolises were created. Even during the 1930s, Dallas' proximity to the East Texas oil fields insulated it against the Great Depression. Throughout the 20th century, the oil industry has helped Dallas maintain its position as an international commercial center.

The city's reputation was further secured and spread by the Texas Centennial Exposition of 1936, which, along with the construction of a $1 million auditorium downtown and the development of Elm Street's theater row, helped Dallas become a center for conventions and tourism, not to mention an entertainment and cultural mecca. The Majestic, which opened in 1921, was the queen of theater row and, after major renovations, still proudly stands as a beautiful venue for outstanding artistic performances.

By the time its own centennial rolled around in 1941, Dallas had become a regional medical center and a major wholesale market. The economy of this city of 350,000 prospered from World War II, as Dallas became the manufacturing capital of the Southwest. The postwar years brought Texas Instruments, and with it the beginning of high technology. When joined by other high-tech firms in the years to come, Dallas would gain the nickname Silicon Prairie.

Over the next few decades, the city's business sector was strengthened even more by the addition of successful enterprises, and in the 1980s, as an already strong international city, Dallas continued its march toward cosmopolitanism. An energetic Office of International Affairs, 27 foreign consulates, and a number of strategic sister-city relationships have helped attract visits from Great Britain's Queen Elizabeth, President Muhammad Hosni Mubarak of Egypt, and other heads of state. Another initiative that is helping the city reach its international aspirations is the annual Dallas Ambassadors Forum and International Ball, spearheaded by the mayor and the Greater Dallas Chamber of Commerce. Honoring members of the International Diplomatic Corps and focusing attention on the abundance of business opportunities in Big D, this is one of the city's most successful events.

Other examples abound: The Health Industry Council promotes Dallas' wealth of medical and biotechnology services; the sports commission was largely responsible for bringing the 1994 World Cup Soccer Games and International Broadcast Center to the city; the cultural commission has helped acquire world-renowned art exhibits; and in 1996, Dallas became the first U.S. city to host a major event that celebrates Japanese culture—the widely heralded Sun & Star festival.

There's no doubt that the city benefits from these worldwide connections. The Dallas-Fort Worth Metroplex, a highly successful regional partnership between the two cities and their suburbs, is the Southwest's focal point for international trade; it ranks third nationally in the number of Fortune 500 companies, and ninth in the world as a headquarters site for the largest multinational corporations. Dallas is indeed a "player," and, in most cases, it's setting the rules for the game.

ALTHOUGH SWIMMING IS NO LONGER PERMITTED IN WHITE ROCK LAKE, THESE BATHERS TOOK THE OPPORTUNITY TO COOL OFF FROM THE HOT TEXAS SUN AT THE SPILLWAY IN 1952 (ABOVE). BUILT A FEW MILES EAST OF DOWNTOWN AT THE TURN OF THE CENTURY, THE LAKE WAS DALLAS' FIRST RESERVOIR.

The Spirit of the Centennial (OPPOSITE), WHICH GREETS VISITORS TO FAIR PARK, IS JUST ONE REMNANT OF THE TEXAS CENTENNIAL EXPOSITION OF 1936, A STATEWIDE CELEBRATION THAT GAVE DALLAS ONE OF THE FINEST COLLECTIONS OF PUBLIC ART DECO STRUCTURES AND DECORATIONS IN THE WORLD.

SHOWING ITS TRUE SPIRIT OF TEXAS-TOUGH DETERMINATION, DALLAS has prevailed and endured despite some terrible blows to its stability. The city was on an upswing in 1960, when the National Football League granted it an expansion franchise and the Dallas Cowboys team was born. Not only did the cheerleaders become a sensation, but the team actually played great football and became synonymous around the world with this most American of sports, even earning the nickname America's Team. More devout fans call the 'Boys "God's Team." Well, why else do you think there's a hole in the roof of Texas Stadium?

Just as it seemed that the city's fortunes were on an inexorable upward trajectory, however, one of the country's greatest tragedies occurred, bringing Dallas the kind of attention that no city wants. On November 22, 1963, President John F. Kennedy was assassinated here. Determined not to let this fateful incident permanently scar the city, local leaders united behind Goals for Dallas, a long-range plan that would pull people together and rebuild the city's spirit. Fulfillment of the group's goals led to great achievements, such as the central library system, the Dallas community college system, and what would come to be the region's greatest economic engine, Dallas/Fort Worth International Airport (DFW).

Slowly, in the decades after the assassination, Dallas gained national repute as an "Emerald City," a place where you could realize the American dream. As recession hit northern communities, new business and industry flocked to Dallas, and within a short period of six years, 15 new buildings changed the face of the city's skyline. Dallas/Fort Worth International Airport, home base for American Airlines, became a powerful business magnet serving millions of passengers annually. Today, DFW is the world's second-busiest airport, and is predicted by the Federal Aviation Administration to become the busiest by the year 2000.

In 1984, when Dallas hosted the Republican National Convention, the city was again thrust squarely into the international spotlight. Magazines like *Time*, *National Geographic*, and *Fortune* heaped praise on Dallas as "the city that works." The Dallas-Fort Worth Metroplex was touted as "the best place in the nation to do business." Dallas had reached yet another high-water mark. Residents and admirers from across the country had a sense that the boom of the 1980s would go on forever. (It should come as no surprise that this was also the period when J.R. Ewing was at his most popular, bringing yet another layer of attention to the city.)

And then, just as everything appeared to be going well, life dealt the city another blow: The national recession of the mid-1980s hit Dallas hard, while the energy and real estate crises caused numerous individual bankruptcies and crippled financial institutions. The city's economy was set back on its heels. Scores of companies laid off their workers; others shut their doors for good. The downtown business district suffered greatly, and only a handful of longtime players remained. Devastating problems like crime, drugs, teen pregnancies, unemployment, racial strife, and homelessness changed the look and sound of the city—as they did in other urban centers across the country.

▲ LAYNE MURDOCH

TROY AIKMAN IS THE LATEST IN A LONG LINE OF GREAT DALLAS COWBOYS QUARTERBACKS, GUIDING HIS TEAM TO THREE SUPER BOWL VICTORIES IN THE 1990S (ABOVE). TWO OTHER NOTABLE COWBOYS INCLUDE LARRY HAGMAN AND STEVE KANALY, WHO PLAYED J.R. EWING AND RAY KREBBS ON *Dallas* (OPPOSITE). ONE OF THE MOST POPULAR TELEVISION SHOWS EVER, THE PRIME-TIME DRAMA WAS AIRED IN MORE THAN 100 COUNTRIES AT ITS PEAK.

Nonetheless, even during these tough times, and even as its tax base eroded, Dallas maintained its can-do attitude and hands-on policies, never losing sight of its priorities. More police officers patrolled the streets. Housing, health, and human services were strengthened. The city's parks, libraries, and cultural institutions were improved. But citizen morale remained low through the late 1980s and the beginning of the 1990s. Jobs were scarce, emotions ran high, friction grew among the different socioeconomic classes, and race relations deteriorated.

In an effort to restore racial harmony, Dallas Together, an 88-member, blue-ribbon committee, was appointed. After months of heated debate, the committee concluded that the first priority must be a more inclusive form of government that reflected the city's broad diversity. And so it was that, in the early 1990s, an era of political empowerment for all citizens was launched. The Dallas City Council was restructured, with 14 members elected from single-member districts and the mayor chosen in a citywide election. This breakthrough in minority representation helped lead to the election of the city's first African-American mayor, Ron Kirk, in 1995.

Policies of diversity, openness, and inclusion are now being embraced by the private business sector as well as government, an achievement that, for the most part, can be credited to a covenant developed by local civic leaders who are members of the Dallas Together Forum. Participants include more than 150 companies that have set broad goals for hiring, promoting, and contracting minorities. Members of this group and the Women's Covenant of the Dallas Glass Ceiling Working Committee, which has adopted a similar pact to enhance economic opportunities for women, have volunteered to publish their records on hiring and purchasing.

All of these initiatives have been noticed and lauded: In December 1996, for example, Dallas became the first recipient of Turner Broadcasting System's City of Harmony award for its determination to tackle racism and prejudice. While there are still battles to be fought and won, the award provided affirmation that the city's programs are paying off. In addition, Dallas' nonpartisan council-manager form of government has garnered recognition from several respected national publications, including *Financial World*, which have consistently rated Dallas first or near the top among the nation's best-managed cities.

Today, there is a resurgence in Dallas' fortunes, economically as well as politically. Once again, the city is a national leader in corporate relocations, business expansion, job growth, and retail sales—key indicators of financial strength. As Dallas' population has cracked the million mark, a newly rediscovered sense of community, so much a part of Dallas since its earliest days, can be felt throughout the area. In keeping with this, the Dallas Plan, a new long-range strategy being implemented by the city, offers a vision for the city's growth over the next three decades and features a citizens' approach similar to Goals for Dallas. Everywhere you turn, Dallas is on the move again.

As the hub of American Airlines, Dallas/Fort Worth International Airport, opened in 1974, is currently the second-largest airport in the world, handling nearly 60 million passengers each year.

Drivers make their way to and from downtown Dallas in a blur of light and color (opposite). Although the city operates an extensive bus system and a spanking-new light-rail network, a car is still the easiest way to get around and see the sights.

NE PLACE WHERE CHANGE IS PARTICULARLY EVIDENT IS DOWNtown, which, in recent years, has begun to reclaim its glorious past. Public improvements are visible throughout the downtown district; renovated older office buildings are finding tenants; and residents are choosing to live downtown where apartments and lofts are plentiful. Pegasus Plaza, completed in 1994, is perhaps the best example of the rebirth of an area that, at the same time, continues to honor its heritage. Located in the center of downtown, the plaza features a magnificent fountain that pays homage to a longtime Dallas landmark, the bright red Pegasus that sits atop the Magnolia Building. At the time it was completed in 1923, the building, then home to Mobil Corporation, was the tallest structure south of Washington, D.C.

A walking tour of downtown reveals an entire laundry list of amenities, cultural and otherwise. Deep Ellum in the east end is an inspired blend of Dallas culture, with an eclectic mix of artists, poets, designers, and musicians, along with a sampling of trendy restaurants. Meanwhile, at downtown's opposite corner, the West End Historic District—with its imaginative shops, first-run movie theaters, arcades, and dining options to satisfy any appetite—has transformed what was once a conglomeration of boarded-up, century-old commercial warehouses into a colorful destination for entertainment and tourism. On any given night, the bustling crowds add a lift to this area of downtown. Nearby, the city-owned Reunion Arena offers the best in sports throughout the year, hosting the NBA's Dallas Mavericks, the NHL's Dallas Stars, and the Dallas Sidekicks professional indoor soccer team, as well as a variety of top entertainment.

On downtown's southeast edge, the recently renovated, 50-year-old Dallas Farmers Market is the world's largest of its kind. And on the northeast side, the Arts District, a vibrant, urban cultural center that is the largest in the United States, is home to the Dallas Symphony Orchestra, which performs in the I.M. Pei-designed Morton H. Meyerson Symphony Center; the recently enlarged Dallas Museum of Art, which features an excellent collection of contemporary, pre-Columbian, African, Asian, and New World and Pacific Cultures art; Artists Square, an open park for music and dance; and the Arts District Theater, a second venue for productions of the Dallas Theater Center. In addition, a one-of-a-kind sculpture garden, scheduled to open in 1999, will contain superb pieces amassed by Ray Nasher, who is considered to have one of the finest privately owned sculpture collections in the world. Adjacent to the Arts District is a thriving area of excellent restaurants, galleries, and specialty shops—all of which are happily served by the McKinney Avenue Trolley, a group of carefully restored streetcars that help enhance the area's old-time atmosphere.

At the southern border of downtown is another state-of-the-art, Pei-designed building—Dallas City Hall. And across the street is the magnificent Dallas Convention Center, which, as one of the country's largest and most versatile event locales, contributes significantly to the business district's vitality. With more than 3 million conventioneers each year, and a wide variety of first-class restaurants and hotels, it's no wonder that Dallas is the nation's second-ranked convention city. Nearby is Pioneer Plaza, a popular destination for tourists. The park's impressive bronze statues of longhorns and cowboy wranglers, the world's largest monument in that medium, depict an old west cattle drive on the site of an actual 1850s cattle trail. A short distance away, Union Station, built in 1916, is still the city's main rail station.

AUTHENTIC RODEOS, SUCH AS THE ANNUAL MESQUITE CHAMPIONSHIP RODEO AND THE SOUTHWESTERN EXPOSITION AND LIVESTOCK SHOW AND RODEO IN FORT WORTH, ARE REGULAR EVENTS IN AND AROUND THE METROPLEX (BELOW). FOR "FLYING" HORSES OF ANOTHER KIND, LOCALS CAN LOOK TO THE NEON PEGASUS, A FAMILIAR SYMBOL OF DALLAS' PROGRESSIVE SPIRIT. FOR DECADES, THE WINGED CREATURE HAS CROWNED THE SKYLINE FROM ITS POSITION ATOP THE BEAUX ARTS MAGNOLIA BUILDING (OPPOSITE).

DONOVAN REESE

Several other areas of downtown also attract crowds. Old City Park—Dallas' first park—consists of wonderful small historic buildings that hark back to the city's early years. Dealey Plaza, named for George Bannerman Dealey, founder of the *Dallas Morning News*, looks out on the site of the Kennedy assassination and continually draws visitors from all over the world. Across from the plaza is Dallas' most visited historic site, the Sixth Floor Museum, located in the infamous Texas School Book Depository building. The museum contains a comprehensive exhibit that details the life, death, and legacy of President Kennedy, focusing on the Warren Commission theory of his assassination. Down the street, "Old Red," a former county courthouse erected in 1890, is a splendid architectural example of the city's past. And especially convenient for those who work or live in the downtown area, Thanks-Giving Square is a tranquil spot where people of different faiths come together in prayer.

Not far away is the world's only theater designed by Frank Lloyd Wright, the Dallas Theater Center, which is best known for its superior experimental works. Likewise, Theatre Three, a distinctive theater-in-the-round; the distinguished Booker T. Washington Arts Magnet High School; and the unique Sammons Center for the Arts are all respected arts facilities in the downtown area.

Bolstering the ease with which Dallasites can get into and out of downtown is a new light-rail transportation system, Dallas Area Rapid Transit, the first of its kind in the Southwest. A 12-mile starter line provides access from North Dallas to downtown and Oak Cliff, and when complete, the 90-mile commuter rail network will offer a direct link between downtown, Dallas/Fort Worth International Airport, and suburban cities.

But the flurry of activity downtown is by no means the only indicator of Dallas' resurgence. With the influx of corporate relocations, the city's business base has continued to grow, and now includes financial services, telecommunications, warehousing and distribution, health care, and fashion. This rapid movement toward a world economy has given global recognition to Dallas as an international center of commerce and culture, as well as a dependable metropolitan market. The city's boundaries appear endless.

ADJACENT TO THE DALLAS CON-VENTION CENTER, THE 4.2-ACRE PIONEER PLAZA IS ONE OF DOWNTOWN DALLAS' NEWEST—AND MOST POPU-LAR—ATTRACTIONS, FEATURING *The Trail Drive*, A HERD OF MORE THAN 40 BRONZE STEERS GUIDED BY THREE MOUNTED COWBOYS. THE MONUMENT, DESIGNED BY TEXAN ROBERT SUM-MERS, NOT ONLY VIVIDLY RE-CREATES A 19TH-CENTURY CATTLE DRIVE UP THE SHAWNEE TRAIL, BUT IT ALSO SERVES AS A MAKESHIFT JUNGLE GYM FOR LOCAL YOUNGSTERS.

▲ CAROLYN BROWN

O f Dallas' wealth of assets, residents value most its high quality of life. This is a wonderful place to live, and there are an infinite number of reasons why. Health care for all is a must, and Dallas' hospital centers are among the world's best. For example, there are more Nobel laureates on the staff of the University of Texas Southwestern Medical Center at Dallas than at any of the world's other medical institutions.

To further enhance the quality of life in the area, special priority has long been given to the city's schools, libraries, parks, and cultural facilities. Strong local belief in the importance of education has resulted in the top-notch downtown library and its 20 neighborhood branches, which are often described as "dependable banks where we deposit our children and withdraw our future." With the slogan Looking Ahead—Moving Forward, the city's public schools have been making record gains in student achievement and attendance, and Dallas' private schools are among the nation's finest. Dallas has a passion for higher education and, together with its suburbs, boasts excellent colleges and universities, including a seven-campus community college district, Southern Methodist University, the University of Texas at Dallas, the University of Dallas, Paul Quinn College, Dallas Education Center, Dallas Baptist University, and the Dallas Institute of Humanities and Culture.

People in Dallas have long believed that a healthy cultural climate is also of the utmost importance. In the past 15 years alone, a mutually advantageous partnership between the city and individual citizens has created both the internationally acclaimed Meyerson Symphony Center and the superb Dallas Museum of Art. These first-rate facilities, which anchor the Arts District, are merely the latest in a long line of endeavors that define the city's strong alliance with the private sector. On the drawing board is a splendid hall for the grand Dallas Opera and the highly respected Fort Worth/Dallas Ballet, as well as other performing arts groups.

◄ MOSES OLMOS

A WONDERLAND OF CULTURAL OPPORTUNITIES, BIG D IS HOME TO NUMEROUS FIRST-CLASS PERFORMING ARTS GROUPS, INCLUDING THE RENOWNED DALLAS SYMPHONY ORCHESTRA, LED BY CONDUCTOR ANDREW LITTON (ABOVE).

ALLIE TENNANT'S *Tejas Warrior* GREETS VISITORS TO THE HALL OF STATE, A COMPREHENSIVE MUSEUM LOCATED IN FAIR PARK'S 277-ACRE COMPLEX (OPPOSITE). ONCE INSIDE, PATRONS ARE TREATED TO MASSIVE MURALS THAT SUMMARIZE TEXAS HISTORY FROM 1519 TO THE 1930S.

The city also takes great pride in excellent small performing arts groups like the Greater Dallas Youth Orchestra and the Turtle Creek Chorale, and in such minority arts organizations as the Anita Martinez Ballet Folklorico, Dallas Black Dance Theater, Junior Black Academy of Arts and Letters, Mexican Cultural Center, Teatro Dallas, Philippine Arts Theater, Dallas Chinese Youth Orchestra, and Japan-American Touring Program. This artistic diversity enriches the city and has made it the cultural center for the region.

To show just how much Dallasites appreciate the fine arts, consider this: Dallas is the only U.S. city that actually owns a radio station dedicated to classical music. And recently, carrying on its tradition of building for the arts, Dallas voters approved a bond issue that will enable the city, with citizen financial support, to construct a new Hispanic cultural center.

As if to remind us that our love of the arts did not just develop in the last few years, there is Fair Park, Dallas' unique cultural and entertainment center that has become a landmark in its own right. Now more than 60 years old, this area is a virtual directory of prestigious, publicly and privately owned and operated cultural facilities. Located in the midst of one of the best and largest collections of art deco buildings anywhere are the new African-American Museum; the Hall of State, the city's repository for Dallas and Texas history; the Museum of Natural History; the Dallas Aquarium; the Fair Park Music Hall, home to the Dallas Summer Musicals; the Dallas Civic Garden Center; the Age of Steam Railroad Museum; the Science Place, with its state-of-the-art IMAX theater; and the Starplex Amphitheater, where well-known recording artists perform. This list of remarkable arts and educational facilities near the heart of the city is completed by the innovative South Dallas Cultural Center, located directly across the street from Fair Park.

One of Fair Park's most popular entertainment attractions is the renowned Cotton Bowl, Dallas' host stadium for the 1994 World Cup Soccer Games; the home field for the Dallas Burn major-league outdoor soccer team and the Southern Methodist University Mustangs football team; and the site of several high school football games. Two college football classics are also played there, including the Al Lipscomb State Fair Classic and the matchup between the Texas Longhorns and the Oklahoma Sooners, an annual contest for bragging rights that constitutes one of the nation's hottest football rivalries. Good attendance at both games is guaranteed, and helps ensure the success of the annual State Fair of Texas, which draws millions of visitors to the city.

The quality of life in Dallas has long been enhanced by its outstanding park system. Always looking for ways to make life easier, safer, and brighter, as Dallas grew, parks were carefully planned to ensure that grass, trees, and recreational facilities would be easily accessible to every neighborhood. With more than 21,000 acres of public space that includes 406 parks, 16 lakes, and numerous sports facilities, the city's residents don't have to go far to find just the right spot for family picnics, all kinds of recreational opportunities, and even free performances by the Shakespeare Festival of Dallas.

The most beautiful of these parks is the Dallas Arboretum and Botanical Garden. These 66 acres on the eastern shore of White Rock Lake display a myriad of seasonal flowers year-round, and provide a perfect respite from the city's sometimes hectic pace. The Dallas Zoo in Oak Cliff is another star of the park system and has become an outstanding destination for fun, education, and research. The zoo's Wilds of Africa exhibit was the first anywhere to include replicas of an entire continent's major animal habitats.

Dallas is widely and correctly known as a shopper's paradise, with more shopping centers per capita than any other U.S. city. In addition to Neiman Marcus' flagship store downtown, which celebrated its 90th anniversary in July 1997, more than 20 area malls and retail centers indulge the most enthusiastic shopping addict. Included among them are Northpark, the nation's first climate-controlled, enclosed-court shopping center; the Galleria, Prestonwood, and Valley View in North Dallas; the Shops and Galleries of the Crescent Court in the uptown area; Highland Park Village, often considered to be the oldest shopping center in the United States; and Red Bird Mall in southwest Dallas. Such retailers attract customers from, literally, the world over.

Finally, it's no secret that Dallasites love sports, and the abundance of professional teams gives the city an added dimension of fun. Of course, there are the Cowboys, who play at Texas Stadium in nearby Irving, but there are several other exciting teams too. Along with the Mavericks, the Stars, the Sidekicks, and the Burn, the Texas Rangers baseball team plays just a few miles from downtown at The Ballpark in Arlington. Locals' loyalty to their home teams is legendary, and it's only equaled by loyalty to their hometown.

DALLASITES CELEBRATE WITH AN ENTIRE CALENDAR OF EVENTS AND FESTIVALS. EACH YEAR, THE CITY'S HISPANIC CITIZENS OBSERVE CINCO DE MAYO, THE DAY IN 1862 WHEN AN OUTMANNED MEXICAN ARMY TRIUMPHED OVER HOSTILE FRENCH FORCES IN THE CITY OF PUEBLA, MEXICO (ABOVE).

IN THE FALL, MILLIONS OF VISITORS ENJOY THE 24-DAY TEXAS STATE FAIR, THE LARGEST OF ITS KIND IN THE UNITED STATES (OPPOSITE). THE FAIR'S MYRIAD ATTRACTIONS INCLUDE THE TEXAS STAR, THE TALLEST FERRIS WHEEL IN THE WESTERN HEMISPHERE, AS WELL AS BIG TEX, WHO, AT 52 FEET, IS THE WORLD'S TALLEST COWBOY, GREETING FAIRGOERS WITH AN ENTHUSIASTIC "HOWDY, FOLKS!"

NONE OTHER THAN WILLIAM SHAKESPEARE ASKED, "What is the city but the people?" Dallas *is* its people. The city's greatest resource has always been the people who live here—hardworking, friendly, caring individuals with a true benevolence of spirit. The people of Dallas are known for giving of themselves for others. Dedicated volunteers raise millions of dollars each year to help the disadvantaged among us. The city supports these private endeavors with substantial financial subsidization of housing, health, and human services. Certainly, Dallas deserves its reputation as being a city with a heart.

Dallas has always been a city whose leaders and followers have confronted their challenges with vision, hard work, spunk, and in-

genuity, their efforts marked by inspirational and entrepreneurial drive. Propelled by an indomitable will to succeed and immeasurable confidence in the future, the citizens of Dallas are continuing to build a strong foundation for more good years ahead.

The symbols that are so visible to the outside world *are* meaningful. The stars on the Cowboys' helmets and the smirk on J.R.'s face offer a glimpse into the city's unmistakable spirit. Just as John Neely Bryan and the earliest settlers knew when they stumbled upon the tiny settlement, there is absolutely no better place to live, learn, work, and play than in this community of promise and pride. Dallas is daring and dynamic, comfortable and enduring. And, most of all, it is world class. ✱

DALLAS MAY BE CALLED THE CITY OF DREAMS, BUT THIS NORTH DALLAS KITE FLYER KNOWS IT'S OK SOMETIMES TO JUST LIVE FOR THE MOMENT (OPPOSITE). ALSO FLYING HIGH, THE FLAG WITH THE UBIQUITOUS LONE STAR (ABOVE) HAS BEEN A SYMBOL OF TEXAS' UNMISTAKABLE SPIRIT SINCE 1836, WHEN THE REPUBLIC DECLARED INDEPENDENCE FROM MEXICO. TEXAS BECAME A STATE NINE YEARS LATER, IN 1845.

Since the 1970s, a construction boom has resulted in several dramatic office towers scattered throughout the city, including the light-colored Texas Commerce Tower and the Plaza of the Americas (OPPOSITE), the Mary Kay Building in Far North Dallas (TOP), and the vaulted roofline of the post-International Style Bank One Center (BOTTOM). The city's status as a financial center has ensured more than its share of glass towers. The geometric, 60-story Fountain Place, formerly the First Interstate Bank Tower (PAGE 30), dominates the Dallas skyline, while 3100 Monticello Avenue houses several of Dallas' successful organizations (PAGE 31).

MCMXXII

MAGNOLIA BUILDING

One of the best ways to see downtown Dallas is from atop Reunion Tower, where a revolving restaurant affords spectacular—and panoramic—views from 50 stories up (PAGE 32). The neoclassical turret of the 19-story Davis Building, built in 1925, continues to make its mark on the Dallas skyline (PAGE 33).

Several ornate, beaux arts landmarks also call downtown home. The 27-story Magnolia Building was the city's tallest structure from its completion in 1923 until 1943 (PAGE 34), while the posh Adolphus Hotel, built by beer baron Adolphus Busch in 1912, is among the city's finest places to stay (PAGE 35).

PAGE 32: DONOVAN REESE

PAGES 33, 34, AND 35: STEWART CHARLES COHEN

ORNAMENTATION IS THE icing on Dallas' architectural cake. The balcony grilles at the elegant Crescent Center, a combination office tower/hotel/retail complex overlooking downtown, evoke the spirit of its namesake New Orleans (OPPOSITE). The sleek lines of the 2 million-plus-square-foot Dallas Convention Center (TOP), one of the largest facilities of its kind in the world, contrast with an arched walkway at the historic Magnolia Building (BOTTOM).

A STORM-INDUCED RAINBOW
and the setting sun take
turns touching the city skyline.

I N THE RIGHT LIGHT—AND from the right angle—the city's towers can appear forbidding. At 72 stories, NationsBank Plaza is the city's tallest building— a fact that, along with its dramatic, argon-outlined structure, guaran- tees its dominance of downtown (OPPOSITE). Nearby is the I.M. Pei-designed Fountain Place, a chisel-shaped glass tower sur- rounded by a terraced water garden (ABOVE).

A BRIGHTLY LIT BUS STOP faces the august Adolphus Hotel on Commerce, while a downtown worker strides past a store window with a familiar neon outline.

THE GLORY WINDOW IN THE tiny, snail-shaped Chapel of Thanksgiving is the focal point of Thanks-Giving Square, a spiritual oasis in the center of downtown's financial district (ABOVE). A different kind of oasis can be found at Dallas Alley in the West End Marketplace. Home to dozens of shops, nightclubs, restaurants, and fast-food vendors, the scene is loud and lively every night of the week (OPPOSITE).

OFFICE BUILDINGS CREATE A distinctive backdrop for large public sculpture—a fitting metaphor for the role the business community plays in the area's thriving arts scene. In Thanks-Giving Square, the *Ring of Thanks* and the *Bells of Thanksgiving* inspire quiet contemplation among visitors who stroll through its landscaped gardens (ABOVE), while in Far North Dallas, three undulating structures rise dramatically outside the Anthem Health Building, one of many large office complexes that stretch along the Dallas North Tollway (OPPOSITE).

RICK YEATTS ▲   ▲ CAROLYN BROWN

TWO STUNNING, I.M. PEI-designed edifices bookend downtown Dallas. When City Hall was completed in 1978 on the district's southern edge, it was so ahead of its time that the jutting structure and its ceremonial plaza made an appearance in several science-fiction movies (ABOVE). To the north looms the Morton H. Meyerson Symphony Center—the crown jewel of the Arts District—which claims the finest acoustics of any music center in the country (OPPOSITE).

CAROLYN BROWN

Many of the city's prominent residents have given generously of their time and money to make Dallas a better place to live. Current Mayor Ron Kirk, overlooking downtown from City Hall, has won plaudits for his thoughtful, fair-minded approach to satisfying the city's diverse population (TOP), while Dallasite Robert Strauss has served as a U.S. ambassador to Russia and as Democratic national chairman (BOTTOM RIGHT). U.S. Senator Kay Bailey Hutchison maps out the day's itinerary with her assistant and two pilots (BOTTOM LEFT). Once a newscaster in Austin, Hutchison later became Texas' first female state treasurer.

▶ STEWART CHARLES COHEN

HOLDING THE ORIGINAL deed to the city that was given to John Neely Bryan in 1854 is civic leader and businessman Ross Perot, who is nationally recognized for his unwavering business and political vision (TOP). In 1962, Perot founded Electronic Data Systems, a Dallas company that has prospered under the leadership of Lester M. Alberthal Jr. since 1986 (BOTTOM RIGHT). Both men are generous benefactors of the local arts community.

The fountain in Pegasus Plaza, created by the Dallas Institute of Humanities and Culture, symbolizes the importance of the myth of Pegasus and the nine muses to the city. Instrumental to the development of the monument were Brad Goldberg, sculptor; Dr. Gail Thomas, Institute director; Mary Ellen Degnan, Institute development officer; and Michael Kendall, landscape architect (BOTTOM LEFT).

DALLAS HAS ITS FAIR SHARE of entrepreneurs who have brought success to themselves and the city. The marketing genius of Stanley Marcus and his family has made Neiman Marcus one of the nation's leaders in fashion and high-quality mail-order shopping for more than half a century (TOP LEFT), while over the last quarter-century, American Airlines Chairman and CEO Robert Crandall has helped develop his innovative company into one of the nation's premier air carriers (TOP RIGHT). Real estate giant Trammell Crow opened a small warehouse in Dallas in 1948 and transformed it into one of the nation's most successful real estate development companies (BOTTOM).

WITH A FACULTY THAT boasts four Nobel laureates—including Michael S. Brown, M.D.; Johann Deisenhofer, Ph.D.; Joseph Goldstein, M.D.; and Alfred G. Gilman, Ph.D. (TOP LEFT)—the University of Texas Southwestern Medical Center at

Dallas has emerged as one of the world's leading medical institutions. Dr. Kern Wildenthal, who has devised several revolutionary procedures in cardiology, became the center's president in 1986 (TOP RIGHT).

Caroline Rose Hunt enjoys high tea in the Lady Primrose Tea Room of the Crescent Court (BOTTOM LEFT). One of the city's cultural leaders, Hunt is the principal in a vast real estate empire that includes the Crescent.

Robert Decherd, a mainstay in city planning and philanthropy, is chairman, CEO, and president of the A.H. Belo Corporation, one of the nation's media giants and publisher of the *Dallas Morning News* (BOTTOM RIGHT).

THE RAYMOND AND PATSY Nasher collection of modern and contemporary sculpture—including works by Jean Dubuffet, Auguste Rodin, Henry Moore, Willem de Kooning, and Roy Lichtenstein—is among the world's finest (TOP). In 1997, Nasher agreed to lend his holdings to the Nasher Sculpture Garden, which will open at the Dallas Museum of Art (DMA) in 1999. This acquisition elevates the DMA, directed by Jay Gates (BOTTOM LEFT), to the world-class level.

Dr. Harry Robinson Jr. serves as president and CEO of the African-American Museum in Fair Park, which contains one of the largest collections of African-American folk art and historical documents in the country (BOTTOM RIGHT).

JOAN SHEAHAN

With the help of dedicated local citizens, Dallas' performing arts community grows stronger by the day. Morton H. Meyerson, chairman of the board of Perot Systems, is a committed civic leader and the namesake for the city's renowned symphony center (TOP). Richard Hamburger, director of the Dallas Theater Center, has garnered a national reputation for his original reworkings of classic theatrical pieces and his stylish productions of new work (BOTTOM RIGHT). As the executive producer and director of Theatre Three, known for its diverse repertoire and top-notch interpretations, Jac Alder is a major contributor to the arts (BOTTOM LEFT).

▶ CAROLYN BROWN

O VERSIZED URBAN MURALS have become popular in cities nationwide, and Dallas is no exception. Painted on the Renaissance Tower parking garage, *Mass Transit*, by Jeff Garrison and Chris Arnold, adds a little fun to an otherwise normal workday downtown.

S INCE IT OPENED IN 1984, the Dallas Museum of Art, with its collection of abstract expressionist paintings and pre-Columbian and African art, has become one of the state's finest cultural attractions. Claes Oldenburg's massive *Stake Hitch* also finds a home in the DMA.

BEFORE WORLD WAR II, more than a dozen large theaters inhabited Elm Street, but the Majestic, built in 1921, is the only one that remains. In its in- fancy, the Renaissance-revival theater, which was home to vaudeville shows, drew many col- orful patrons and performers. Converted to films in the 1930s, the sumptuously designed, 1,570- seat auditorium was donated to the city in the late 1970s and to- day hosts touring dance, theater, and music companies.

OLD RED IS ONE OF THE
few 19th-century build-
ings still standing in Dallas. Built
in 1892, it was the fifth courthouse to occupy the site.

WHEN IT WAS BUILT IN 1931, Highland Park Village was one of the country's first suburban retail centers and purportedly the first in which the stores faced inward. Still one of the city's finest shopping locales, the Village houses plenty of upscale retailers and a newly renovated movie theater, constructed in the Spanish eclectic style.

A STRETCH OF LAND FEW Americans are *not* familiar with is downtown's Dealey Plaza, which is home to the Dallas County Administration Building, formerly the Texas School Book Depository (TOP). Best known as the location from which Lee Harvey Oswald allegedly fired at John F. Kennedy, it now houses the Sixth Floor Museum, which is dedicated to the life and assassination of the former president (OPPOSITE BOTTOM). A half-block away is the starkly modern John F. Kennedy Memorial (BOTTOM).

64

▶ DOUGLAS NEWBY

BROOKLYN MAY HAVE BEEN known as the City of Churches at the turn of the century, but Dallas could lay claim to that title today. Nearly 2,000 houses of worship are sprinkled throughout the city, including (FROM OPPOSITE LEFT) the Gothic-style Cathedral Santuario de Guadalupe, St. Edward's School, St. Edward's Catholic Church, and Grace United Methodist Church.

THE LAVISH HOMES OF THE mile-long Swiss Avenue Historic District recall the affluence of East Dallas just after the turn of the century (TOP). A litany of deed restrictions and construction requirements helped ensure the neighborhood's stability and success as one of the city's first planned suburbs.

Another of Dallas' early suburbs is Highland Park, which, along with University Park just to its north, remains one of the city's most desirable addresses (BOTTOM).

▲ EMANUEL BOROK

WATER HAS NEVER PLAYED a big part in the fortunes of landlocked Dallas, but the city boasts several spectacular liquid showcases nonetheless. The I.M. Pei-designed Fountain Place is sur-rounded by a landscaped water garden complete with cascading falls and a grid of choreographed "dancing" fountain jets that make for a spectacular water-and-light show (OPPOSITE). Conner Park and its sinkhole are among the many scenic spots along Turtle Creek, which flows through the Park Cities (ABOVE).

▲ CAROLYN BROWN

LOCATED ON THE SHORES OF White Rock Lake in East Dallas, the 66-acre Dallas Arboretum and Botanical Garden, opened in 1985, features spectacular floral displays, botanical exhibits, and a natural lakeside amphitheater. Visitors come from across the country to see the 44-acre, 1930s DeGolyer House and Gardens, listed on the National Register of Historic Places, as well as the Johnson and Palmer Fern Dell Gardens, which boast one of the country's largest azalea collections.

JAN WILSON JOROLAN / GEOIMAGERY

Wᴵᴸᴰ ᴀɴɪᴍᴀʟꜱ ꜰɪɢᴜʀᴇ ɪɴ several popular Dallas attractions. A lifelike mammoth named Jumbo, modeled by sculptor Tom Tischler after a fossil found within the city limits, "roams" the grounds outside the Dallas Museum of Natural History in Fair Park (ᴏᴘᴘᴏꜱɪᴛᴇ). Next door, the Science Place houses lifelike animatronic dinosaurs that chill the spines of children and grown-ups alike (ʟᴇꜰᴛ).

Just south of the Trinity River is the Dallas Zoo, home to more than 2,000 animals, including this lowland silverback gorilla, which lives in one of six African habitats that can be seen via the Wilds of Africa monorail ride (ʀɪɢʜᴛ).

It's more common than you'd think to see animals roaming the streets of Greater Dallas. Robert Glen's *The Mustangs of Las Colinas*, the largest equestrian sculpture in the world, is so lifelike that the horses actually create splashes as they "gallop" through Williams Square Plaza in Las Colinas (TOP), while each bronze steer in Pioneer Plaza's massive monument has "Big D" branded into its side (BOTTOM). Every time the Ringling Bros. and Barnum & Bailey Circus rolls into town, half the entertainment comes during the elephant walk to Reunion Arena (OPPOSITE BOTTOM).

▲ CAROLYN BROWN

THE BLUEBONNET IS THE state flower of Texas, and although it's illegal to pick them, it's within every citizen's right to enjoy their beauty. Each spring, the blooms fill Texas roadsides with color.

DALLAS

A LTHOUGH THE DALLAS Arboretum's collection of tulips is one of the best floral displays around, the clusters of bluebonnets and other wildflowers scattered throughout the city can be equally inspiring.

THE PRODUCE AT EATZI'S, an upscale market and bakery in Oak Lawn, is just about as fresh as it gets (OPPOSITE). But if you want your food direct from the farm, go to Dallas' Farmers Market, four blocks of open-air sheds packed with fresh and cold-storage fruits and vegetables from North Texas (BOTTOM). For a sinful version of an otherwise healthy treat, sink your teeth into a sumptuous caramel or candied apple at one of the many area festivals (TOP).

HALLOWEEN IS MORE THAN just pumpkins at the Farmers Market, where hot peppers add their own spice to the holiday.

THERE ARE PLENTY OF WAYS to have a good time at the annual Texas State Fair, and dining on "fair food" is one of the best. Classic treats include butter-drenched corn on the cob; award-winning desserts; and cotton candy, a staple in every fairgoer's diet.

▶ RICK YEATTS

LIGHTING UP THE MIDWAY at the State Fair are the ever popular Ring of Fire and the dramatic Texas Star, the largest Ferris wheel in the Western Hemisphere (OPPOSITE). Some rides are a blur of color for riders and viewers alike.

N O TRIP TO FAIR PARK IS complete without a visit to the Hall of State. Highlights include the Great Seal, which depicts the six flags that have flown over Texas (TOP), and the golden-skinned *Tejas Warrior*, who guards the entrance to the magnificent building (bottom).

DALLAS BOASTS ITS SHARE of "stellar" attractions, including the Texas Sesquicentennial seal at Fair Park (TOP) and the seal of the City of Dallas outside City Hall (BOTTOM).

DESIGNED AS A PERMANENT display of state history, beginning with Texas' discovery by the Spanish in 1519, the Hall of State is home to the Great Hall of Texas (ABOVE) and Eugene Savage's massive murals (OPPOSITE).

THE HALL OF STATE WAS built of materials native to Texas, and all its details—light fixtures, doors, and floor and wall patterns—are symbolic of the state's flora, fauna, history, or industries (BOTTOM). Across Fair Park's Court of Honor is Centennial Hall, which is fronted by a 700-foot-long reflecting pool (TOP).

ACH OF THE OPEN PORTICOS OF Centennial Hall shelters one of six statues representing the nations that have ruled the Lone Star State, including (FROM OPPOSITE BOTTOM) the Confederacy, Spain, Texas, France, Mexico, and the United States.

THE ANNUAL COTTON BOWL matchup between Texas and Oklahoma—one of the great rivalries in college football—caps the 24-day Texas State Fair in style. Opened in 1930, the partially sunken stadium holds approximately 72,000 spectators.

SINCE 1960, WHEN THE franchise was born, the Dallas Cowboys have justifiably earned the moniker America's Team, sometimes attracting more fans on the road than the home team. Three of the 'Boys perennial All-Pros include Emmitt Smith, arguably the most celebrated player in the team's storied history (OPPOSITE); Troy Aikman, the most accurate passer in NFL postseason history (TOP LEFT); and Deion Sanders, who may be the best coverage defensive back ever (TOP RIGHT). With so many greats to choose from, fans often have a tough time picking their favorite player.

THE DALLAS COWBOYS cheerleaders have been popular since their showbiz makeover in 1972, but it wasn't until Super Bowl X in 1976, when one member winked at a TV camera, that the squad gained worldwide fame. Equally recognizable are some other legends of the franchise, including Tom Landry, the first—and longtime—coach of the team (OPPOSITE, BOTTOM LEFT, WITH HIS WIFE), and "Captain Comeback" Roger Staubach, the quarterback who exuded Cowboys class and cool (OPPOSITE, BOTTOM RIGHT). Jerry Jones, who bought the club in 1989, has redefined the NFL owner's role with his savvy marketing ability and has positioned the Cowboys to enter the next century in winning fashion (BOTTOM).

BECOMING A COWBOYS FAN starts early. Each summer, the team holds its summer training camp at St. Edward's University, 200 miles down the road in Austin, where crowds of onlookers, including this serious fan, gather to watch the 'Boys work out (OPPOSITE).

These two youngsters fish around at the annual festival in Valley Ranch, the suburb northwest of Dallas where the Cowboys make their home (LEFT).

▶ LAYNE MURDOCH

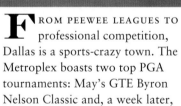

FROM PEEWEE LEAGUES TO professional competition, Dallas is a sports-crazy town. The Metroplex boasts two top PGA tournaments: May's GTE Byron Nelson Classic and, a week later, the MasterCard Colonial, won by Corey Pavin in 1996 (LEFT). Hurler Nolan Ryan, a native Texan whose stellar career with the Rangers lasted from 1989 to 1993, is the only player to have his number retired by the team. No other pitcher in major-league history has thrown seven no-hitters (RIGHT).

W ITH THEIR BEAUTIFULLY landscaped fairways and manicured greens, area golf courses are irresistible to most players. Each year, professional tournaments draw such crowd pleasers as Tiger Woods, pictured here at the 1997 MasterCard Colonial (LEFT).

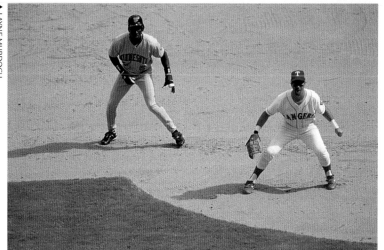

MAKING THE PLAY-OFFS for the first time in 1996, the Texas Rangers have finally come into their own, boasting a full roster of talented players. Juan Gonzalez, the American League's Most Valuable Player in 1996, wields one of the most dangerous bats in the majors (OPPOSITE), while Ken Hill, one of baseball's steadiest starters, is the team's perennial Opening Day pitcher (TOP LEFT). Each game, Ivan "Pudge" Rodriguez proves himself to be the best catcher in baseball (TOP RIGHT), while Will "the Thrill" Clark lives up to his nickname (BOTTOM RIGHT).

When The Ballpark in Arlington opened its portals in 1994, its mix of old and new design elements prompted several baseball experts to call it the best stadium in the majors.

P ERPETUALLY GRINNING— and leaping and cheer-leading—Mavs Man debuted in 1996 as the new Dallas Mavericks mascot and quickly became a crowd favorite (OPPOSITE LEFT). But Mavs Man was not the only new face during the 1996-1997 season, which saw a major over-haul of the team's roster. Swing-man Michael Finley, who came to Dallas from the Phoenix Suns, is known for his electrifying moves and glovelike defense (OPPOSITE RIGHT). Here, former New Jersey Nets guard Khalid Reeves drives to the basket to score against the Minnesota Timberwolves (LEFT).

N O MATTER THE SPORT, Dallas hosts its fair share of the action, from a high-reaching contest featuring the University of North Texas basketball team (OPPOSITE) to a match between the U.S. Women's National Soccer Team and the Canadian team (TOP) to the 1995 Western U.S. Rugby Football Club Championship, won by the Dallas Harlequins (BOTTOM).

I N BIG D, SOCCER FANS HAVE plenty of chances to enjoy the game. The Burn, Dallas' outdoor professional team, has drawn a strong local following since its inaugural season in 1996. Competing in the Cotton Bowl, the Burn adds top world players to its ranks each season.

▲ RICK YEATTS

FOLLOWERS OF INDOOR soccer—a confined, high-scoring sport likened to human pinball—can catch the Dallas Side-kicks at Reunion Arena, where the two-time Continental Indoor Soccer League champs are led by flashy forward Tatu (LEFT).

As a host city for the 1994 World Cup games, Dallas saw action on a global scale, including this exhibition match that pitted the U.S. team against Bolivia (RIGHT).

L OCAL POLICE AND FIRE departments provide their cadets with rigorous training, the result of which can be seen in Dallas' finest, who patrol the city on their various "mounts." Many men and women in blue continue their conditioning by participating in such competitions as the Police Athletic League boxing matches (OPPOSITE, TOP LEFT).

▲ LAYNE MURDOCH

A LTHOUGH ICE HOCKEY MAY seem a bit out of place in Texas, the Dallas Stars, who moved here from Minnesota in 1993, have risen to the top of the National Hockey League. Leading the team are defenseman Derian Hatcher (OPPOSITE), high scorer Mike Modano (LEFT), and wing Bob Bassen (RIGHT).

THE ANNUAL YMCA TURKEY Trot is a chance for local runners to strut their stuff, and some 15,000 hearty souls show up every Thanksgiving morning to run through downtown and across the Trinity River into Oak Cliff (RIGHT). The Grand Prix of Dallas street-racing festival, which has also visited the city several times over the past few years, temporarily turned the Reunion area into a premier racetrack in 1996 (OPPOSITE).

AN OVERPASS IN THE DALLAS "mixmaster" dissects the city's spectacular skyline, separating the Renaissance Tower and NationsBank Plaza from the Hyatt Regency and Reunion Tower (PAGES 120 AND 121).

PAGES 120 AND 121: DONOVAN REESE

P LANES, TRAINS (COMPUTER-controlled passenger trams, anyway), and automobiles converge at Dallas/Fort Worth International, one of the world's largest and busiest airports. The airfield is also a favorite of pilots, who appreciate its oversized, parallel runways and long, unobstructed approach paths.

DALLAS' AIRPORTS AREN'T the only reason Big D is such a destination city. An extensive highway system, featuring five interstate and 19 other U.S. and state highways, makes travel to and from the Metroplex easy and convenient.

▲ CHRIS REGAS

O F COURSE, PLENTY OF
highways means plenty of
cars. This auto-parts puller visits
one of the many junkyards on the
outskirts of the city (TOP), while a
proud Cadillac owner poses with
his customized ride (BOTTOM).

IN 1917, DALLAS' CHAMBER of commerce bought a small piece of land south of Bachman Lake so the War Department could train pilots for World War I. Called Love Field, it later began passenger service and became the city's municipal airport in 1927. For many years, the airport was home to such flight schools as the Dallas Aviation School.

▶ LOUIS DELUCA

Today, Love Field is the hub of the enormously successful Southwest Airlines. Headquartered in Dallas since 1971, the carrier is run by Chairman and Cofounder Herb Kelleher (LEFT). The airport's location, smack-dab in the middle of the city, makes it easy to get close to the runway for a cheap thrill.

RICK YEATTS

BIG IS A POPULAR THEME IN Dallas, as evidenced by Big Tex, the world's tallest cowboy (OPPOSITE); the annual Plano Hot-Air Balloon Festival, which attracts all manner of innovative balloon designs (LEFT); and downtown's annual AmeriFest international celebration, which offers this Texas-sized chair for weary walkers (RIGHT).

BLESSED WITH GOOD weather nearly year-round, Dallas is home to a number of outdoor events, including the Valley Ranch Festival (LEFT), the Prairie Dog Chili Cookoff (TOP RIGHT), and the bonnet contest at the Easter Parade (BOTTOM RIGHT). Oak Lawn's Pooch Parade in Reverchon Park is one of the city's more unusual events (OPPOSITE).

ACH DECEMBER, THE Neiman Marcus Adolphus Children's Parade, benefiting the Children's Medical Center, winds through downtown Dallas and past the Adolphus Hotel (TOP). In recent years, highlights have included Deputy Dan, a cowboy who gives Big Tex a run for his money (OPPOSITE, TOP LEFT); the Trinity Valley Community College Cardettes dance team, dressed as dalmatians (OPPOSITE BOTTOM); and an ever festive group of holiday well-wishers (BOTTOM).

▲ APRIL B. KAO

DALLAS ACKNOWLEDGES ITS rich ethnic heritage with several festivals, including (CLOCK-WISE FROM OPPOSITE) the popular Cinco de Mayo celebration at Fair Park; the Asian Festival, featuring authentic music, food, and crafts in downtown's Artists Square; the International Festival, which brings people of diverse cultures to North Dallas; and a colorful Native American powwow in Artists Square.

ONE OF THE LARGEST AND most innovative school systems in the nation, the Dallas Independent School District offers a variety of educational opportu- nities, from remedial studies to award-winning programs for hearing- and vision-impaired students to specially designed magnet schools.

THE CITY'S OLDEST AND MOST prestigious center of higher education and one of the nation's top private universities, Southern Methodist University (SMU) boasts a 600-plus-acre campus that is peppered with distinguished neoclassical buildings. Here, President Gerald Turner stands in front of Dallas Hall, completed in 1915 as the school's first building (TOP).

SMU has earned international renown for its geological sciences and anthropology departments, thanks to such distinguished professors as Louis Jacobs, Ph.D., who examines a fossil at the Shuler Museum of Paleontology with two of his research associates (BOTTOM LEFT), and Dr. Lewis Binford, who revolutionized the modern disciplines of archaeology and anthropology (BOTTOM RIGHT).

▼ CAROLYN BROWN

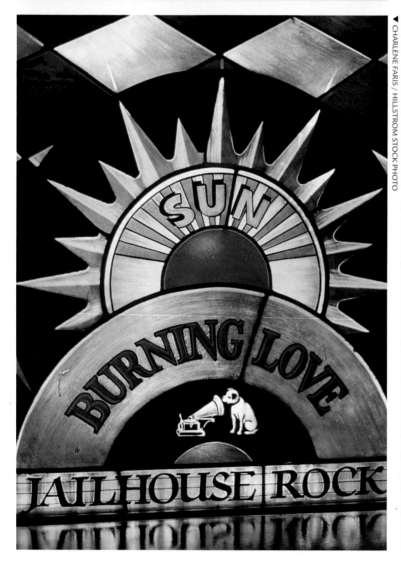

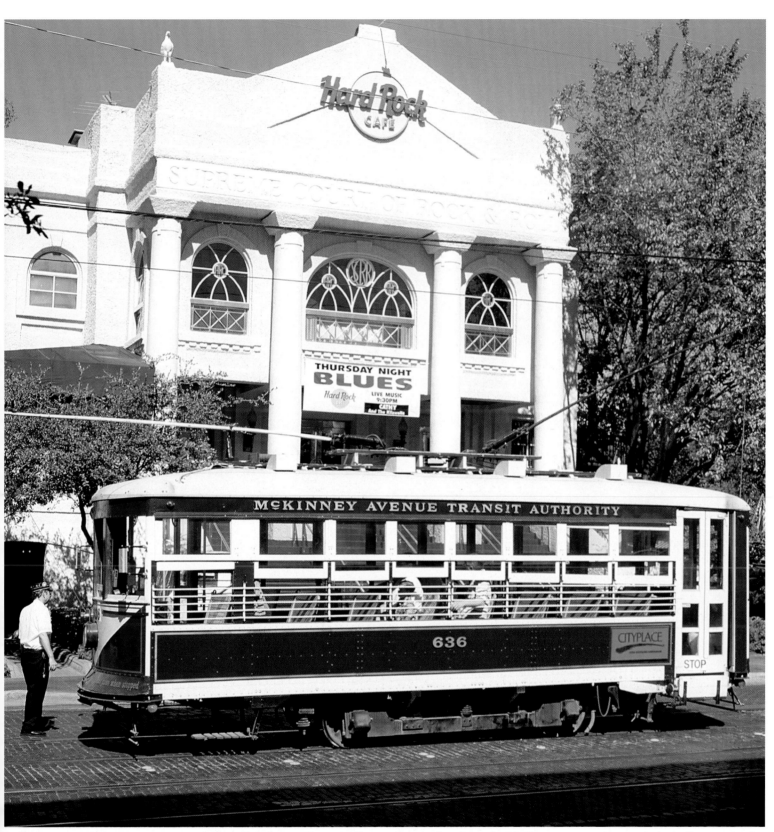

ᴀFTER DARK, DALLAS OFFERS a variety of options for movie buffs, rock and rollers, and folks just out for a good time. The showpiece of downtown's West End Marketplace is Planet Hollywood, opened in 1994. Dallas' Hard Rock Cafe, considered by many aficionados to be the finest in the country, is housed in a former church on the McKinney Avenue trolley line that runs uptown from the Arts District. The Hard Rock offers an extensive array of memorabilia, tributes, and artwork, including a stained glass window honoring Elvis Presley and a mirror imprinted with eloquent lines from one of the Beatles' last songs.

JAMES BLAND

Iᴛ ᴛʜᴇ ᴘᴀsᴛ sᴇᴠᴇʀᴀʟ ʏᴇᴀʀs, Dallas has gained a wide-spread reputation for fostering new music, as several local bands have made it big on a national scale. In addition to Steve Miller, Edie Brickell, and Jackopierce, a few groups who call Dallas home include punk popsters Hagfish (ʟᴇꜰᴛ); frenetic rockers the Reverend Horton Heat (ʀɪɢʜᴛ); and the gone-but-not-forgotten Loco Gringos (ᴏᴘᴘᴏsɪᴛᴇ).

APRIL B. KAO

APRIL B. KAO

ONCE A FREEDMEN'S TOWN that became an important African-American commercial district known as the Harlem of the Southwest, Deep Ellum fell into disuse after the construction of Central Expressway in 1949. Having experienced a resurgence in the 1980s, the district is today packed with art galleries, theaters, hip nightclubs, eateries, and body-piercing establishments.

AS ONE OF THE NATION'S foremost fashion meccas, Dallas boasts more shopping per capita than any other city in the United States. Contributing to this statistic is the enormous Dallas Market Center, the world's largest wholesale mart. The center consists of five buildings, including the International Apparel Mart, which hosts fashion shows throughout the year.

T EXAS' WESTERN HERITAGE is primarily kept alive by Texans themselves, who proudly drink Lone Star Beer and sport 10-gallon hats, dust-filled ban- danas, and oversize belt buckles. One of the state's all-time-great folk heroes is the late Hondo Crouch (LEFT), who was once the owner and self-proclaimed mayor of Luckenbach, Texas, a tiny town located south of Dallas near San Antonio.

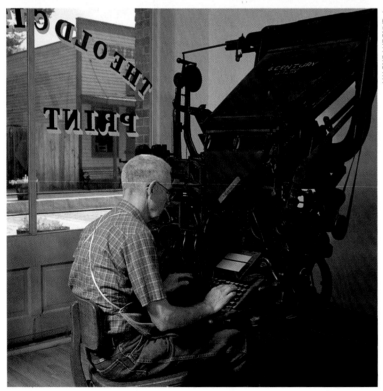

AN INVALUABLE PICTURE of life in the second half of the 1800s, Old City Park is a priceless collection of 19th-century houses, shops, and other structures, many of which feature period furnishings and craft demonstrations. The buildings, which were relocated to the park from various sites around North Texas and painstakingly restored, include (CLOCKWISE FROM TOP LEFT) a covered wagon and rough cabin; the Queen Anne-style George House, built by David George as a wedding present for his wife in 1900; a detached log kitchen, where Virginia Jackson prepares food as it was cooked 150 years ago; and a print shop and bookstore, where Richard Mauk fills visitors' orders on an 1885 job press. A turn-of-the-century business district rounds out Old City Park's walk through local history (OPPOSITE).

DALLAS

DALLAS MAY BE A COSMO-politan city, but it's still a Texas town. These images of western wear evoke the spirit of the Lone Star State that lives deep in the hearts and minds of its people.

A TRADITION BORN IN 1981, the Ranch Rodeo draws teams from working ranches in and around Dallas each Memorial Day to showcase their talents.

156 DALLAS

AS THEY RIDE OFF INTO THE sunset each evening, Texas cowboys take pleasure in knowing that a hard day's work is behind them.

▲ DONOVAN REESE

BRIGHT FLOWERS, BIG CITY:
A glance at the skyline over
a hillside coated with Indian paint-
brush reveals the scope of this
world-class city.

PROFILES IN EXCELLENCE

A LOOK AT THE CORPORATIONS, BUSINESSES, PROFESSIONAL GROUPS, AND COMMUNITY SERVICE ORGANIZATIONS THAT HAVE MADE THIS BOOK POSSIBLE. THEIR STORIES—OFFERING AN INFORMAL CHRONICLE OF THE LOCAL BUSINESS COMMUNITY—ARE ARRANGED ACCORDING TO THE DATE THEY WERE ESTABLISHED IN THE DALLAS AREA.

ABT EXECUTIVE SUITES ✱ ADLETA AND POSTON, REALTORS ✱ AT&T ✱ BAYLOR UNIVERSITY MEDICAL CENTER AND BAYLOR HEALTH CARE SYSTEM ✱ BRINKLEY SARGENT ARCHITECTS ✱ BRINK'S HOME SECURITY, INC. ✱ BYRNE JOHNSON INC. ✱ CANMAX INC. ✱ CapRock COMMUNICATIONS CORPORATION ✱ CARRINGTON COLEMAN SLOMAN & BLUMENTHAL L.L.P. ✱ CHAMPION PARTNERS, LTD. ✱ CHICAGO TITLE INSURANCE COMPANY ✱ CH2M HILL ✱ CLUB CORPORATION INTERNATIONAL (CLUBCORP) ✱ COLUMBIA HEALTHCARE CORPORATION, NORTH TEXAS DIVISION ✱ CORRIGAN REAL ESTATE SERVICES ✱ CRESCENT REAL ESTATE EQUITIES COMPANY ✱ DALLAS AREA RAPID TRANSIT ✱ DALLAS COUNTY COMMUNITY COLLEGE DISTRICT ✱ DALLAS THEOLOGICAL SEMINARY ✱ DARLING INTERNATIONAL ✱ RICHARD DRUMMOND DAVIS, ARCHITECT ✱ DDB NEEDHAM DALLAS

✱ DESIGN QUORUM ✱ DOCTORS HOSPITAL ✱ EL CHICO RESTAURANTS, INC. ✱ FAISON-STONE, INC. ✱ GRACE PRESBYTERIAN VILLAGE ✱ HALL FINANCIAL GROUP, INC. ✱ HEARTPLACE ✱ HICKS, MUSE, TATE & FURST INCORPORATED ✱ HILB, ROGAL AND HAMILTON COMPANY OF DALLAS ✱ JACKSON WALKER L.L.P. ✱ KAISER PERMANENTE ✱ KIMBERLY-CLARK CORPORATION ✱ KPMG PEAT MARWICK LLP ✱ KYNG-FM "YOUNG COUNTRY®" ✱ THE L&B GROUP ✱ LOCKWOOD GREENE ✱ MCI COMMUNICATIONS CORP. ✱ MCKESSON CORPORATION ✱ MRS BAIRD'S BAKERIES, INC. ✱ NATIONSBANK ✱ NEIMAN MARCUS ✱ NORTHPARK CENTER ✱ PARK PLACE MOTORCARS ✱ PRESBYTERIAN VILLAGE NORTH ✱ RAPP COLLINS WORLDWIDE ✱ THE REAL ESTATE COUNCIL ✱ REES ASSOCIATES, INC. ✱ ROCKWELL AVIONICS & COMMUNICATIONS ✱ RUSHMORE FINANCIAL GROUP ✱ SOUTHERN METHODIST UNIVERSITY ✱ STRASBURGER & PRICE, L.L.P. ✱ SUMMERFIELD SUITES HOTEL ✱ TEXAS WOMAN'S UNIVERSITY ✱ TURNER CONSTRUCTION COMPANY ✱ UICI ✱ THE UNIVERSITY OF DALLAS ✱ UPTOWN REALTORS ✱ U.S. RISK INSURANCE GROUP, INC. ✱ WINSTEAD SECHREST & MINICK P.C.

1887-1964

1887
JACKSON WALKER L.L.P.

1901
TEXAS WOMAN'S UNIVERSITY

1903
BAYLOR UNIVERSITY MEDICAL CENTER AND
BAYLOR HEALTH CARE SYSTEM

1907
NEIMAN MARCUS

1911
SOUTHERN METHODIST UNIVERSITY

1915
KPMG PEAT MARWICK LLP

1923
DDB NEEDHAM DALLAS

1924
DALLAS THEOLOGICAL SEMINARY

1928
MRS BAIRD'S BAKERIES, INC.

1939
STRASBURGER & PRICE, L.L.P.

1940
EL CHICO RESTAURANTS, INC.

1951
ROCKWELL AVIONICS & COMMUNICATIONS

1956
THE UNIVERSITY OF DALLAS

1957
CLUB CORPORATION
INTERNATIONAL (CLUBCORP)

1959
DOCTORS HOSPITAL

1961
GRACE PRESBYTERIAN VILLAGE

1962
HEARTPLACE

JACKSON WALKER L.L.P.

HE FIRM, TRACING ITS ROOTS TO 1887, HAS CHANGED DRAMATIcally throughout the past century, expanding until it became known in 1958 as Jackson, Walker, Winstead, Cantwell & Miller, and more recently as Jackson Walker L.L.P., with five offices throughout Texas. Over the years, however, one thing hasn't changed: the firm's commitment to helping the business and civic communities of the cities in which its offices are located.

Today, Jackson Walker is one of the oldest and largest Texas-based law firms with one of the region's most distinguished legal traditions. The continual development of a broad base of practice areas has enabled the firm to attract a diverse group of domestic and international clients. The firm offers expertise in virtually every area of the law through a strong regional base of over 170 attorneys in Dallas, Fort Worth, Houston, San Antonio, and Austin.

Since opening its doors, Jackson Walker has helped create and sustain the leading industries in Texas from the early days of railroads, banking, oil and gas, and newspapers. The firm broadened its scope at mid-century to include insurance, broadcasting, and aviation, and today offers additional expertise in litigation, finance, corporate and securities, employee benefits and executive compensation, energy, environmental, estate planning and administration, health care, labor and employment, real estate, tax, transportation, bankruptcy, intellectual property, and international law.

By continuing to expand its practice areas, Jackson Walker has become a full-service firm representing individuals, public and private corporations, estates, trusts, and partnerships, ranging in size from start-up operations to Fortune 500 companies.

Recognizing that the demands of companies headquartered in this region have assumed international proportions, Jackson Walker was one of the founding members of Globalaw, a worldwide network of law firms throughout the United States and over 55 countries. These affiliates are a major presence in each of their markets, thus extending the excellence in service and business standards that are reflected by Jackson Walker.

As part of the firm's commitment to excellence, a common characteristic stands out: a focus on practical, cost-effective solu-

JACKSON WALKER L.L.P.: TRADITION, DIVERSITY, AND QUALITY LEGAL SERVICES FOR MORE THAN 100 YEARS

◄ DAVID BLACK

tions to legal problems that add value and emphasize what works for clients based on the highest professional standards. "Jackson Walker played an important role in making The Ballpark in Arlington a reality," says Tom Schieffer, president of The Texas Rangers Baseball Club. "From the initial negotiations with the city through the project's completion, the firm's legal expertise and commitment were crucial to the successful completion of The Ballpark. In addition to being a valuable resource and business partner, Jackson Walker has made a difference in our community through its involvement in numerous civic and charitable activities."

The firm's business success is mirrored by a commitment to charitable and public service causes. While continuing to provide superior legal representation, Jackson Walker has always encouraged its attorneys and employees to be involved in the community. Numerous individuals in the firm have established a long-standing tradition of serving as representatives of city, state, and federal government or as members of the boards of civic, charitable, and trade organizations. "Over the years, Jackson Walker has understood the importance of being a good corporate citizen to the community," says Deedie Rose, president of the board of trustees of the Dallas Museum of Art. "And they continue to make a major difference through their support of the Dallas Museum of Art."

I N 1901, THE TOWN OF DENTON, JUST TO THE NORTH OF DALLAS, consisted of vast ranches and little else. But forward-thinking Texas legislators, long committed to building a school that would "prepare women for the industries of the age," decided

Denton would be home to the College of Industrial Arts.

As Dallas has grown, over the years, into a major metropolis, Denton has been transformed into a burgeoning city. And the College of Industrial Arts, which opened its campus in 1901 with 186 students and 14 teachers, is now Texas Woman's University (TWU). The institution boasts 9,800 undergraduate and graduate students—of which 9 percent are men—and 500 full-time and 200 adjunct faculty plus staff members, for a total of 1,200 employees and an annual budget of $80 million. It is the largest state-supported school primarily for women in the United States.

FROM LIBERAL ARTS TO PRE-MED

The TWU campus is a mixture of the quaint—Georgian architecture of columns, pediments, cupolas, and domes—and the modern, which includes a 23-story dormitory high-rise and a new, 186,000-square-foot Movement Sciences Complex.

Courses of study at the university include a broad spectrum of disciplines—ranging from sociology to dental hygiene to textiles—and degrees are offered at bachelor's, master's, and doctoral levels. TWU's Institute of Health Sciences is nationally recognized as a leader in the fields of nursing, occupational therapy, and physical therapy. The university remains abreast of modern developments by cultivating corporate and business partnerships, which play a critical role in providing access to resources and technology.

TWU has a long tradition of preparing the future teachers of Texas. In recent years, the school became one of only 20 in the country to introduce the Reading Recovery Program. This program teaches educators how to identify at-risk first graders and target them for special tutoring. TWU's Spanish version of the program also is used by other schools in the Southwest.

Community outreach, from free health care to literacy for children, is a long-standing TWU tradition. For example, MCARES—the university's mobile van (with the help of the Mattel Foundation)—serves children at five Head Start sites in Dallas to improve their access to health care, including screenings, immunizations, and health education.

The emphasis TWU has placed on academics is demonstrated in the 3.3 grade point average of the student athletes attending on athletic scholarships. It is important also to note that TWU's gymnastics team is the four-time NCAA Division II national champion. The average student age is 31, as many of the women return to school determined to complete their education after beginning families and careers. The campus environment supports women with children, from the availability of day care to after-school programs. The Denton Independent School District also provides transportation to area elementary, middle, and high schools.

"I view with pride the dedication that this university has to its mission," says Dr. Carol D. Surles, the third TWU woman president and the first African-American to hold the post. "We welcome all students who choose to learn and live in our unique environment. They, like our faculty and staff, experience our vital and vibrant mission: to educate and empower primarily women. The momentum is ours as we grow and look forward to new challenges ahead."

RONDA CORLEY

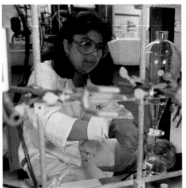

CHAD WINDHAM

RONDA CORLEY

DALLAS THEOLOGICAL SEMINARY

N 1921, LEWIS SPERRY CHAFER HAD A VISION OF A NEW KIND OF school to train students for the ministry: "The major study should be centered on the Bible," Chafer wrote in detailing the focus a new school should maintain. Three years later, on October 1, 1924, the first 13 students of what is known today as Dallas Theological Seminary met in a leased apartment building in downtown Dallas.

by sending forth ministers into the churches and communities. Since the school's founding, some 8,000 graduates have gone on to serve as presidents

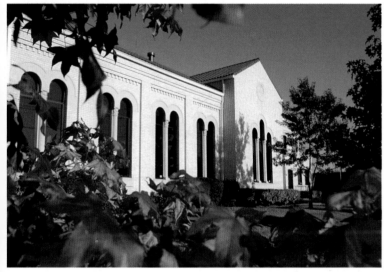

Today, the seminary is housed on a lush, landscaped, 17-acre campus in a village of 20 red-tile-roofed buildings on the outskirts of downtown Dallas near Baylor University Hospital. The 1,500 students, representing 50 states and 42 countries, learn from 80 of the most respected instructors in the world.

Since 1994, the nondenominational, nonprofit seminary has been headed by Charles R. Swindoll, its fourth president. Known to hundreds of thousands from his 18-year-old daily syndicated radio broadcast, *Insight for Living*, as well as through his best-selling books, Swindoll has guided the seminary to its next level of success by attracting a world-class faculty to conduct the school's five degree programs, including its doctoral programs.

LEARNING TO TEACH AND PREACH

The seminary contributes to the city of Dallas in the same manner as it impacts the world at large—

of 88 schools, deans of 43 schools, and 548 faculty members across the United States; 77 percent are in education, churches, and para-church organizations; and 17.4 percent are in secular occupations. Current students may be found working in churches or serving as volunteers in Dallas-area civic and nonprofit organizations.

While the school remains contemporary in its approach to biblical application, the seminary's course of study is rooted in the

Bible; as a result, ancient Hebrew and Greek remain a core part of the four-year Th.M. degree. There is no better example of this dual emphasis than the Center for Christian Leadership, which develops leaders with character, vision, and skill through study and faith in the Bible. Similarly, Dallas Theological Seminary's master of arts degree in corporate chaplaincy is the only one of its kind, combining biblical and theological studies with practical workplace relationships.

Many facets of the seminary are open to the public, including the large and remarkably specialized Turpin Library, the noncredit Center for Biblical Studies courses, and many continuing education programs. By opening its campus to the public and by bringing top scholars and diligent Bible students from around the country and the world to the city, Dallas Theological Seminary has been an important part of Dallas' spiritual life for nearly 75 years.

"Dallas Seminary is a place where God is manifested in significant ways, shaping and equipping students for a lifetime of ministry," says Swindoll. "For this reason and many more, we are honored to call Dallas home."

CLOCKWISE FROM TOP LEFT: THE MITCHELL MINISTRIES CENTER ADDS BEAUTY TO THE 17-ACRE CAMPUS.

THE SUN RISES OVER WALVOORD STUDENT CENTER.

AUTUMN LEAVES FRAME THE TOWER OF CHAFER CHAPEL ON THE CAMPUS OF DALLAS THEOLOGICAL SEMINARY.

PRESIDENT CHARLES R. SWINDOLL TALKS WITH A GROUP OF STUDENTS ON CAMPUS.

BAYLOR UNIVERSITY MEDICAL CENTER AND BAYLOR HEALTH CARE SYSTEM

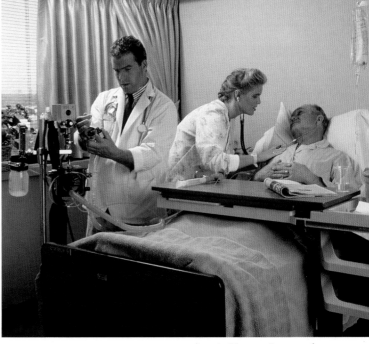

BAYLOR IS A FAMILIAR AND RESPECTED NAME IN TEXAS, APPEARING on many Texas institutions. And two of those institutions—Baylor University Medical Center and Baylor Health Care System—have emerged as leaders in the new world of American health care.

The Baylor story is as big as the story of Texas itself, and Baylor's roots in Dallas go back to the turn of the century. In 1900, a young physician named Charles McDaniel Rosser believed Dallas was large enough to support its own school of medicine. He met with opposition, though, from those who were not convinced the town, which in those days still had livestock wandering the streets, could sustain a school.

BAYLOR'S MISSION IS A COMMITMENT TO QUALITY PATIENT CARE, MEDICAL EDUCATION, RESEARCH, AND COMMUNITY SERVICE AS AN EXTENSION OF ITS CHRISTIAN MINISTRY (TOP).

SINCE ITS HUMBLE BEGINNINGS IN 1903, BAYLOR UNIVERSITY MEDICAL CENTER (BUMC) HAS ATTRACTED NATIONALLY RECOGNIZED MEDICAL TALENT TO ITS STAFF AND TO DALLAS, INCLUDING MANY OF THE FIRST SPECIALISTS IN DALLAS (BOTTOM).

The doubters fought his proposal every step of the way; but with the help of the pastor of the First Baptist Church of Dallas, Dr. George W. Truett, and wealthy benefactors, the 25-bed Texas Baptist Memorial Sanitarium opened in a converted 14-room house on Junius Street in 1903. The hospital expanded in 1909 after an adjacent five-story building was completed, and in 1921, the teaching hospital was renamed Baylor Hospital to emphasize its relationship with Baylor University in Waco.

A LEGACY OF ATTRACTING NOTABLE PHYSICIANS

Since its humble beginnings in 1903, Baylor University Medical Center (BUMC) has attracted nationally recognized medical talent to its staff and to Dallas, including many of the first specialists in Texas. Among them are counted J.B. "Daddy" Shelmire, the city's first dermatologist, also said to be the first Dallas physician to have a microscope in his office; J.M. Martin, considered the father of radiology in the Southwest; James T. Mills, the first plastic surgeon in Dallas; Curtice Rosser, the city's first colon and rectal surgeon; Robert Shaw, the first thoracic surgeon in Dallas; Albert P. D'Errico, the first formally trained neurosurgeon in the Dallas area; and Ruth Jackson, the first woman in the United States to be certified by the American Board of Orthopedic Surgery. Today, BUMC's transplantation cardiology, orthopedic, and oncology programs continue to draw top medical specialists.

That legacy continues, as more than 250,000 patients come to BUMC each year seeking treatment from world-renowned specialists working within a network of hospital clinics and outpatient programs.

In all, there are nearly 3,000 licensed beds and 12,500 employees working within the Baylor network. Baylor Health Care System recently was identified as one of the top 100 integrated delivery systems in the United States.

In patient satisfaction surveys, both outpatient and inpatient consumers rated Baylor University Medical Center and many of its community hospitals the best in North Texas in quality, personalized care, doctors, and nurses. Ninety-eight percent said they would recommend Baylor University Medical Center to others. BUMC was accredited by the Joint Commission on Accreditation of Healthcare Organizations in 1996 with an "ac-creditation with commendation" rating, which only 4 percent of hospitals in the United States achieve. And *U.S. News & World Report* said BUMC was among the top in the fields of physical rehabilitation, urology, gynecology, gastroenterology, geriatrics, and ophthalmology.

The expansive medical center stays abreast of the latest technological developments to such a degree that *Health Care Informatics* magazine named BUMC's laboratory among the most advanced in computer applications in America.

MORE THAN A HOSPITAL
A commitment to service has helped build trust in Baylor for nearly a century, so it was only natural that in 1981, long before "managed care" became an industry buzzword, Baylor Health Care System (BHCS) was created. Innovation in health care was not new to Baylor: In 1929, the hospital devised the Baylor Plan, the first prepaid hospital insurance program that later became known as Blue Cross.

In 1980, Ennis Community Hospital joined BHCS, and Grapevine, Waxahachie, and Garland hospitals changed their names to become Baylor Medical Centers in Grapevine, Garland, and Ellis County. Other community hospitals followed their example and today, in addition to other hospitals built by Baylor, there are more than two dozen Baylor locations throughout North Texas, including family health centers, senior health centers, and specialized centers.

BHCS takes Baylor from being a multihospital system to a fully integrated health care delivery system that provides high-quality care.

Today, BUMC and BHCS are headed by Boone Powell Jr., who has been president and chief executive officer since 1980. He is the son of Boone Powell Sr., who first came to Baylor Hospital in 1945 as its business manager and served as administrator and CEO for 30 years. Boone Powell Jr. is committed to leading the health care system into the next century with the same success his father did with the hospital.

The Baylor story is one of conflict, courage, and accomplishment, written by people with the wisdom to learn from the past, the energy to serve the present, and the vision to face the future. As Baylor continues to create the trends in health care, the Baylor system will continue to grow and improve by adding new facilities and introducing new technologies.

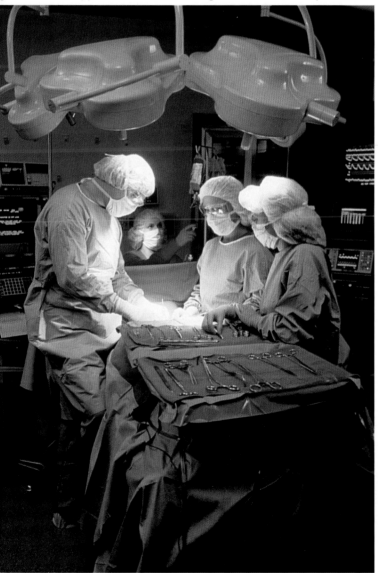

BAYLOR UNIVERSITY MEDICAL CENTER IS A MAJOR REFERRAL CENTER FOR THE SOUTHWEST AND BEYOND.

I N 1907, HERBERT MARCUS SR.; HIS SISTER, CARRIE MARCUS Neiman; and her husband, A.L. Neiman, opened the doors to what would quickly become a Dallas institution—the first Neiman Marcus store. ✱ The store, described by its owners as "an exclu-sive shopping place for fashion-able women," garnered headlines, not only for its high-end, high-quality merchandise, but also because of its geography. The fashion retailing industry was un-derstood to be centered in New York, so what were these Texas upstarts—all three still in their 20s—trying to do in Dallas?

As it turned out, Neiman Marcus changed retailing by opening up the high-fashion market beyond New York and Paris. Along the way, the store pioneered personalized gift wrap-ping, weekly fashion shows, and customer loyalty programs, and was the first retailer outside New York to advertise in national fash-ion magazines.

"Had we been located in Cleveland or Indianapolis, we wouldn't have received a fraction of the attention," says Burton Tansky, the firm's chairman and chief executive officer. "But the very fact that we were located in Texas made the difference, and Neiman Marcus was suddenly thrust into the position of being the best-known name from the state since the Alamo."

NINETY YEARS OF REVOLUTIONIZING RETAILING

"It would be better for someone else to evaluate our contribution to retailing, but I suggest that this is a unique business that was founded on the operating prin-

ciples that were expressed on opening day, September 10, 1907," says Stanley Marcus, who is the son of Herbert Marcus and who joined the company in 1926. "From that year to the present time, those principles are still the guiding beacons. This can be said about very few other businesses with similar longevity."

Herbert Marcus assured cus-tomers nearly a century ago that Neiman Marcus "will be known as the store of quality and superior values. We shall be hypercritical in our selections. Only the finest productions of the best garment makers are good enough for us. Every article of apparel shown will bear evidence—in its touches of exclusiveness, in its chic and grace and splendid finish—to the clever-est designing and the most skillful and thorough workmanship." Nearly a century after his father coined these watchwords, Stanley Marcus points out, "The integrity of Neiman Marcus has never been challenged."

There are 30 Neiman Marcus stores in the United States, and the elegant, 269,000-square-foot downtown Dallas store serves as the company's flagship. The larg-est-volume store is also in Dallas at NorthPark Center, and together

Clockwise from top left: Neiman Marcus' largest volume store is NorthPark in Dallas.

Luxury merchandise is the hall-mark of Neiman Marcus.

Neiman Marcus is known for visually striking interiors that feature an impressive art collec-tion of more than 6,000 pieces.

The first Neiman Marcus store opened in downtown Dallas on September 10, 1907.

been responsible for legendary customer service stories, including an instance when a customer had the store re-create an entire store-window Christmas display in his home.

Over the years, Stanley Marcus—who became store president in 1935, chairman and CEO in 1950, and finally chairman emeritus in 1975—conjured many attention-getting sales promotions. Among them were 30 internationally themed Fortnight expositions that involved schools, museums, and performing arts groups throughout North Texas, and the famous His and Hers gifts in the annual *Neiman Marcus Christmas Book*, with the first matching Beechcraft airplanes offered for $176,000 in 1960.

In 1996, the company launched *the book*, which combines the image of a high-fashion magazine with the selling power of a catalog. Published eight times a year, *the book* instantly set new standards in customer communication for all upscale retailers.

BUILDING FROM HISTORY FOR A PROMISING FUTURE

"Just as our past shapes us in the human arena, so too does the past influence the corporate spirit," says Tansky. "A company that stays true to its original mission while adapting to changing market conditions is a company that not only will be successful, but also will likely be a leader in its industry. Neiman Marcus has stayed true to its original mission: a tradition of merchandise leadership, a reputation for extraordinary customer service, and a commitment to constant innovation. These elements have put Neiman Marcus at the pinnacle of American retailing."

As Neiman Marcus celebrates its 90th anniversary, the company recognizes that its strong heritage is key to ensuring a successful future.

the book, PUBLISHED BY NEIMAN MARCUS, IS A PRIME EXAMPLE OF INNOVATIVE MARKETING (TOP).

A FANTASY PET PALACE IS AMONG THE MORE UNUSUAL OFFERINGS IN THE *Neiman Marcus Christmas Book* (BOTTOM).

with a third store at Prestonwood Mall, each location is a popular destination for locals and visitors alike. New locations in Honolulu and Coral Gables are under way.

Significantly, the downtown Neiman Marcus store has been targeted as the anchor in an effort to invigorate retailing in the Dallas business district. City leaders have been working with Neiman Marcus executives in an effort to use the store's continuing legacy to help revitalize the area by attracting new businesses.

People are drawn to Neiman Marcus because of its philosophy of exceeding the customers' expectations. Sales associates become familiar with their customers and build long-term relationships. Some of these associations have

OUTHERN METHODIST UNIVERSITY'S PARTNERSHIP WITH Dallas dates back to 1911, when a group of citizens pledged land and money to help establish the university on a prairie site just five miles north of downtown. From this vantage point, as the turn of the century approaches, SMU "finds itself with unique opportunities because Dallas increasingly is becoming a gateway to the global community," says SMU President R. Gerald Turner.

Since opening in 1915, SMU has grown to include 75 buildings on 163 acres. But its outreach—like that of Dallas—extends far beyond the boundaries of its parklike campus of collegiate neo-Georgian buildings. Nonsectarian in its teaching, SMU includes six degree-granting schools, offering a comprehensive education centered in the liberal arts and interwoven with professional and graduate studies. A new Strategic Plan, introduced in 1996, outlines SMU's direction for the next millennium.

AN INTERNATIONAL FUTURE

And a far-reaching direction it is. The university's goal is to prepare students for the global society they are inheriting by incorporating an international dimension into academic programs and campus life. Toward that end, a new interdisciplinary major has been introduced in international studies. Foreign language programs are being expanded, most recently with the addition of Chinese to the curriculum. And opportunities for study abroad are being enhanced. With programs throughout Europe and in Mexico, Japan, and Australia, SMU ranks ninth among comparable universities in the number of students who study abroad. Foreign students make up more than 5 percent of SMU's enrollment of 9,000, and efforts are under way to recruit more students from such areas as the Pacific Rim and Latin America.

The university contributes its expertise to Dallas and the region through several specialized centers, among them the John Goodwin Tower Center for Political Studies, which focuses on international issues, and the new Center for Pacific Rim Legal Studies in the School of Law. Another new center, the Cary M. Maguire Center for Ethics and Public Responsibility, engages business, professional, civic, and church leaders in an ongoing dialogue regarding ethical issues of the city, region, and world. To increase understanding of the history and cultures of the American Southwest, SMU has opened the Clements Center for Southwest Studies, offering under-graduate and graduate programs, sponsoring seminars, and producing major publications on the region. The center draws upon special resources such as the SMU-in-Taos program at Fort Burgwin in New Mexico. The summer campus offers classes in the humanities, sciences, and arts, and includes an archaeological dig of a 13th-century Anasazi Indian pueblo.

The diversity of SMU's student body itself provides a fertile training ground for understanding the world's cultural, social, and political issues. Minority students make up about 20 percent of total enrollment, compared with only 9 percent 10 years ago. Although

CLOCKWISE FROM TOP: FOUNDED IN 1911, SMU OPENED IN 1915 WITH 706 STUDENTS—MORE THAN TWICE THE NUMBER EXPECTED.

THE PARKLIKE CAMPUS OF 163 ACRES IS JUST FIVE MILES NORTH OF DOWNTOWN DALLAS. SMU ENJOYS A CLOSE RELATIONSHIP WITH THE METROPLEX.

DALLAS HALL, SMU'S FIRST BUILDING, WAS NAMED IN HONOR OF AREA RESIDENTS WHO PROVIDED LAND AND MONEY TO HELP ESTABLISH THE UNIVERSITY.

60 percent of SMU undergraduates list home addresses in Texas, the university also enrolls students from all 50 states and some 95 foreign countries.

The Inter-Community Experience (ICE) Program is an excellent example of the way education and community service intersect at SMU. Under the program, SMU professors offer urban studies

ternships at area churches. And increasingly, countless volunteer service projects are getting students off campus and into the neighborhoods of Dallas, where they combine their classroom instruction with practical experience. Some 2,000 students perform volunteer work each year through programs such as Community Service Day and Alternative Spring Break, which takes students to areas ranging from inner-city homeless shelters to Native American reservations.

THE DALLAS COMMUNITY AS CAMPUS

SMU's Strategic Plan also calls for increasing its historically strong ties to the Dallas community. The relationship has never been closer. Many of the city's major corporations provide mentors to students in SMU's Edwin L. Cox School of Business, or participate in the co-op program of the School of Engineering and Applied Science. The School of Law's legal clinics provide free legal representation for low-income area residents. Numerous other partnerships link SMU students and professors with projects at area medical schools and health care centers. Perkins School of Theology sponsors in-

courses not on campus, but at an inner-city community center to bring students face-to-face with issues being discussed. Students in the classes provide daily tutoring to neighborhood children. Of their own volition, some students live in the neighborhood in a house they and other volunteers built with the help of Habitat for Humanity. Not only do ICE participants learn firsthand about urban issues, but the children benefit from the one-on-one attention provided by the SMU students, who also introduce them to the possibilities of a college education. Under SMU's Strategic Plan, the university will expand student opportunities for service learning.

Other contributions to the Dallas community include the Meadows Museum, which houses one of the finest collections of Spanish art outside of Spain and is open to the public. The Meadows School of the Arts sponsors more than 400 concerts, performances, and exhibits each year. Programs such as the Willis M. Tate Distinguished Lecture Series bring world-renowned speakers to the campus and community.

TRANSCENDING CAMPUS BOUNDARIES

Recognizing that many older-than-average students need educational resources closer to home and work, SMU has extended its offerings both north and south: The School of Engineering and Applied Science offers programs in the Telecom Corridor of Richardson and in Houston; the Division of Continuing Education has opened a North Dallas Education Center; the Edwin L. Cox School of Business is offering graduate courses in Plano; and the Perkins School of Theology sponsors an extension program in the Houston/Galveston area.

Just as Dallas leaders acted to secure a major university for their city, SMU aims to strengthen the community by educating those who will lead as professionals and as citizens of this region and beyond. SMU's more than 70,000 alumni hold many of the most influential positions in a variety of professions, not only in Dallas, but throughout the world.

Steeped in a rich and colorful history, SMU moves into the new millennium with a singular vision: to enhance its students' intellectual, social, moral, and religious development by capitalizing on its dynamic relationship with Dallas. At the dedication of Dallas Hall, the university's first building, then President Robert S. Hyer was asked when the university would be completed. He replied, "After the city of Dallas is completed."

SMALL CLASSES PROVIDE STUDENTS WITH PERSONAL ATTENTION, MENTORING OPPORTUNITIES, AND HANDS-ON RESEARCH EXPERIENCE (TOP).

SMU'S STUDENT BODY OF MORE THAN 9,000 INCLUDES STUDENTS FROM ALL 50 STATES, THE DISTRICT OF COLUMBIA, AND 95 FOREIGN COUNTRIES (BOTTOM).

KPMG Peat Marwick LLP

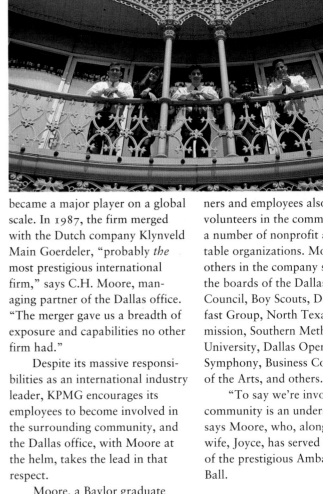

HE FIGURES ARE IMPRESSIVE: 77,000 EMPLOYEES, 147 COUNTRIES, and $8.1 billion in worldwide revenues. Without a doubt, KPMG Peat Marwick is the premier Big Six international accounting firm, with 400 more offices around the globe than its closest rival, and a client list that includes 2,500 of the world's top companies.

But the whole is only as strong as the sum of its parts—in this case, its regional offices—and the Dallas office of KPMG is regarded as one of the foremost in the international partnership. It's in Dallas that the company recently opened its new firmwide, 50,000-square-foot business processing center.

Because it's located in an area rich with high-tech corporations, the 1,000-employee Dallas practice is known and respected for its strong technical and innovative capabilities. And it's been that way for nearly a century.

HISTORIC
TRANSFORMATION

James Marwick and Roger S. Mitchell founded Peat Marwick in England in 1897 as a public accounting firm. Gradually, the company spread throughout the United States—the Dallas office opened in 1915—and eventually became a major player on a global scale. In 1987, the firm merged with the Dutch company Klynveld Main Goerdeler, "probably *the* most prestigious international firm," says C.H. Moore, managing partner of the Dallas office. "The merger gave us a breadth of exposure and capabilities no other firm had."

Despite its massive responsibilities as an international industry leader, KPMG encourages its employees to become involved in the surrounding community, and the Dallas office, with Moore at the helm, takes the lead in that respect.

Moore, a Baylor graduate who joined the Dallas office of Peat Marwick in 1963, points out that the firm's roots run deep in the Metroplex. Not only does KPMG serve such local international leaders as JC Penney, Hunt Oil, Electronic Data Systems, Brinker International, Frito Lay, Caltex, NCH, and FINA on a professional basis, but the part-ners and employees also work as volunteers in the community for a number of nonprofit and charitable organizations. Moore and others in the company serve on the boards of the Dallas Citizens Council, Boy Scouts, Dallas Breakfast Group, North Texas Commission, Southern Methodist University, Dallas Opera, Dallas Symphony, Business Committee of the Arts, and others.

"To say we're involved in the community is an understatement," says Moore, who, along with his wife, Joyce, has served as cochair of the prestigious Ambassadors Ball.

THE LOB
TRANSFORMATION

For such a large company, KPMG is uniquely flexible in the way it does business. Four years ago, under the guidance of Jon C. Madonna, the former U.S. chairman, KPMG Peat Marwick underwent a firmwide transformation, leaving behind traditional opera-

TOP: AMONG THE MEMBERS OF KPMG's STAFF COUNCIL ARE (FROM LEFT) JAMES LEE, MARIA GANT, JEFF HOFFMAN, TIFFANY GREEN, AND GREG HALL. NOT PICTURED ARE STEPHANIE CARSON, ANNA CONLEY, AND LEAH HAGMAN.

BOTTOM: WITH THE INTRODUCTION OF FUTURE DIRECTIONS, THE FIRM UNITED ITS DOMESTIC AND INTERNATIONAL OPERATIONS, LINKING TOP PROFESSIONALS IN THE FIELD TO DELIVER THE BEST CLIENT SERVICES KPMG CAN PROVIDE.

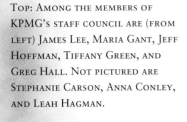

tional methods and adopting a never before attempted strategy of market-focused professional services.

"Before, there was a network of 100 local offices that operated under more of a franchise mentality," Moore says. In March 1992, the KPMG Future Directions initiative was introduced. "The restructuring was significant, but I can tell you it was a result of listening to our clients," Moore says. "Again and again, we heard the clients ask for more people who knew their businesses and their industries. So we, in effect, reinvented the firm. Our entire focus is on the client's line of business . . . It's completely different from the way the competition operates."

KPMG's transformation created teams in geographic areas. These teams are made up of industry-trained partners who are aligned into five industry-specific lines of business (LOBs) to deliver value-added services. These LOBs include manufacturing, retailing, and distribution; financial services; information, communications, and entertainment; health care and life sciences; and public services. As a result of the change, KPMG clients understand risk, plan strategically, and continually improve the way they operate, not simply to stay in business today, but to thrive as an industry leader tomorrow.

With the introduction of Future Directions, the firm united its domestic and international operations, linking top professionals in the field to deliver the best client services KPMG can provide. "It has been overwhelmingly gratifying to see the spirit of teamwork taking hold throughout our network worldwide," Moore says.

With integrated teams concentrating on a single LOB, training is more important than ever before. In response, KPMG implemented a business school for all those participating in the LOBs.

Professionals from all levels attend seminars presented by the top speakers in the field and gain experience firsthand by serving in their particular industries in the field.

"We're learning from each other as well as the speakers," says Moore. "We realize our assets go home every night—our

assets are not the bricks and mortar that people can see around the world; our assets are our people."

Working with the biggest and best companies in the world, and serving the charitable organizations of the city, KPMG Peat Marwick enriches all involved—employees, clients, and the communities in which it operates.

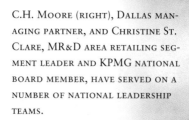

C.H. MOORE (RIGHT), DALLAS MANAGING PARTNER, AND CHRISTINE ST. CLARE, MR&D AREA RETAILING SEGMENT LEADER AND KPMG NATIONAL BOARD MEMBER, HAVE SERVED ON A NUMBER OF NATIONAL LEADERSHIP TEAMS.

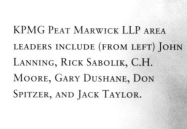

KPMG PEAT MARWICK LLP AREA LEADERS INCLUDE (FROM LEFT) JOHN LANNING, RICK SABOLIK, C.H. MOORE, GARY DUSHANE, DON SPITZER, AND JACK TAYLOR.

W HO NAMED 7-ELEVEN FOR THE SOUTHLAND ICE COMPANY? WHO introduced Dr Pepper and its familiar "10, 2, and 4" jingle to the world? Who coined the word "Metroplex" to describe the Dallas/Fort Worth region? One advertising agency is responsible for creat-

ing these and hundreds of other well-known images and words—DDB Needham Dallas.

Operating with a philosophy of Better Ideas Better Results,™ the Dallas office of the world's second-largest advertising agency network has created lasting impressions for American Airlines, Borden, *The Dallas Morning News*, Dillard Department Stores, Embassy Suites Hotels, Environ-

The more he learns about things like snakes and weasels and *rats and leeches*, the less likely he is to hang out with them after school.

mental Protection Agency (EPA), FOOTACTION USA, Frito-Lay, Imperial Sugar, Interstate Batteries, the McIlhenny Company (makers of Tabasco® brand pepper sauce), Mrs Baird's Bakeries, Phillips Petroleum Company,

and dozens of other nationally recognized corporations.

The advertising created by the 250 professionals at DDB Needham's offices and studios are seen and read by millions worldwide. In 1996, the Dallas agency was honored at every major creative show, including the International Advertising Festival in Cannes, the Art Directors Club, the American Advertising Awards, and the CLIO Awards. And the agency was the only DDB Needham office of 202 in 80 countries to be so recognized.

THE RIGHT WAY, RIGHT AWAY

The company that has grown to become one of the Southwest's largest advertising agencies was founded in 1913 in Oklahoma City by Shelley E. Tracy and Raymond P. Locke. The agency, known as Tracy-Locke until 1996, quickly gained a reputation for having the ability to take a brand and sell it the right way, right away, to the right consumer. The Borden Company was the first of the agency's major clients.

In 1923, the burgeoning agency moved to Dallas, adding Dr Pepper to the client list. In 1937, Morris L. Hite joined the firm and greatly expanded the client list, recruiting such blue-chip clients as Haggar Slacks, Imperial Sugar, Mrs Baird's Bakeries, and Textan and Geophysical Services—the forerunner to Texas Instruments. It was Hite who named Southland Ice Company's convenience stores 7-Eleven, reflecting the stores' operating hours of 7 a.m. to 11 p.m. Hite recently became only the second advertising executive from the Southwest to be named to the American Advertising Federation's Hall of Fame.

In 1992, determining that its future success would be linked to its ability to deliver advertising services on a worldwide basis, Tracy-Locke joined the DDB Needham Worldwide Communications Group Inc. Today, the Dallas office is one of the driving forces in advertising throughout the Southwest, and its client tenure is double the industry average.

The full-service agency offers a wide array of marketing communication services. Its interactive communications division—DDB Interactive—is critically acclaimed as one of the top Internet resources in the world, and its broadcast production group—Teleworks—is among the largest in the Southwest. The firm's SpotPlus media buying service purchased more than $350 million in media in 1996, making it one of the largest centralized spot buying organizations in the country.

EXTENDING CREATIVITY INTO THE COMMUNITY

As an outreach to the community that has supported the agency's

growth, DDB Needham Dallas annually donates the talents of its staff to more than 20 community groups, including the Boy Scouts of America, the American Heart Association, the Greater Dallas Chamber of Commerce, the Dallas Independent School District, and the Retina Foundation.

In 1996, the agency adopted the Colonial Learning Center for the school year—not to provide it with advertising or marketing services, but to donate supplies and tutoring for the underprivileged children who attend the school.

"Many clients today look to advertising agencies for expertise in three key areas: providing sound, strategic thinking that will help further differentiate their brands; producing effective advertising that delivers results; and executing campaigns on a global basis," says Jake Schroepfer, president and chief executive officer of the Dallas agency.

"At DDB Needham Dallas, we're committed to delivering better ideas that yield better results in the marketplace," says Schroepfer. "And we've assembled a team of professionals who are leaders in the Dallas community, as well as leaders in the advertising community, to ensure we fulfill our commitment."

OPERATING WITH A PHILOSOPHY OF BETTER IDEAS FOR BETTER RESULTS, DDB NEEDHAM DALLAS, PART OF THE WORLD'S SECOND-LARGEST ADVERTISING AGENCY NETWORK, HAS CREATED LASTING IMPRESSIONS FOR (CLOCKWISE FROM TOP) AMERICAN AIRLINES, *The Dallas Morning News*, MCILHENNY COMPANY (MAKERS OF TABASCO® BRAND PEPPER SAUCE), PHILLIPS PETROLEUM COMPANY, AND DOZENS OF OTHER NATIONALLY RECOGNIZED CORPORATIONS.

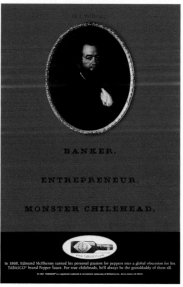

EW THINGS IN TEXAS ARE AS FAMILIAR OR AS COMFORTING AS A loaf of Mrs Baird's bread. Generations of Dallas residents have grown up on Mrs Baird's bakery products and have come to consider those loaves, buns, cakes, and other baked goods as sym-

bols of home.

After nearly 90 years as a family business, Mrs Baird's is facing the future with a new outlook and a new slogan: From a family business to a business with a family heritage. But no matter how things change, there are some things that Mrs Baird's will never alter.

"We have built our business based on three core values—quality, freshness, and service. And that's what we will grow the company on in the future," says Larry Wheeler, president and chief executive officer since 1995 and the first nonfamily member to serve in those capacities. "New products continue to be a strong part of our focus in the future. And we are well positioned for growth and expansion that could involve acquisitions as well as internal growth."

FROM KITCHEN STOVE TO MODERN FACTORIES
Mrs Baird's began in 1908 in the Fort Worth kitchen of Ninnie L. Baird. "Grandmother" Baird baked bread for her family in a four-burner, wood-fired stove and often gave extra loaves of her fresh bread to friends as gifts. When those friends insisted that she bake bread for them on a

regular basis, the young widow began selling her baked goods as a way to support her family.

With the help of her four sons, who delivered her bread, and her daughters, who helped with the household chores, Ninnie Baird soon outgrew her tiny stove and bought a commercial oven, paying $25 cash and the balance in bread and rolls. Her sons, who made deliveries at first on foot and later on bicycle, were swamped with orders, and the family buggy was converted into a delivery wagon. Even the family horse, Ned, was brought into the business to pull the wagon.

By 1928, with deliveries now made by motorized vehicles,

Ninnie Baird made her first expansion out of Fort Worth, opening a plant in Dallas. Ten years later, another plant was opened in Houston, and four months later the Fort Worth bread plant was constructed. The Dallas bakery, now located on Mockingbird and Central Expressway, still offers tours through the baking facility, just as it has since the day the company began baking bread there in 1952. Tours are also offered at the south Fort Worth facility.

Ninnie Baird's hardworking family systematically opened bakeries throughout Texas—from Abilene to Lubbock to San Antonio—each meeting with encour-

MRS BAIRD'S FIRST COMMERCIAL OVEN HAD THE CAPACITY FOR 40 LOAVES OF BREAD (LEFT).

MRS. NINNIE L. BAIRD FOUNDED MRS BAIRD'S BAKERIES IN 1908 (RIGHT).

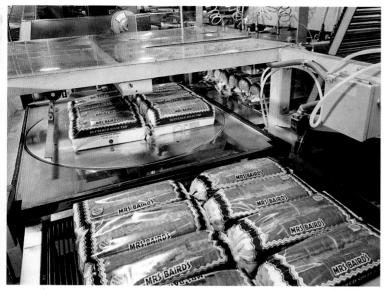

aging success. At present, the regional company has 10 production facilities and more than 3,000 employees throughout the state, baking some 150 different products.

Over the years, Mrs Baird's has been an industry leader in innovation, including establishing such landmarks as the first assembly line to automatically seal the packages and the first air-conditioned baking facility. In 1992, the new Fort Worth bakery was hailed by industry specialists as the world's most advanced bread plant.

The company product line consists of a full range of baked goods, including multiple varieties of breads and cakes. In recent years, the company has added Mrs Baird's Texas Tortillas, which met with immediate acceptance. And the introduction of Mrs Baird's Bagels in 1996 made headlines across the state.

FROM HOME BUSINESS TO MARKET FORCE
Annual sales for Mrs Baird's are more than $290 million, with 1,000 vehicles serving some 24,000 grocers, satisfying a customer base that includes most of Texas and parts of New Mexico, Oklahoma, and Louisiana.

Mrs Baird's continues to grow and prosper as it enters its second century of business and boasts several generations of Bairds in various capacities throughout the company. Janet Baird Quisenberry, general manager of the Dallas bakery, is the first woman to head a bakery since Ninnie Baird. Several grandchildren, great-grandchildren, and great-great-grandchildren of the original Mrs. Baird also work in the company.

Those family members serve with an impressive array of experienced and influential corporate officers and board members drawn from various fields. Wheeler, who spent 17 years with Pillsbury before his appointment at Mrs Baird's in May 1995, speaks for them when he says, "What sets Mrs Baird's apart is the steadfast dedication to our core values: quality, freshness, and service. We have an uncompromising commitment to those values, and we will not compromise them in order to lower costs."

That's been the Mrs Baird's way for generations, and it will be the Mrs Baird's way for generations to come.

CLOCKWISE FROM TOP LEFT: TODAY, MRS BAIRD'S BAKERIES BAKE MORE THAN 150 VARIETIES OF BREAD AND CAKE PRODUCTS.

THE DALLAS BAKERY, NOW LOCATED ON MOCKINGBIRD AND CENTRAL EXPRESSWAY, STILL OFFERS TOURS THROUGH THE BAKING FACILITY, JUST AS IT HAS SINCE THE DAY THE COMPANY BEGAN BAKING BREAD THERE IN 1952.

MRS BAIRD'S BEGAN IN 1908 IN THE FORT WORTH KITCHEN OF NINNIE L. BAIRD.

STRASBURGER & PRICE, L.L.P.

HEN A CLIENT SEEKS COUNSEL FROM THE SAME LAW FIRM FOR more than five decades, the law firm becomes a valued partner in the company's leadership team. It goes beyond being a provider of legal services and instead becomes a trusted adviser. The Dallas-based law firm of Strasburger & Price, L.L.P. has been the firm of choice for some of the largest and most prominent companies in the world. It is a relationship the partners of Strasburger & Price do not take lightly.

A LEGACY OF TRUST

Strasburger & Price was founded in 1939 by Texans Henry Strasburger and Hobert Price, law school classmates who came to Dallas after graduating from the University of Texas. Henry Strasburger was a colorful attorney, whose courtroom style is legal legend.

Hobert Price had a photographic memory that turned many court decisions in his favor with his impressive ability to instantly cite case precedents supporting his position. Together they created a charismatic combination. Throughout the years, Strasburger & Price has grown from seven lawyers to more than 180, with offices in Austin, Houston, and Mexico City, as well as in Dallas, serving some of the largest high-profile clients nationally and internationally.

The civil law practice of Strasburger & Price is comprehensive. The firm's corporate and trial law practice includes expertise in commercial litigation, corporate and securities, energy, environmental, franchising and distribution, governmental, health care, insurance litigation, intellectual property, international, labor and employment, personal injury, product liability, professional liability, real estate, and tax. When the Dallas/Fort Worth International Airport began its overdue runway expansion, it chose Strasburger & Price to contest limitation efforts by surrounding jurisdictions. Legislation authorizing the expansion was found to be constitutional, resulting in a new runway opening in 1996. As Dallas continued its boom, attracting more families and businesses for relocation, it needed more land for residential and commercial sites. Strasburger & Price was retained to acquire valuable land sites for future development in Dallas and the surrounding communities of Lewisville, Coppell, and Southlake.

Companies such as Bristol-Myers Squibb Co.; Columbia/HCA Health Care Corporation; Dallas/Fort Worth Airport; DDB Needham Dallas, Inc. (formerly Tracy-Locke); Dell Computer Corporation; General Motors Corporation; International Business Machines Corporation; Maguire/Thomas Partners; Mobil Land Development Company; Mobil Oil Corporation; NationsBank of Texas, N.A.; Nissan Diesel Motor Company, Ltd.; Rolex Watch U.S.A., Inc.; Schepps and Oak Farms Dairies, Inc.; The Southland Corporation; and Texas Commerce Bank, N.A. are but a few of the clients Strasburger & Price represents.

A LEGACY OF LEADERSHIP

As an integral part of the Dallas legal community, four members of Strasburger & Price have served as presidents of the Dallas Bar Association, and nine have

LAWYERS AT STRASBURGER & PRICE INCLUDE (FROM LEFT) MIKE JOPLIN, NEIL RAMBIN, DAVID KITNER, KELLY ALLBRITTON, AND BOB THOMAS

◀ ALEX MINOR

been elected to the prestigious American College of Trial Lawyers in recognition of their trial excellence. Others have served as directors of the State Bar of Texas and as officers of such professional organizations as the Texas Association of Defense Counsel, Federation of Insurance and Corporate Counsel, International Association of Defense Counsel, Defense Research Institute, and Product Liability Advisory Council.

With attorneys representing 33 law schools from across the country, Strasburger & Price is renowned for recruiting academic excellence. Much of the firm's reputation for unprecedented service and prestige is a result of the continuous training lawyers receive throughout their careers. New litigation attorneys participate in the Strasburger & Price Trial Academy so that junior members learn trial skills from seasoned litigators. New attorneys in business law practice areas are given comprehensive instruction in the techniques of negotiation, drafting, and examining transactions from the client's perspective. Strasburger & Price leaders learned long ago that sustained efforts to develop new attorneys create the high

caliber of professional service upon which its clients rely.

A LEGACY OF COMMUNITY INVOLVEMENT

Just as Strasburger & Price weaves itself into the fabric of the giants of industry, so too does it infuse its energies into the surrounding

Dallas community. Partners and employees of Strasburger & Price are involved in such events as the Dallas Adopt-a-School program, Genesis Women's Shelter, the Dallas "Can" Academy, Community Day, and various holiday programs. Partners and associates give their time to such nonprofit institutions as the YWCA, Ronald McDonald House, Habitat for Humanity, Make-A-Wish Foundation, Victims Outreach, Dallas Community of Churches, University of Dallas, and Communities Foundation.

For nearly 60 years, Strasburger & Price has prided itself on remaining true to the philosophical cornerstones established by its founders: develop trust, instill confidence, generate innovation, and do what is best for the client. It is a philosophy that will carry Strasburger & Price into the next century as a leader in the legal community.

THE STRASBURGER & PRICE TRAINING ACADEMY INCLUDES MOCK TRIALS AND VIDEOTAPED CROSS-EXAMINATION (TOP).

FIRST OFFICER LEGRAND BLOUNT OF DELTA AIRLINES AND MIKE BUCHANAN, ATTORNEY AT STRASBURGER & PRICE, CELEBRATE T.J'S WISH COME TRUE—A TRIP TO WALT DISNEY WORLD PROVIDED BY THE MAKE-A-WISH FOUNDATION (BOTTOM).

NOT CERTIFIED BY THE TEXAS BOARD OF LEGAL SPECIALIZATION

El Chico Restaurants, Inc.

T HE HISTORY OF THE EL CHICO SLOGAN, "NO ONE KNOWS TEX-MEX like El Chico," began in 1926, when Adelaida "Mama" Cuellar began selling enchiladas and tamales from a stand at the Kaufman County Fair in Texas. Fourteen years later, the Cuellar family opened its first El Chico restaurant in Dallas, thus beginning the era during which El Chico has become synonymous with one of the world's favorite cuisines: Tex-Mex.

By combining recipes from popular Mexican dishes with those of Texas, the Cuellars popularized a cuisine that met with immediate success. Now there are almost 100 full-service restaurants operated by El Chico and its franchisees in 14 states—including 20 in the Dallas area—with more than 4,000 employees. Those figures make El Chico one of the top two full-service Mexican food restaurant chains in the country. El Chico is now a pub-

licly traded corporation listed on the NASDAQ exchange. According to President and CEO Wallace Jones, "Each of the El Chico restaurants continues the 57-year-old tradition of serving fresh, authentic Tex-Mex dishes based on the closely guarded recipes created by Mama Cuellar and her sons: Frank, Mack, Gilbert, Alfred, and Willie Jack."

El Chico has a rich heritage. In 1964, El Chico introduced its Tex-Mex specialties to celebrities, luminaries, and visitors from around the world at New York's World's Fair. In 1966, Princess Grace of Monaco requested the Cuellars to add spice to a royal banquet in Monaco. In both 1985 and 1988, President and Mrs. Reagan requested an El Chico picnic at the White House (the only time an encore has ever been requested). In 1988, El Chico sponsored the Mexican bobsled team in the Calgary Winter Olympics. And, in 1990, El Chico served President Bush and other world leaders at the Economic Summit of Industrialized Nations in Houston.

The founding Cuellar family has had an important impact on civic affairs around the Metroplex. In 1991, the Cuellars were named the Family of the Year by the YMCA, and the family has been inducted into the Hall of Honor by the Texas Restaurant Association. The family has also been cited as Outstanding Minority Businessmen of the Year by the Interracial Council of Business Opportunities, and U.S. Secretary of Commerce Malcolm Baldrige presented the Cuellars with a spe-

cial award for exceptional accomplishment and leadership in the development of minority business in 1984. In 1996, the Dallas Independent School District honored the memory of founder Gilbert Cuellar Sr. by naming a school after the business and community leader.

Just as El Chico is often given credit for inventing the cuisine, the Dallas-based firm is reinventing the way it is presented by investing millions of dollars each year on updating and invigorating its restaurants with new decor and menu graphics, as well as modern floor plans. In addition, the company, which reported $104 million in revenues in 1996, is adding new restaurants each year in order to feed a nation hungry for authentic Tex-Mex fare.

For almost six decades, El Chico has earned a reputation for great food. As the next century approaches, El Chico's new physical image will give an increasing number of restaurants a new look to keep the image as fresh as the food. The reimaging effort, being conducted in 15 to 20 percent of the restaurants in the chain each year, is improving the atmosphere in which consumers can enjoy El Chico food. This new image program has attracted much attention and has caused many consumers to rediscover that El Chico truly is the best restaurant option for authentic Tex-Mex food. El Chico Restaurants, Inc. operates two other upscale Mexican concepts in Dallas under the names of Cantina Laredo and Casa Rosa. "El Chico Restaurants has a history rich in tradition and respect for food," says Jones, "and we intend to continue that history as we build more El Chico and Cantina Laredo restaurants in the future."

SINCE OPENING IN 1940, EL CHICO HAS BECOME SYNONYMOUS WITH ONE OF THE WORLD'S FAVORITE CUISINES: TEX-MEX (TOP).

AS THE NEXT CENTURY APPROACHES, EL CHICO'S NEW PHYSICAL IMAGE WILL GIVE AN INCREASING NUMBER OF RESTAURANTS A NEW LOOK TO KEEP THE IMAGE AS FRESH AS THE FOOD (BOTTOM).

THE UNIVERSITY OF DALLAS

HE UNIVERSITY OF DALLAS BELIEVES THAT AN EDUCATED HUMAN being possesses a universal understanding of the world and its workings. To achieve this goal, the university combines rigorous programs in the liberal arts and sciences with an innovative graduate school of business to prepare students for life and work in our changing world.

THE LIBERAL ARTS: AN EDUCATION FOR LIFE

The University of Dallas celebrated its 40th anniversary in 1996, but its traditions reach back to the roots of Western civilization. In conferring accreditation upon the university, the American Academy of Liberal Education praised the school for its "clear commitment to the highest standards of teaching."

Class size is strictly limited at both Constantin College (the undergraduate school) and Braniff Graduate School, and classes are taught only by regular faculty, 95 percent of whom hold a PhD or terminal degree in their field. Students also benefit from professional career counseling, athletics, community service activities, and work-study programs at local businesses.

DEVELOPING INSIGHTFUL, EFFECTIVE, AND ETHICAL BUSINESS LEADERS

From full-time residential studies on the main campus to distance-learning transmissions in remote areas, the Graduate School of Management (GSM) prepares students for leadership roles in business and the professions. Offering 11 MBA and 10 master of management programs with a choice of nearly 30 concentrations, GSM confers more advanced business degrees than any other institution in the Southwest.

One objective of GSM is to make sound MBA programs accessible to employed professionals. Some 75 percent of GSM students attend part-time programs on the Irving campus, at satellite campuses, or in the facilities of major employers across the Metroplex.

HIGH ACADEMIC STANDARDS, SUPERIOR PERFORMANCE

The university boasts exceptionally high acceptance rates to medical, law, and graduate schools. Incoming freshman Scholastic Aptitude Test (SAT) scores average 200 points above the national norm, and in 1988, Dallas was one of the youngest universities ever to be granted a chapter of Phi Beta Kappa. Recently, the university was cited by *Peterson's Guide* as one of the top 190 schools in the nation for science and mathematics.

A memorable experience for University of Dallas undergraduates is their semester at the Eugene Constantin Campus near Rome, Italy, where they integrate academic studies with their own observations of the cultural treasures of Europe. The curriculum also includes lecture tours throughout Italy, a 10-day trip to Greece, and opportunities for individual travel.

OPEN TO ALL

While affiliated with the Roman Catholic Church, the University of Dallas welcomes students of all beliefs and nationalities. The 1,100 undergraduates, 300 liberal arts graduate students, and 1,500 students in the Graduate School of Management together represent every region of the United States, nearly every faith, and more than 50 nations.

Located in the beautiful Las Colinas area of Irving, the university's main campus occupies the highest point of a secluded 1,000-acre holding and commands a panoramic view of the metropolitan area. Both Dallas/Fort Worth International Airport and Love Field are within a 20-minute drive.

The Dallas campus radiates from 188-foot Braniff Memorial Tower, a major landmark. Planned additions include an expansion of the Fine Arts Center, a new library, and a performing arts center, where world-class performances will draw audiences from across the region.

Young, small, and dynamic, the University of Dallas sees growth and even greater achievement and renown in its future—a realistic expectation for this outstanding institution.

CENTRALLY LOCATED IN THE BEAUTIFUL LAS COLINAS AREA OF IRVING, THE UNIVERSITY OF DALLAS CAMPUS RADIATES FROM 188-FOOT BRANIFF MEMORIAL TOWER, A MAJOR LANDMARK (LEFT).

A MEMORABLE EXPERIENCE FOR UNIVERSITY OF DALLAS UNDERGRADUATES IS THEIR SEMESTER AT THE EUGENE CONSTANTIN CAMPUS NEAR ROME, ITALY, WHERE THEY INTEGRATE ACADEMIC STUDIES WITH THEIR OWN OBSERVATIONS OF THE CULTURAL TREASURES OF EUROPE (RIGHT).

A S THE WORLD CHANGES, THE GLOBAL MARKETPLACE IS CHANGING. And Rockwell is changing right along with it. Since its inception, the Richardson-based Communication Systems Division of Rockwell Avionics & Communications has provided the U.S. military with revolutionary products, systems, and services, and has been recognized as the industry leader in very low frequency systems, radio-frequency networks, and satellite communications.

With the 1996 sale of Rockwell's Aerospace and Defense businesses (with the exception of government and military avionics and communications) to Boeing, the company entered a new phase of its history and a new realm of possibilities.

Now Rockwell is expanding its Collins brand name further into the commercial world, providing its groundbreaking products, systems, and services to public and private companies around the world. As a result of this expansion, the company projects half the business of the "new" Rockwell will be conducted on an international level.

FROM AMATEUR RADIO TO SATELLITE COMMUNICATIONS

The history of the original Collins Radio Company begins with youthful radio pioneer Arthur A. Collins, an electronics genius who began developing new methods of radio communication at an early age. The Iowa boy gained national attention at age 15 when he established radio contact with the Macmillan expedition during its scientific expedition to Greenland by using an amateur radio he built. The navy's sophisticated communications gear couldn't make contact due to atmospheric conditions, but young Collins' homemade equipment maintained contact with the explorers throughout their mission.

In 1931, Collins began making radios in the basement of his home, designing circuits, fabricating chassis wiring in components, and testing each unit. He established then, two years before he would incorporate his eight-employee company, the philosophy of building quality into each Collins product.

Collins continued to garner headlines and build his company, using innovation as a guiding principal. Among other highlights, Collins made the radios for Admiral Richard Byrd's exploration of the South Pole in 1933.

There were other milestones for Collins—for whom Collins Boulevard in Richardson is said to be named—and his fledgling Collins Radio Company. The first

ROCKWELL PROVIDES UNIQUE CAPABILITIES FOR THE U.S. NAVY'S NEW E-6A AIRCRAFT.

airborne application of a Collins radio came in 1934, when the Goodyear Tire Company's blimp, *Enterprise*, was launched with a Collins transmitter on board. In 1935, Collins invented the Auto-tune, a device that permitted rapid radio band switching and tuning; with that product, Collins entered the world of aviation, and the armed forces came calling.

In May 1951, Collins announced he was building a $1 million, 50,000-square-foot plant to build microwave equipment in an unheard of northern suburb of Dallas. At the time, Richardson was considered a remote outpost, which suited Collins just fine. His complex grew as the orders came in, and his plant came to be considered a major site for avionics and communications discoveries.

In 1960, using equipment pioneered in Richardson, the company achieved the first two-way radio voice transmission via artificial satellite, and it was in Richardson that the first photograph was transmitted between two sites—a photograph of President Eisenhower was transmitted from Richardson to Cedar Rapids.

In 1973, Collins Radio Company merged with Rockwell International Corporation, thus providing Collins and his team of scientists and engineers with unprecedented support to develop new products and systems, and to realize the firm's fullest potential.

ROCKWELL AVIONICS & COMMUNICATIONS

Today there are some 800 people, nearly half of them engineers, working at Rockwell's sprawling Communication Systems Division in Richardson. The two buildings constitute 487,000 square feet of high-tech laboratory space where research and development for the world continues.

The Communication Systems Division is expanding its domain into the private sector in a number of fields directly related to the innovations the company first pioneered for the military. With solid leadership positions in communications, navigation, and surveillance products, the company is taking a leading role in the development of next-generation air traffic management systems and is aggressively entering markets in Russia, the Commonwealth of Independent States, China, and other countries. The company is also capitalizing on its reputation as the leader in ground-based and satellite communications, becoming a key supplier of communications and data management systems for industrial users, as well as the military.

Additionally, the company continues to develop global positioning system technology, which Rockwell developed for the military and successfully introduced into a number of commercial arenas.

Rockwell's Richardson campus continues to provide solutions to the U.S. defense industry, but remains focused on the challenge of exploring new industries within the expanding global marketplace. Yet in the light of the changing world, Rockwell's Communication Systems Division charges, "Deliver the best . . . Commit to better"—an indication that the values on which Arthur Collins founded the company in the 1930s will remain with the new Rockwell Avionics & Communications well into the next century.

ROCKWELL'S 487,000-SQUARE-FOOT FACILITY IS LOCATED IN THE NORTHEAST CORNER OF RICHARDSON'S TELECOM CORRIDOR (TOP).

ROCKWELL'S SEVERAL CHANNEL ANTI-JAM MANPORTABLE (SCAMP) RADIO IS IN PRODUCTION NOW FOR THE U.S. DEPARTMENT OF DEFENSE (BOTTOM).

ON A VISIT TO AN EXCLUSIVE COUNTRY CLUB IN PALM SPRINGS, California, a young Dallas attorney named Robert H. Dedman noticed that land prices immediately surrounding the golf course were rising at an astonishing rate. Acres that cost $2,000 five years before were selling for as much as $200,000.

The year was 1957, and Dedman, convinced that the presence of the golf course and club accounted for the rise, returned to Dallas with an ambitious idea. Dedman concluded that real estate developers could be persuaded to include a country club in the middle of the residential properties they were building. But he added some important variations that would appeal to home buyers across the board: Instead of targeting the ultrarich, he wanted to put clubs "in reach of the top 10 percent of the population, not the top 1 percent."

MISSION HILLS COUNTRY CLUB IN RANCHO MIRAGE, CALIFORNIA, A CELEBRATED 54-HOLE COMPLEX, IS HOME TO THE DINAH SHORE TOURNAMENT, CONSIDERED BY MANY TO BE THE WOMEN'S MASTERS (TOP).

THE HOMESTEAD RESORT IN HOT SPRINGS, VIRGINIA, ESTABLISHED IN 1766, BECAME A CLUB RESORT IN 1993 (BOTTOM).

Dedman began to fulfill his plan in Dallas, with the development of Brookhaven Country Club, a 400-acre country club complex within a 1,100-acre mixed-use development. Now, 40 years later, there are some 250 clubs and affiliated properties owned through Dedman's north Dallas-based company, Club Corporation International, or ClubCorp, as it is called. And there are 225,000 members and 26,000 employees worldwide.

Dedman altered the way country clubs previously had operated by using logic to streamline overhead while maximizing facility usage. For example, instead of one swimming pool, ClubCorp properties might have five; instead of one 18-hole golf course, there might be three. And all facilities used the same clubhouse, which reduced operating costs. To take the concept even further, Dedman decided that members at one ClubCorp affiliate would have membership privileges at any of the other ClubCorp affiliates outside a certain radius of their home clubs. And these clubs would not discriminate on the basis of sex, race, religion, or national origin.

BRANCHING OUT OF THE SUBURBS AND INTO THE CITIES

Developers of the nation's burgeoning suburbs in the 1950s and 1960s were open to the ClubCorp concept, but Richard Poole, the first manager of Brookhaven and later the director of development, saw opportunities in cities, where affluent young Americans were finding it difficult to socialize without leaving the city limits.

Poole pioneered the city club concept, which created venues where members could socialize and enjoy fine dining within the inner cities. In addition, members also were provided full Associate Club privileges. Developers of high-rise office towers were amenable to the idea, since having the clubs on the premises attracted tenants. The first city club was the Lancers Club, which opened in Dallas in 1965 and has since merged with the Tower Club.

Between 1970 and 1985, more than 90 city clubs were

opened, including the first city athletic club, the University Club of Houston. Constructed in conjunction with the city's famous Galleria, the athletic club featured the first indoor climate-controlled tennis complex in the world, as well as workout facilities, squash and tennis courts, and swimming pools, along with fine dining and Heart Healthy™ cuisine.

Expansion also continued in the suburbs. In 1975, Inverrary Country Club in Fort Lauderdale, a ClubCorp subsidiary, hosted its first tournament on the Professional Golfers' Association tour. In 1984, the company purchased its first major resort, Pinehurst Resort & Country Club in North Carolina. Now the Club Resorts subsidiary operates eight major resort properties in the United States and Canada.

AT HOME IN DALLAS
In 1987, the company established a Dallas-based central clearinghouse for member charges at nearly 200 Associate Clubs. From its headquarters on LBJ Freeway, the firm began publishing *Private Clubs* magazine, which communicates membership benefits and the private club lifestyle to club members. ClubCorp also has a toll-free ClubLine, which members can call to make dining and golf reservations, as well as receive directions to and information about clubs they may want to visit.

In 1993, the privately held ClubCorp acquired $100 million worth of properties around the world, and now its subsidiaries operate clubs in China, Germany, Indonesia, Mexico, South Africa, Singapore, and Thailand. Other developments are under way in many parts of Latin America and Asia.

CONTINUING THE LEGACY
Founder Robert Dedman's legacy is recognized throughout the Dallas area: The Dedman College of Southern Methodist University (SMU) and the Dedman Center for Lifetime Sports at SMU are named after him; 800 Dedman Merit Scholars at the University of Texas at Austin benefit from scholarship

funds donated by Dedman; and Dedman Memorial Hospital and Dedman Medical Center are testimonies to his service.

In 1987, Dedman was inducted into the Texas Business Hall of Fame; he received the Entrepreneur of the Year Award for Texas in 1976. He also was named Humanitarian of the Year in Dallas in 1980, Outstanding National Business Leader in 1985, and Marketer of the Year in 1986. And in 1989, he received the Horatio Alger Award.

Today his son, Bob Dedman Jr., serves as chairman of the board of Club Corporation of America and as president and chief operating officer of Club Corporation International, ensuring that the elder Dedman's vision endures. "Our goal is to be the world-class leader in hospitality," says Bob Dedman Jr. "We hope to establish a presence in all major markets. We foresee half of our growth occurring internationally, with the other half occurring in North America, and we hope to enlist our members in helping us achieve that growth. We will work hard to preserve the pride that accompanies belonging to a ClubCorp affiliated club by emphasizing service. Our philosophy, values, and culture come down to that—service."

CLOCKWISE FROM TOP RIGHT: AT COUNTRY CLUBS SUCH AS GREENBRIER COUNTRY CLUB IN CHESAPEAKE, VIRGINIA, THERE'S MORE TO LIFE THAN GOLF.

PINEHURST RESORT & COUNTRY CLUB IN NORTH CAROLINA FEATURES EIGHT GOLF COURSES, INCLUDING THE WORLD-RENOWNED NO. 2, SITE OF THE 1999 U.S. OPEN.

THE CITY CLUB OF WASHINGTON, D.C., IS AN ELEGANT RETREAT FOR POWER BROKERS FROM CAPITOL HILL.

BOB DEDMAN JR. IS CARRYING ON THE VISION FOR CLUBCORP THAT WAS FOUNDED BY HIS FATHER, ROBERT DEDMAN.

HERE IS A WINDOW ON THE FIFTH FLOOR OF DOCTORS HOSPITAL with a view of a small brick building a few blocks away. Longtime Dallas physicians sometimes glance out the window and, taking in the view, recall the days when the hospital—some 50 beds in size—occupied just one floor of that small building on nearby Garland Road. Staff physicians occupied a second floor.

These days, Doctors Hospital is a 268-bed, acute care community hospital nestled amid the trees of White Rock Park on the banks of White Rock Lake, within view of downtown Dallas. And that small building where the hospital was born is now Professional Building II.

Today, Doctors Hospital has more than 800 employees and approximately 400 doctors, according to Rosemary Rayburn, chief operating officer. What began with a $500,000 investment in September 1959 is now a four-building complex with total assets of $103 million. In 1996, a $40 million top-to-bottom renovation and expansion was completed.

"It really was a substantial updating of the hospital, from the structure on up," says Nelson Forsyth, MD, who has been practicing internal medicine at Doctors Hospital for 24 years. The West Tower, which houses hospital administration, was added to the campus, and new radiology and cardiopulmonary departments, as well as additional parking, were completed in 1994.

"Until 1977 we were totally an inpatient facility," says Rayburn. "With the remodeling, we now have a considerable new emphasis on outpatient care. The bulk of the expansion was outpatient care and medical office space. That certainly reflects the trend in modern health care."

A SUCCESSFUL OPERATION

The white stone structures of Doctors Hospital—with their inviting curvilinear interior design and soft mauve and teal color scheme—do not form an intimidating, sprawling complex or a crowded highrise tower. The four professional buildings are situated to allow patients and family members to park their vehicles close to the buildings they need. The main hospital building is designed in an H shape. Although its departments are located in different wings, the smoothly flowing layout makes them easily accessible.

"Patients can access the care quickly," says Charles R. Cain, MD, an internist who joined the staff in 1962. "And there is convenience for the family. People are concerned about being visited when they go to the hospital. Well, here we make it as easy as possible to have visitors, and we don't even charge for parking, which is unusual in Dallas."

Dr. Louis R. Turbeville, a pediatrician and the moving force behind the hospital in the late 1950s, led a group of Dallas physicians in 1957 to begin a hospital on the fringes of the city. Following the death of Turbeville in 1970 Dr. Bob Smith took the helm and helped bring the hospital into the modern era.

Doctors Hospital continues to modernize. The hospital has one of only 60 Apache III inten-

AN AERIAL VIEW SHOWS THE DOCTORS HOSPITAL CAMPUS WITH WHITE ROCK LAKE IN THE BACKGROUND (LEFT).

MARCH OF DIMES' WALKAMERICA IS JUST ONE OF THE WAYS IN WHICH DOCTORS HOSPITAL GIVES BACK TO THE COMMUNITY BY PROVIDING FIRST-AID STATIONS THROUGHOUT THE ROUTE AND SERVING AS SPONSOR FOR THE START/FINISH LINE (RIGHT).

◀ LAURIE CAMPBELL

sive care diagnostic units in the country—the only one in Texas. The 29,000-square-foot Sports & Industry Care Center has advanced equipment for rehabilitation of the growing number of workplace injuries: "The diagnostic equipment is all new, it just doesn't get any better," says Rob Freymuller, the youthful and energetic chief executive officer.

Because of the top-notch equipment on the premises, Doctors Hospital attracts an impressive spectrum of subspecialists. "Ultrasound, MRI, CT, nuclear medicine—there really is no radiological diagnostic testing that we don't have," says Steve LaGrone, director of business development.

There are some 5,000 surgeries performed at the hospital each year, ranging from neurosurgery, cardiac, open heart, and orthopedics to simple cosmetic surgery. Physicians specialize in everything from cardiology to obstetrics to psychiatry, and there is a nine-bed, 24-hour emergency room that can manage advanced cardiac life support. "The attitude and integrity of the medical and hospital staffs— that stands out in my mind as one of our strongest attributes," says Freymuller. LaGrone adds that this confidence in the hospital's personnel can be found throughout the greater Dallas community.

"I think it's significant that the people who work here, no matter where they live in the region, seek care from the physicians here," he says. "That says a lot for what they think of the staff."

The hospital remains involved in community activities in several ways: Civic groups often use hospital facilities for neighborhood meetings, there are frequent public seminars, and the hospital is a major local sponsor of the March of Dimes, and the American Heart Association.

And in turn, the community gives back to the hospital. More than 125 volunteers donate 35,000 hours each year to help the hospital perform at its peak.

MODERN MEDICINE, MODERN POLICIES

Today, Tenet Healthcare Corporation, the second-largest investor-owned health care services company, owns Doctors Hospital, giving the hospital significant additional recognition on a national—and particularly on a regional—basis.

According to Freymuller, "The renovation positioned the hospital for outpatient care in which there was a tremendous need in this area. But we also added more diagnostic equipment, designed the hospital to be more efficient, and made it more user friendly. It truly is a hospital for the '90s—and beyond."

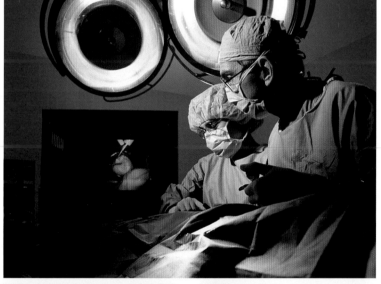

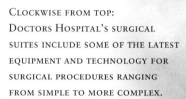

CLOCKWISE FROM TOP: DOCTORS HOSPITAL'S SURGICAL SUITES INCLUDE SOME OF THE LATEST EQUIPMENT AND TECHNOLOGY FOR SURGICAL PROCEDURES RANGING FROM SIMPLE TO MORE COMPLEX.

IN ADDITION TO TRADITIONAL REHABILITATION, AQUATIC THERAPY IS AVAILABLE TO PATIENTS WHO HAVE BEEN GIVEN PHYSICIAN APPROVAL TO USE THIS TREATMENT METHOD.

DOCTORS HOSPITAL PROVIDES TOURS TO SCHOOL-AGE CHILDREN TO HELP THEM FEEL MORE COMFORTABLE IN A HOSPITAL SETTING SHOULD THEY REQUIRE HOSPITALIZATION.

HEREVER EXCELLENCE IS FOUND, THERE ARE PEOPLE DEDICATED TO making a difference. For more than 30 years, the people at Grace Presbyterian Village have held fast to the simple belief that they can make a difference every day in the quality of retirement living

and nursing care for each of its residents. Grace Presbyterian Village has built its reputation on excellence, and it shows in the respect each resident receives, and in the attention given to individual needs.

Grace Presbyterian's medical and administrative staff brings to each resident as much compassion as competence. Many have been on the Village staff for years, with the average length of service exceeding 10 years. Whatever level of care is required, all residents at Grace Presbyterian Village find a level of caring that is truly exceptional.

COTTAGES, RESIDENTIAL WINGS, AND PERSONAL CARE

The Village offers a variety of living arrangements to suit the individual needs of each resident. For the active retiree capable of fully independent living, spacious cottage apartments offer safe, secure surroundings with around-the-clock protection and no maintenance worries. Conveniences include all-electric kitchens, washer and dryer connections, carports, well-lit walking paths, and nearby patios with gas grills for entertaining family and friends. For emergencies, medical attention is just a push button away.

In the residential wings, a comfortable room in the main complex offers privacy and independent living for those who require no daily assistance with medications or health needs. Furnished and decorated by the resident, these private rooms offer the convenience of three meals a day in a nearby dining room. Weekly housekeeping and laundry services are available, providing all the comforts of home without all the chores.

The Personal Care Unit is designed for those who are largely independent but require some help with daily living. Assistance is provided with medications and daily needs by 24-hour, on-site licensed staff.

NURSING AND DEMENTIA CARE

For those who require nursing care, the Village offers a range of highly acclaimed programs and services, ranging from intermediate to full-time skilled care, in its Medicare-certified area, all under the supervision of registered nurses. Nursing care offers close monitoring of health conditions and physical, occupational, and speech therapies.

At the Village, a continuum of care is provided for residents with Alzheimer's disease and related disorders. Camellia Wing is a state-of-the-art, personal care unit offering "secured freedom" in a home-like setting. The second unit, One South, is a special care unit offering compassionate, consistent nursing care for more advanced needs.

ACTIVITIES AND SERVICES FOR EVERY LIFESTYLE

Residents' freedom to create their own lifestyles includes the freedom to choose from a range of activities and programs open to all Village residents. Shopping excursions, theater outings, worship services,

arts and crafts, exercises, dances, picnics, and celebrations are just a few of the events that fill the Village calendar each month.

Towering trees and gentle rolling hills make the Village seem miles away from city life. But just beyond the sound of rustling leaves and serenading birds lies Dallas. Nearby Interstate 35 offers access to downtown within 10 minutes, or nearly anywhere else in the Dallas area in little more than half an hour.

But the only way to fully appreciate Grace Presbyterian Village is to see it. For visitors, the quality of life and commitment to excellence are immediately apparent, from award-winning innovations in retirement living to the warm bonds between staff and residents.

GRACE PRESBYTERIAN VILLAGE HAS BUILT ITS REPUTATION FOR EXCELLENCE BY WORKING DILIGENTLY EVERY DAY TO FIND NEW AND BETTER WAYS TO ENRICH THE QUALITY OF LIFE AND THE QUALITY OF CARE FOR EVERY RESIDENT.

I N A TIME OF CRISIS, A CARDIOLOGIST NEEDS IMMEDIATE ACCESS to patient information. If the physician is one of HeartPlace's 36 cardiologists, he or she has access to every piece of information in the patient's medical record, retrievable from locations through-

out North Texas and southern Oklahoma. This total access to critical information is an industry first, but it's not the first time HeartPlace has broken new ground in health care. Since its inception in 1962, Dallas-based HeartPlace has become the industry's dependable pioneer and recognized leader in cardiovascular care.

HeartPlace physicians established the first cardiology training program and the first specialized coronary care unit at Baylor University Medical Center in 1963. Many of the staff members were the first in the Dallas region to perform such procedures as cardiac catheterization, balloon angioplasty, cardiac laser and stinting, transesophageal echocardiography, thrombolytic clot-busting therapy, implantable cardiac defibrillation, and electrophysiologic ablation. Other Metroplex milestones include permanent pacemaker implants, radial angiography and radial angioplasty, and transradial approach for balloon angioplasty.

EDUCATING PATIENTS FOR BETTER HEART HEALTH CARE

While technological innovation in cardiac care is crucial, what's important to thousands of HeartPlace patients is the high quality of the personalized medical care they receive. HeartPlace is committed to educating the public about the importance of a "heart healthy" lifestyle. The message is conveyed throughout the community by means of ancillary services, including risk appraisals, stress and weight management, and smoking cessation courses.

HeartPlace patients are afforded same-day appointments,

24-hour phone access, and thorough follow-up to postprocedure care; outpatient testing is available at select clinics; and every location offers free, easy parking. And HeartPlace participates in all major health plans and Medicare assignments. By using HeartPlace's state-of-the-art information systems, all findings, recommendations, and records are presented to referring physicians within 24 hours, or as needed.

HeartPlace's 36 cardiologists, a cardiothoracic surgeon, and 190 support staff members communicate regularly with patients about the quality of service, and an internal Quality Improvement and Utilization Management program constantly checks standards. "Excellence is more than just a goal," says HeartPlace president Kevin Wheelan, MD. "It is our normal operational standard. Everyone involved with HeartPlace realizes the importance of a well-coordinated, cooperative effort." This effort is managed by Cardiovascular Provider Resources, L.P. (CPR), which was formed in 1995 to become a premier physician practice management company. CPR and HeartPlace share a common goal in pioneering quality patient care.

HeartPlace's ambitions are not confined to just the organization. Currently, a HeartPlace foundation is in the planning stages that will allow HeartPlace doctors to donate cardiac care to the indigent of the Metroplex, an extension of existing charitable programs for patients.

In the future, HeartPlace will make its services available to health care providers in the Midwest and East, linking patients and physicians to its cardiology network. Additionally, an initial public offering will be extended to capitalize further expansion, as well as underwrite important exploration and research in cardiology.

HEARTPLACE'S 38 CARDIOLOGISTS, A CARDIOTHORACIC SURGEON, AND 190 SUPPORT STAFF MEMBERS COMMUNICATE REGULARLY WITH PATIENTS ABOUT THE QUALITY OF SERVICE (TOP).

SINCE ITS INCEPTION IN 1962, DALLAS-BASED HEARTPLACE HAS BECOME THE INDUSTRY'S DEPENDABLE PIONEER AND RECOGNIZED LEADER IN CARDIOVASCULAR CARE (BOTTOM).

1965-1979

1965
DALLAS COUNTY COMMUNITY
COLLEGE DISTRICT

1965
NORTHPARK CENTER

1970
CARRINGTON COLEMAN SLOMAN &
BLUMENTHAL L.L.P.

1971
MCI COMMUNICATIONS CORP.

1972
LOCKWOOD GREENE

1973
WINSTEAD SECHREST & MINICK P.C.

1975
BRINKLEY SARGENT ARCHITECTS

1977
CHICAGO TITLE INSURANCE COMPANY

1977
RICHARD DRUMMOND DAVIS, ARCHITECT

1977
U.S. RISK INSURANCE GROUP, INC.

1978
THE L&B GROUP

1978
RAPP COLLINS WORLDWIDE

1979
ADLETA AND POSTON, REALTORS

1979
KAISER PERMANENTE

CITIZENS OF DALLAS HAVE ALWAYS SUPPORTED THE DALLAS County Community College District (DCCCD) with financial as well as people support. With an enrollment of more than a million students since 1965, DCCCD has become an important fixture in the Dallas community, and it is an investment that has paid off well.

"The community college system is one of the things used to sell Dallas when businesses move here," says Chancellor J. William Wenrich. "Companies want to know that they can get a viable workforce quickly and that their employees will be trained properly. We are able to assure both. In addition, the physical facilities we have are as nice as those found at any higher education institution in Texas."

In May 1965, voters approved the initial $41.5 million bond issue that financed the first stages of DCCCD's development. El Centro, located in the heart of downtown Dallas' business district, opened first in 1966, with Eastfield and Mountain View colleges enrolling their first students in 1970. In 1972, the Richland campus began accepting students.

Today, following an $85 million sale of bonds in 1972, the DCCCD is the largest institution for higher learning in Texas and is the sixth-largest community college system in the nation—with seven colleges strategically placed throughout the county, including Cedar Valley and North Lake colleges, which opened in 1977, and Brookhaven College, which began enrolling students in 1978. It was at this point that DCCCD fulfilled its ambitious mission of making a college available within 15 minutes of any resident. The residents are responding: DCCCD now enrolls more than 45,000 students for credit each semester, with another 60,000 taking noncredit courses offered seven days and five nights a week throughout the year.

LEARNING FROM A DISTANCE

DCCCD's open-door admissions policy makes higher education available to anyone with an interest, despite their previous academic history. DCCCD also makes it easy to attend classes, even if the student can't be in a traditional classroom in person.

DCCCD is one of the largest producers of broadcast-quality instructional television courses in the country. Taking advantage of its own television studio, microwave network, and satellite transmitters and receivers located at the 28,000-square-foot R. Jan LeCroy Center for Educational Telecom-

munications, DCCCD has created an industry-leading program that allows students to earn an associate's degree via distance learning. Students can view DCCCD's live television programs from their homes or business sites, or tape telecourses for viewing anytime. Students with computers also can enroll in numerous classes on-line in DCCCD's system of virtual, or electronic, classrooms. Students with demanding travel schedules, full-time careers, and/or family commitments can take distance learning courses for credit and continue to fulfill their other responsibilities.

CLOCKWISE FROM TOP:
THE LEARNING RESOURCE CENTER LOCATED ON EACH DALLAS COUNTY COMMUNITY COLLEGE DISTRICT (DCCCD) CAMPUS PROVIDES AN ATMOSPHERE FOR RESEARCH AND LEARNING.

HANDS-ON LEARNING APPLICATIONS ARE A COMMON PART OF STANDARD CURRICULUM IN TECHNICAL COURSES THROUGHOUT THE DCCCD.

BIOLOGY IS ONE OF THE BASIC COURSES REQUIRED FOR AN ASSOCIATE OF ARTS DEGREE FROM THE DCCCD.

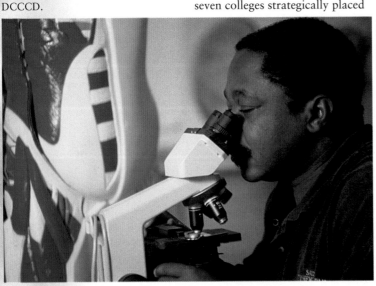

◀ KEN BROCK

In addition to telecourses, live television courses, and on-line courses, the DCCCD's flexible-entry courses allow students to proceed at their own pace, and cooperative-work-experience courses let students earn credits through on-the-job experience.

Currently, DCCCD is putting an emphasis on its workforce development program. An employer can arrange with the DCCCD to create and execute a program that, in the end, will upgrade the current staff of employees through a tailor-made educational program that fits the specific needs of that business.

The DCCCD draws 31 percent of its revenue base from local taxes, 44.5 percent from the state, and just 21.3 percent from student tuition. This balance keeps the cost of higher education for the individual at an enticingly low level. Dallas residents can change their lives through education for less than $5 a day. A poll taken by the Texas Higher Education Coordinating Board revealed the DCCCD has the lowest tuition rate among community colleges in the state.

FROM ASTROLOGY TO ZOOLOGY

Seventy-five percent of the students enrolled in DCCCD credit classes intend to pursue a bachelor's degree. At DCCCD, they find a wide range of courses

in the natural, physical, computer, and social sciences; English; mathematics; humanities; and business that will readily transfer to other colleges and universities. In addition, the colleges offer more than 100 technical/career programs in fields where labor demands are high, including intensive cardio-vascular technology, criminal justice, technical engineering, robotics, microchip manufacturing, nursing, travel and tourism, computer information systems, and performing arts. More than 1,000 noncredit courses are offered each semester for the student who simply wants to explore a new topic or update skills for a career.

Not surprisingly, the median age of a DCCCD student is 29, indicating that most of the students already have workforce experience and realize that continuing education is vital to their careers.

DCCCD also is preparing the Dallas workforce for today's global market, offering bid assistance and counseling on how to do business with government agencies at the Center for Govern-

ment Contracting; a counseling and reference center for importers and exporters at the International Small Business Development Center; and Teaching Spanish for Business at the International Language Institute.

"Education is changing," observes Wenrich, "and as a national leader in the use of television and the Internet for class credit, we continue to overcome obstacles. Currently, we are dealing with the details that will define the methods of education of the future. And we are working on ways to provide quality student support services and academic processing and testing, whether the student is on campus, at work, or at home."

CLOCKWISE FROM TOP LEFT: A DEGREE IN FASHION OR PATTERN DESIGN OFFERS STUDENTS THE LATEST IN COMPUTER TECHNOLOGY FOR CREATIVE DESIGN.

CHEMISTRY IS A POPULAR COURSE AMONG STUDENTS ENTERING THE ALLIED HEALTH PROFESSIONS.

MANY OF DALLAS' LEADING CHEFS ARE GRADUATES OF THE FOOD AND HOSPITALITY SERVICES PROGRAM AT EL CENTRO COLLEGE.

DISTANCE LEARNING VIA COMPUTER MODEM AND THE INTERNET MAKES LEARNING MORE CONVENIENT FOR STUDENTS WHO ARE UNABLE TO MAINTAIN A TRADITIONAL EDUCATIONAL SCHEDULE.

STUDENTS LEARN THE LATEST TECHNOLOGY IN RESPIRATORY THERAPY DURING A TWO-YEAR ASSOCIATE DEGREE PROGRAM AT EL CENTRO COLLEGE.

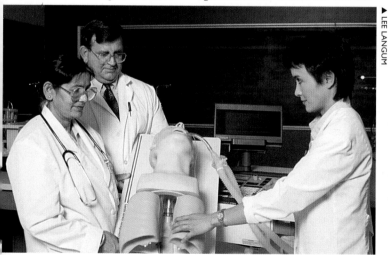

WHEN IT WAS BUILT IN 1965—BEFORE THE WORDS SHOPPING MALL were in general use—NorthPark Center was the largest climate-controlled retail establishment in the world. NorthPark was also the first to bring the outdoors inside, with skylit pavilions and courtyards appointed with fountains, shrubs, and flowering plants.

NorthPark Center was honored by the American Institute of Architects (AIA) with its Best Design of the Decade award in 1965. In 1992, the AIA followed that accolade with its prestigious 25-Year Award, recognizing NorthPark's continuing standard of high quality amid its tasteful elegance.

The success of NorthPark Center is due to the far-thinking vision and enduring efforts of Dallas developer Raymond D. Nasher and his daughter Nancy. It was Raymond who, in the mid-1960s, went against conventional thinking and constructed a mall in a location that many considered too remote for anyone to patronize. Currently, Nancy and her husband, David Haemisegger, are working to bring NorthPark into the 21st century with an ex-

pansion effort that will add 1 million square feet to its existing 1.6 million square feet, making it one of the five largest malls in the country.

MORE THAN STORES

Since the beginning, NorthPark Center has succeeded in its goal of being more than a collection of conveniently located specialty stores. It was intended to be a place where visitors felt comfortable socializing, even if shopping was not on the day's agenda. NorthPark Center, with its plentiful public seating, graceful common areas, and full-service, white-tablecloth restaurants in midcourt, has become a veritable town center.

Beyond that, NorthPark offers its considerable open space and copious customer traffic to Dallas-area nonprofit organizations that may benefit from such popular exposure. For more than a decade, the Dallas County Medical Society has offered services and screenings from 140 health and medical groups in the halls of the mall during its annual health fair. The Dallas Symphony Orchestra has its official box office at the center, as does the Dallas Convention and Visitors Bureau.

Besides offering 160 world-class stores—more than 50 of which are unique to Dallas and Texas, including Barneys New York, Burberry's, FAO Schwarz, Bally of Switzerland, Joan & David, J. Crew, and others—the Center is also adorned with world-class artwork. Raymond Nasher and his late wife, Patsy, provide pieces for exhibit in the mall from their acclaimed private collection. It's not unusual to see original works by Andy Warhol, Roy Lichtenstein, Frank Stella, Tony Smith, Jonathan Borofsky, and Henry Moore on display amid the fountains and shop windows of NorthPark.

Soon, there will be even more to experience at North-Park Center. Explains Nancy Nasher, president of the North-Park Development Company, "Our primary reason for expansion is that we continue to be 100 percent leased with a very strong demand from superb retailers for additional lease space. And with the addition of both flagship Nordstrom and Foley's stores, we believe we have the ability to create one of the premier retail presentations in the country, here in Dallas."

NORTHPARK WAS THE FIRST RETAIL ESTABLISHMENT TO BRING THE OUTDOORS INSIDE, WITH SKYLIT PAVILIONS AND COURTYARDS APPOINTED WITH FOUNTAINS, SHRUBS, AND FLOWERING PLANTS.

Five Hammering Men—1982 BY JONATHAN BOROFSKY IS PART OF THE PATSY R. AND RAYMOND D. NASHER COLLECTION THAT IS ON DISPLAY AMID THE FOUNTAINS AND SHOP WINDOWS OF NORTHPARK CENTER.

JONATHAN BOROFSKY

RICHARD DRUMMOND DAVIS, ARCHITECT

DALLAS NATIVE RICHARD DRUMMOND DAVIS HAS SPENT THE LAST 20 years developing his residential architectural firm to emphasize service, client relationships, and distinguished design. ✱ "We think we can make a house as beautiful as anybody in the busi-

ness," Davis states. "This is self-evident in the appearance of our clients' houses. What we focus on is taking care of our clients through each step of the design and building process."

WATCHING THE DESIGN UNFOLD

Davis does all of the design work right in front of his clients. He then remains intensely involved in overseeing and checking every precise drawing that goes into the construction plans. "I learned that time was wasted sketching by myself in my office without my client," Davis says.

The payment for the services of his firm is established up front as a fixed fee. "After 20 years in business, I have learned that drawing architecture by the hour can create surprising invoices," he says. "We don't like surprises for our clients."

CLASSICAL AND MODERN PREPARATION

After receiving his bachelor of science degree in architecture from the University of Texas in 1972, Davis took his master of

▶ DALTON PHOTOGRAPHY

architecture degree at Princeton University, where he studied with architect Michael Graves, one of the well-known designers of postmodern architecture. He then went to New York City to work for the nationally acclaimed firm of Hardy Holzman Pfeiffer.

Davis opened his own firm in 1977, after returning to Dallas, and began designing residential projects in the Highland Park, University Park, and Preston Hollow communities. Davis says he loves remodeling existing homes, and takes on projects of all sizes, each of which is imbued with his distinctive touches.

Davis has designed a number of well-known estate-sized homes. However, the majority of the residences he designs are between 3,000 and 6,000 square feet. His

reputation has earned him additional residential commissions in New Jersey, Pennsylvania, Colorado, North Carolina, Oklahoma, and the Caribbean.

Davis has built his reputation designing in traditional period and eclectic styles, and his designs remain within the bounds of what is tasteful with regard to proportion and composition.

"To balance and proportion a house and its details to look beautiful takes an eye and a knowledge of what looks correct," Davis says. "That's what makes my homes unique."

RICHARD DRUMMOND DAVIS (ABOVE) HAS DESIGNED NUMEROUS HOMES IN THE DALLAS AREA USING A VARIETY OF STYLES, INCLUDING (TOP LEFT) FRENCH PROVINCIAL; (CLOCKWISE FROM BOTTOM RIGHT) ITALIAN MEDITERRANEAN; LOUIS XV FRENCH CLASSICAL; HOUSE OF NORMANDY, FRANCE; AND HOUSE OF SOUTHERN ENGLAND.

SKED FOR HIS THOUGHTS ON THE NATIONAL RECOGNITION EXTEND-ed to the Dallas law firm of Carrington Coleman Sloman & Blumenthal L.L.P. in peer reviews, the firm's Chairman Jim Coleman says, "We stand accused of being better known in legal circles on either coast than in our home town. Yes, we represent the multinationals from New York, Atlanta, Los Angeles, and San Francisco. But we are the firm of choice for Dallas clients when legal trouble knocks. We live in Dallas, Dallas is our home, and we are proud of our roots."

Seventy years and countless novel, complex, and irresistibly thorny cases ago, Paul Carrington arrived in Dallas from Harvard Law School to practice law. He remained in the city for the rest of his life. His law firm flourished, becoming the advocate of choice for business leaders requiring professional, ethical, intelligent, and tenacious legal representation.

Carrington Coleman lawyers litigate and win cases from complex business controversies to last gasp appeals, and from patent infringements to business split-ups. Some of the state's largest banks beat a path to Carrington Coleman's door to reorganize in the wake of the banking crisis. The firm made law by backing down the Federal Deposit Insurance Corporation (FDIC) in a bank closure for the first time ever and obtaining payment in full of shareholders' equity claims, to boot. The case made history, but making history is secondary at this firm: Winning the case with professionalism is what it's all about.

According to the firm's managing partner, Fletcher Yarbrough, "In the litigation arena, our focus is on the case that challenges, where a claim to an idea or an invention, an employee termination, a merger, or a regulatory problem has erupted into a high stakes lawsuit or a problem heading for the courthouse. Our clients' cases are difficult and unique, and we excel at finding unique solutions."

The firm's other long suit is its interdisciplinary focus in handling complex business mergers, asset deals, reorganizations, and start-up challenges. Carrington Coleman lawyers have presided over the delicate "merger of equals" for regional securities

WITH THE DALLAS SKYLINE CLEARLY IN VIEW, CARRINGTON COLEMAN LEADS THE LEGAL COMMUNITY IN PROVIDING FREE LEGAL SERVICES TO THE NEEDY.

". . . THE FIRM OF CHOICE FOR DALLAS CLIENTS WHEN LEGAL TROUBLE KNOCKS." — CARRINGTON COLEMAN SLOMAN & BLUMENTHAL CHAIRMAN JIM COLEMAN

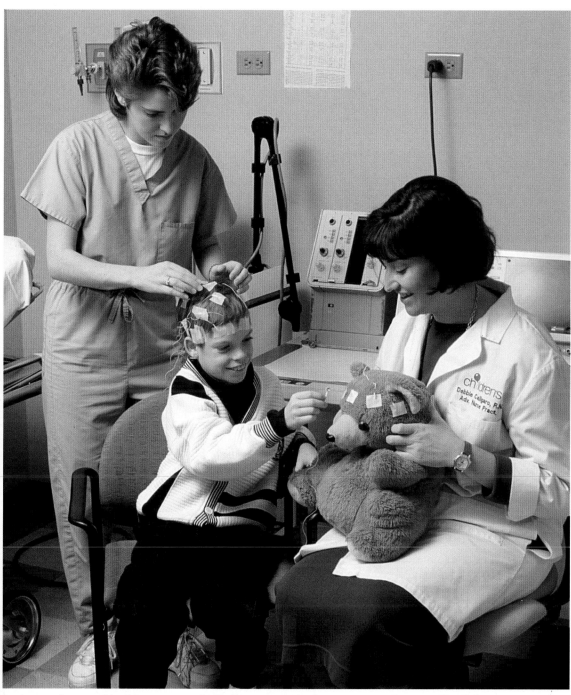

GEORGE FARR, PRESIDENT/CEO OF DALLAS' CHILDREN'S MEDICAL CENTER, STATES, "THE CARRINGTON COLEMAN FIRM IS INTEGRAL TO CARRYING OUT OUR MISSION AT CHILDREN'S: MAKING LIFE BETTER FOR CHILDREN. THESE PEOPLE CARE."

brokerage firms and health care institutions intent on surviving in a new age of competition; the reorganization or liquidation of family-held businesses to assist the transition of leadership, or wealth, from generation to generation; and the genesis of a now-flourishing suburban town that a real estate company once thought of as only a small subdivision on the prairie.

Even the involvement of Carrington Coleman lawyers in the Dallas community has a professional bent. The firm has a long tradition of extending a helping hand. It proudly leads Dallas' legal community in providing free legal services to the needy. The W. Frank Newton Award, from the State Bar of Texas, recognizing dedication to the provision of legal services to the poor, confirms the claim.

Paul Carrington sought, and always found, "lawyers of the highest professional attainments."

In 1996, Jim Coleman was presented with the first ever American Inns of Court Award, given to the lawyer in the Fifth Circuit (made up of Texas, Louisiana, and Mississippi) who best exemplifies the ideals of integrity, ethics, and professionalism. Jim Coleman is a lawyer's lawyer, many will say, and was gratified to be recognized as such. The Dallas firm he built continues to carry on Paul Carrington's tradition: serving clients well.

MCI COMMUNICATIONS CORP.

THE IMPRESSIVE ARRAY OF INDUSTRY-LEADING TELECOMMUNICA-tions services that MCI Communications Corp. delivers every minute of every day to millions of customers around the world originates in the town of Richardson. ✳ It's in Richardson that thousands of engineers develop and test the technology that makes possible voice, data, private line, wireless, and Internet and intranet products, as well as such services as MCI One, the industry's first bundling of long distance, local, cellular, paging, Internet, and other services. And it's where the 55,000-employee, $18 billion-a-year company has its Systems Integration and Technology Laboratory, which continues to create new ways for the world to communicate.

A large part of MCI's history has taken place in the Metroplex. The Washington, D.C.-based company was founded in 1969, and just two years later opened one of its first technical offices in the country in Richardson. And Dallas was one of the three cities where the company inaugurated its first switched long-distance service in 1975. Today, there are more than 300 MCI offices around the country, but Dallas remains one of the corporation's largest and most vital facility centers and home of the company's engineering headquarters.

CLOCKWISE FROM TOP: ENGINEERS IN RICHARDSON SPEND THEIR DAYS CONTINUOUSLY UPGRADING THE BACKBONE IN ORDER TO SPEED UP THE TRANSMISSION OF INFORMATION OVER FIBER-OPTIC LINES.

TODAY, THERE ARE MORE THAN 300 MCI OFFICES AROUND THE COUNTRY, BUT DALLAS REMAINS ONE OF THE CORPORATION'S LARGEST AND MOST VITAL FACILITY CENTERS.

A RICHARDSON EMPLOYEE CONSTRUCTS FIBER FOR THE MCI FIBER-OPTIC NETWORK.

MCI FOR THE NEW CENTURY

Today MCI, which has captured more than 40 percent of the growth in the U.S. long-distance market in the last five years, owns or leases nearly 1.5 million square feet of space in the Dallas region. Of the employees working in the nine area facilities, 80 percent are engineers whose key functions are to develop MCI's information technology and engineer its state-of-the-art telecommunications network. They develop ways of merging systems from around the world and ways to combine the best new technologies. In the 60,000-square-foot raised-floor replica of MCI's network at the company's Integration Lab, MCI engineers test new products in a real-world simulation to ensure that new communication capabilities operate properly.

Over the years MCI has spent approximately $12 billion in developing its network, using the highest level of network intelligence and state-of-the-art monitoring and control systems. Advanced fiber optics, digital microwave, and digital switching technologies have all been pioneered in Richardson.

The developments made in the facilities in the Dallas area have allowed MCI to shift from being an upstart microwave communications company to the status it enjoys today as the world's fastest-growing international carrier, the second-largest carrier in the United States, and the world's third-largest carrier of international voice traffic.

In all, there are 21 million business and residential customers who count on MCI for their communications services.

MCI is also the world's largest provider of Internet access, with MCI's fiber-optic network serving as the "backbone" for hundreds of other telecommunications companies. That's not surprising, since MCI boasts the industry's fastest telecommunications network. And the engineers in Richardson spend their days continuously upgrading the backbone in order to speed up the transmission of information over phone lines.

MCI's 6,000 employees in the Dallas area are held in such high esteem that when British Telecommunications (BT), the fourth-largest telecommunications company in the world, sought to merge with MCI in 1997 to form Concert, the engineers in Richardson were chosen as the technicians who would create the unprecedented global network of services for the newly combined company.

The MCI-BT merger creates the world's first global communications company with transglobal customers, a multinational management team, dual transatlantic headquarters (Washington and London), and shares traded on three international stock exchanges.

THE FUTURE OF COMMUNICATIONS DEVELOPS

As the convergence of communications, computing, and content accelerates, information-centered networks are required to play an even greater role in introducing new products, platforms, and services to the world's users. MCI is dedicated to remaining the industry leader in advancing the technology on which the world depends.

Success in the telecommunications market is no longer simply a matter of price. Success today is about meeting complex customer needs with innovative services, something the engineers at MCI's Richardson campus have been doing since the inception of the company.

In the past, MCI had a transactional relationship with its customers, handling their voice and data traffic. As the company matured, it became a consultant to its commercial customers by helping them design their telecommunications network. Today, as the needs of its customers have changed and MCI's portfolio of services has increased, MCI is now a strategic partner, integrally linked with its customers and their businesses.

The relationship with residential customers has changed as well. Besides enjoying MCI's

traditionally low rates, residential customers are using such sophisticated services as the Internet, electronic mail, cellular telephones, and paging services, all of which are provided via the MCI network.

MCI's founders are credited with breaking up the U.S. long-distance monopoly and making the industry more competitive, to the benefit of the public. In that vein, the company is now leading the charge to bring competition to the $100 billion local market, offering American customers for the first time the freedom to choose their local dial-tone carrier. And the engineering behind those services and others all began at MCI's facilities in Richardson.

CLOCKWISE FROM TOP: CONSTRUCTION WORKERS LAY A FIBER CONDUIT.

WORKERS INSTALL UNDERGROUND CABLES FOR MCI'S TELECOMMUNICATIONS NETWORK.

ADVANCED FIBER OPTICS, DIGITAL MICROWAVE, AND DIGITAL SWITCHING TECHNOLOGIES HAVE ALL BEEN PIONEERED IN RICHARDSON.

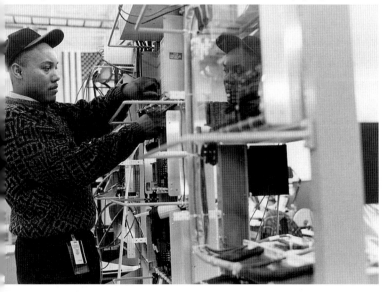

I N BUSINESS SINCE 1832, THE GLOBAL CONSULTING, DESIGN, AND construction firm of Lockwood Greene is a known leader in the industrial and commercial engineering industry, partnering with major technology- and process-based corporations in the planning,

design, and construction of facilities in the microelectronics, chemicals, metals, food and beverage, telecommunications, and health care products industries.

Lockwood Greene's consulting, engineering, architectural, and construction services provide results consistent with clients' expectations to optimize financial return, operational performance, competitive advantage, and global project delivery. These resources are prioritized, aligned, and delivered through a trademarked partnering model that Lockwood Greene developed called Outcomes by Design®. From project conceptualization through training, start-up, and maintenance,

Outcomes by Design® manages the relationship, monitors the process, and measures the results.

A PROMISE WITH
A PROCESS

Realizing that quality is a cyclical concept, Lockwood Greene developed its Outcomes by Design® process to include a three-phase cycle that addresses the continuing standard of quality with regard to client relationships. The process begins with the concept of relationship management, which establishes the parameters of obligation and accountability for the firm and the client. The intention is to avoid miscommunication, misunderstandings, and mistakes

that could be costly in both capital and time.

During the process management phase of the cycle, Lockwood Greene and the client company become a single team with a common goal: to design, fabricate, and implement a facility that will maximize resources and time, as well as achieve a competitive advantage in the marketplace. To that end, Lockwood Greene performs all engineering and architectural work in-house, from inception to completion, so there are no subcontractors to complicate developments.

By the time the team reaches the project management phase, which involves the implementation and management of the newly cre-

CLOCKWISE FROM TOP:
REFINERY LABORATORY OF PHILLIPS
PETROLEUM COMPANY, BORGER,
TEXAS

FABRICATION FACILITY OF THE
MATSUSHITA SEMICONDUCTOR
CORPORATION OF AMERICA,
PUYALLUP, WASHINGTON

H2S LABORATORY OF MOBIL RE-
SEARCH AND DEVELOPMENT COR-
PORATION, DALLAS, TEXAS

ated design, Lockwood Greene has established a meaningful relationship with the client that goes far beyond simply rendering a design. The strategic three-phase cycle has discovered and overcome stumbling blocks, improved original concepts, and, because the process began much earlier than most other design programs, lined up carefully calculated quantities of resources before construction start-up.

PROGRESS MEASURED LOCALLY AND GLOBALLY
Lockwood Greene now has nearly 3,000 employees in 33 offices around the world, with annual sales in excess of $210 million. A subsidiary of Germany-based Philipp Holzmann, the fourth-largest construction conglomerate in the world, Lockwood Greene is able to draw on resources of unparalleled depth, including the vast array of specialists employed by its parent company. One phone call can immediately bring experts from New York, Frankfurt, or Beijing to Dallas.

The Dallas office has been one of the city's best-kept

secrets since 1972, says Michael E. McKelvy, who manages the Texas operations. The company has more than 200 employees in the Geico Insurance building on Spring Valley Road in North Dallas, where past projects have included a $250 million process design for Conoco Oil and a $200 million eight-inch wafer fabrication plant for Samsung in Austin. Placing emphasis on developing relationships with Dallas-area companies has established the

Dallas office as one of the top five consulting, engineering, and architectural firms in the Metroplex.

Companies worldwide have come to rely on the firm not just for engineering services, but for the solid relationships it develops with its clients, knowing that they will receive the responsiveness, flexibility, dependability, quality, and cost effectiveness that have become the hallmarks of Lockwood Greene.

Pneumatic products facility of United Technologies Hamilton Standard, Mesa, Arizona (top)

Wafer fabrication facility of the Matsushita Semiconductor Corporation of America, Puyallup, Washington (bottom)

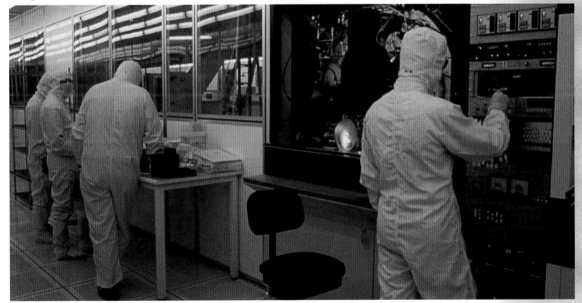

"**B**USINESS LAWYERS WHO UNDERSTAND BUSINESS.**"** THIS STATEMENT defines the driving force of Winstead Sechrest & Minick, one of Dallas' most highly respected, full-service law firms. By understanding its clients' businesses, the firm has earned a distinguished

reputation in the Dallas business and legal communities.

The growth of Winstead Sechrest & Minick mirrors that of Dallas, the city in which it was founded. With Dallas as the principal office, the firm has substantial offices in Austin, Houston,

and Mexico City, ranking the firm among the top 10 largest firms in Dallas.

The firm developed by serving the financial institutions of Dallas, and as the Dallas real estate market actively increased, the firm began representing lenders, developers, and users of all types of

commercial, residential, and industrial projects.

As Dallas has attracted a wide array of new business ventures to the Metroplex, Winstead Sechrest & Minick has itself become more diversified. The corporate/securities practice group handles complex transactions for commercial business and works with issuers, underwriters, and investors of publicly and privately offered securities. The firm continues to represent financial institutions, as well as tax-exempt public entities, in all types of financing and regulatory issues.

During the 1980s, Winstead Sechrest & Minick expanded its bankruptcy, reorganization, and litigation practices to aid both creditors and debtors, as well as broad business interests. Today, this practice group is one of the largest and most experienced in the Southwest.

As the 21st century approaches, the business world is expanding into areas that were unimaginable just a few years ago. Cable television and communications continue to lead the way in technological developments, and Winstead Sechrest & Minick's intellectual property group provides services related to network formation, licensing agreements, rights acquisition, and antitrust matters.

On the international front, the increasing globalization of world economies has led to the passage of a number of history-making trade agreements. To promote such trade, the firm operates in Mexico City as Winstead y Rivera S.C., making it one of the few U.S.-based law firms to have a full-service office in Mexico City.

The firm is organized around two principal groups: Business, which includes corporate employee benefits, energy and environmen-

WINSTEAD SECHREST & MINICK IS ONE OF THE LARGEST TEXAS-BASED LAW FIRMS, WITH ITS PRINCIPAL OFFICE IN DALLAS AND OFFICES IN HOUSTON, AUSTIN, AND MEXICO CITY.

◀ GREG LORING

tal, estate planning and probate, financial institutions, government relations, insurance, international, intellectual property, real estate, securities, tax, and zoning and land use practice areas; and Controversy, which includes litigation, bankruptcy, dispute resolution, construction/surety, and labor practice areas.

Recognizing the challenge of servicing a wide spectrum of clients, Winstead Sechrest & Minick uses a team approach in its representation to ensure that the highest-quality service is provided. Although these practice groups have been formed within the firm to concentrate on the various specialty areas of the law, the firm commits its entire resources to ensure that they remain responsive to clients by focusing on timeliness and results. The firm's internal creed emphasizes its philosophy—We Strengthens Me.

This service-oriented approach also can be witnessed outside the day-to-day operations of the firm. Most Winstead Sechrest & Minick team members, for example, volunteer their time and serve on various boards of nonprofit organizations, charities, societies, and arts and civic groups.

Winstead Sechrest & Minick, the firm of "business lawyers who understand business," is committed not just to the practice of law, but to the service of its clients and the community.

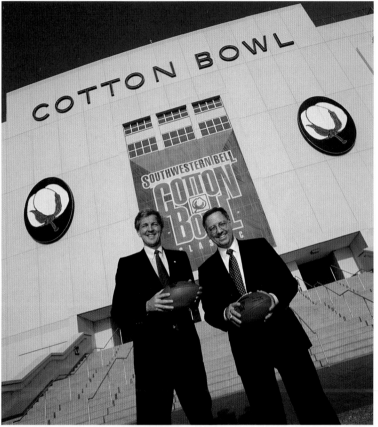

GREG LORING

CLOCKWISE FROM TOP: WINSTEAD SECHREST & MINICK ENCOURAGES COMMUNITY INVOLVEMENT ON AN INDIVIDUAL AND FIRMWIDE BASIS IN NONPROFIT ORGANIZATIONS, CHARITIES, AND CIVIC ORGANIZATIONS.

MANY ATTORNEYS IN THE FIRM SUPPORT PROFESSIONAL DEVELOPMENT AND ACTIVELY PARTICIPATE IN LEADING POSITIONS WITHIN THE LEGAL COMMUNITY.

THE FIRM'S DIRECTOR OF PROFESSIONAL DEVELOPMENT COORDINATES AN EDUCATIONAL PROGRAM FOR THE FIRM'S YOUNG LAWYERS THAT IS DESIGNED TO EASE THE TRANSITION FROM LAW SCHOOL TO LEGAL PRACTICE.

GREG LORING

O NE SHOULD NEVER JUDGE A BOOK BY ITS COVER OR A BUILDING by its facade, for there is more to creating a building than putting up a pretty box. A well-designed building works for all the users of the building. The owner should have a building designed to his or her specifications and budget, the employees should have well-thought-out work flows and atmosphere, and visitors to the building should not feel lost or overwhelmed.

The respected Dallas-based firm Brinkley Sargent Architects is known for providing for each of these users. "Our greatest marketing tool is a satisfied client," says Melissa Brand-Vokey, an architect with the firm. "We are there throughout the entire process to act in partnership with the owner in all aspects of design, through construction, to final move in."

FIRM FOUNDATIONS
The firm was founded as Brinkley & Brinkley in 1975 by longtime Dallas-area resident Dwayne M. Brinkley. Originally, the company offered construction management, as well as architectural services, but in 1984, with the addition of Design Principal Harold Sargent, the firm became Brinkley Brinkley & Sargent and concentrated on just the architectural services. In 1986, the construction management affiliate became a completely independent company. One more name change to Brinkley Sargent Architects in 1991 reflected the addition of Gary Beeman as a principal in this growing firm that is fully capable of handling $1 million renovations to $50 million construction projects from start to finish.

FROM MEDICAL CENTERS TO WATER PARKS
Brinkley Sargent Architects' style defies categorization. No two buildings look alike, a reflection of the philosophy that the site, type of building, and client taste—not a repetitious style imposed by the architect—should dictate the appearance. The firm strives to design timeless buildings that refrain from looking trendy. Along with its diversity in style is its diversity of client base. From Fortune 500 corporations to local city governments, the company has established a proven track record for creative designs that are within budget and on time.

Brinkley Sargent's reputation for world-class design has been recognized by several local, state, and national organizations for design excellence. Its designs have been featured in such publications as the *National AIA Justice Facility Review*, as well as *Modern Healthcare* and *Athletic Business* magazines.

In keeping with the firm's insistence that attention should be focused not on the firm but on

THE RESPECTED DALLAS-BASED FIRM BRINKLEY SARGENT ARCHITECTS IS KNOWN FOR PROVIDING INNOVATIVE AND FUNCTIONAL DESIGNS. THE FIRM HAS DESIGNED SUCH BUILD- INGS AS THE WOMEN'S CENTER AD- DITION TO THE MCCUISTION MEDICAL CENTER (LEFT) AND THE TOPA ONCOLOGY CENTER AT MEDICAL CITY OF DALLAS (RIGHT).

▲ JOHN BENOIST

MARK TREW

its clients, Brand-Vokey explains that Brinkley Sargent's success is based on the trust the client brings to the table. "We're fortunate that our clients allow us to design facilities that become an important part of their business or civic image," she says. "We believe, and try to impress on our clients, that their building makes a statement about who they are."

Sophisticated computers are used for every phase of a project. During the design phase, 3-D imagery is used so that the client can feel comfortable with the design. "It is often hard for a client to

visualize the building from flat plans and elevations," Brand-Vokey notes. "We find that with 3-D models we can walk the client around and through their new building." Computers are then used to create accurate construction documents that facilitate the building process.

But before any such sketches are made, the staff of Brinkley Sargent conducts a thorough investigation into the client needs of the proposed facility. "One of the benefits we bring to a project is our technical knowledge, as well as aesthetic design skills," Brand-

Vokey says. "We pride ourselves in becoming as knowledgeable in the clients' business as they are. Sometimes we know more about their equipment or staff flow than they do."

By understanding what activities occur within a building, Brinkley Sargent is able to design a structure that not only looks good on the outside, but also functions properly for the people and the equipment on the inside. That is what the Dallas area has counted on for more than 20 years, and that is what Brinkley Sargent Architects delivers.

PROJECTS OF THE FIRM INCLUDE (CLOCKWISE FROM TOP LEFT) THE LONGVIEW CANCER CENTER, THE NRH2O WATERPARK, THE WOMEN'S DIAGNOSTIC CENTER AT MEDICAL CITY OF DALLAS, AND THE PLANO JUSTICE CENTER.

CAROLYN BROWN

A LTHOUGH PEOPLE CAN SHOP ON THE INTERNET FOR HOMES LISTED for sale in other states and use computers to help design office towers, the actual process of conducting a real estate transaction has not kept up with the times. Chicago Title Insurance Company is pioneering the strategies that promise to bring the way real estate ownership is transferred into the 21st century. In business since 1847, the firm is no longer content with simply performing the transaction escrows and title history research that are the traditional functions of title companies. Instead, Chicago Title, which handles 20 percent of all residential and nearly 70 percent of all commercial property transactions nationwide, is adding value to the process for its customers (Realtors, lenders, and attorneys) and for their customers (real estate sellers and purchasers).

A HISTORY AND FUTURE OF INNOVATION

Chicago Title and Trust traces its roots to James H. Rees and Edward A. Rucker, who devised a geographic system of property indexes in Cook County, Illinois, in 1847. In fact, after the Great Chicago Fire, the Illinois legislature passed a law designating the company's records that had been saved from the fire as official records since the public records were destroyed. The Title Guarantee and Trust Company issued the first title policy in Illinois protecting the owner against loss if the title was found invalid. Since then, the company has grown significantly and is generally recognized as the leading title insurer in the nation.

The Dallas office of Chicago Title manages more than $5 billion in total escrow proceeds each year in the process of handling some 24,000 transactions. In order to facilitate its customers' transactions, Chicago Title recognizes its responsibility to anticipate its customers' needs and to maintain a close working relationship with those customers in order to ask about special needs or requirements. "Our core purpose is to create value by sharing our talent and expertise," says Michael J. Rooney, vice president and Dallas area manager. "We can create value for our customers by making it easy for them to deal with us and by educating all of the actors in a real estate transaction."

Chicago Title continually adds products and services to its traditional real estate escrow and title functions. The company has recently purchased flood certification, credit reporting, and appraisal operations. National real estate players can access these services electronically or with one telephone call.

A leader in the Dallas residential real estate market, many local Realtors are hot-linked to Chicago Title's Web site. "Our Realtor cus-

"OUR REALTOR CUSTOMERS BENEFIT FROM THE INFORMATION WE PROVIDE AND THEREFORE BETTER SERVE THEIR CUSTOMERS, THE HOME SELLERS AND BUYERS," EXPLAINS CURTIS J. HOFFMAN, RESIDENTIAL OPERATIONS OFFICER.

tomers benefit from the information we provide and therefore better serve their customers, the home sellers and buyers," explains Curtis J. Hoffman, residential operations officer. In the commercial marketplace, the company uses technology as well, providing customized customer service. "For us, the key to technology is improving service to our customers," says J. Scott Sargent, vice president and commercial operations officer.

NEW SERVICES FOR A NEW WAY OF BUSINESS

Intensely personal, customized service is but one result of the availability of technology. "We've discovered that, with all of the real estate information that is available via the Internet, we need to reinvent our industry," says Rooney. "As a local operation of a large, national company, we can create value for our customers, not only by sharing our own talent and expertise, but by tapping into the talent and expertise of the company nationally. Beyond that, we can share that talent and expertise with our customers' customers, sellers and buyers, creating value for them."

In order to strengthen the relationship between the title company, its customers, and their customers, Chicago Title is developing marketing alliances with a broad spectrum of companies that provide consumer services. "We believe that if we create value for people," says Rooney, "we will be rewarded with their loyalty. While we must continue to lead the field in our existing business, we must also be aware of how our customers can drive change in our industry. At Chicago Title Insurance Company, we want to have the foresight to offer these services to our customers before they even ask."

"OUR CORE PURPOSE IS TO CREATE VALUE BY SHARING OUR TALENT AND EXPERTISE," SAYS MICHAEL J. ROONEY, VICE PRESIDENT AND DALLAS AREA MANAGER.

"FOR US, THE KEY TO TECHNOLOGY IS IMPROVING SERVICE TO OUR CUSTOMERS," SAYS J. SCOTT SARGENT, VICE PRESIDENT AND COMMERCIAL OPERATIONS OFFICER.

U.S. RISK INSURANCE GROUP, INC.

STATE'S MENTAL HEALTH AND MENTAL RETARDATION SYSTEM REquired professional liability coverage for its psychiatrists. After nine months of working with several insurance companies and less than one month before the coverage was due to go into effect, suitable coverage had still not been found.

With the deadline rapidly approaching, U.S. Risk Insurance Group, Inc. of Dallas was called upon for consultation. The risk specialists at U.S. Risk listened to the system administrator's concerns and, working with a specific group of underwriters who appreciated the subtleties of the risk exposure, designed a program that was proposed and promptly accepted. U.S. Risk had accomplished in a few weeks what the competition could not do in many months.

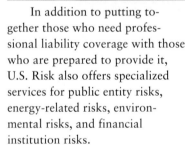

EXPERIENCE LEADS TO CREATIVE SOLUTIONS

The story is not unusual; there are dozens more like it. U.S. Risk has provided coverage for clients as diverse as soft drink bottlers, testing laboratories, government agencies, law firms, banks, architects, developers, and high-tech corporations, when others could not. U.S. Risk thrives when the company is called upon to help clients cover unusual, hazardous, or unique risks.

In addition to putting together those who need professional liability coverage with those who are prepared to provide it, U.S. Risk also offers specialized services for public entity risks, energy-related risks, environmental risks, and financial institution risks.

U.S. Risk, which is headquartered in an elegant, highrise building on North Central Expressway, was founded by a Dallas-based group of business partners who saw a need for an underwriting manager and wholesale brokerage that was determined not just to find coverage, but to add value to the service as well.

The firm is owned by Randall G. Goss, chairman and chief executive officer, who says, "We wish to prove beyond a doubt that, when it comes to designing, underwriting, and placing excess and surplus lines insurance, U.S. Risk provides service second to none."

The operating philosophy of the firm is to "have uncommon knowledge of the marketplace; provide fresh creative approaches, and inventive insurance and risk transfer coverages; and foster a get-it-done-now attitude at every level of the company," says Goss.

The professionals of U.S. Risk begin the coverage process by listening. They work diligently to understand and identify the risks the clients face—whether legal, social, moral, or physical—and then, drawing on the experience of more than 130 staff insurance and risk specialists and support staff, they tailor creative, comprehensive solutions. This diligence in understanding the situations that confront clients makes the difference.

The company also offers its clients professional claims management services, premium financing capabilities, and a host of other value-added products and services. The firm is also known for its expertise with alternative markets, such as risk retention groups, associations, pooling arrangements, and other self-insurance funds. U.S. Risk doesn't eliminate risk, but acknowledging the eventuality of risk demands

DEAN BENTLEY

TOP: U.S. RISK INSURANCE GROUP, INC. IS A HIGHLY PROFESSIONAL, WELL-RESPECTED, INDEPENDENT COMPANY THAT IN 1996 PROCESSED $140 MILLION IN PREMIUMS AND GENERATED REVENUES OF $13 MILLION.

BOTTOM: COMPANY OFFICERS ARE (FROM LEFT) TOM BLOOM, EXECUTIVE VICE PRESIDENT; L.M. "MAC" WESSON, PRESIDENT AND COO; AND RANDALL G. GOSS, CHAIRMAN AND CEO.

complete planning so that the outer boundaries of loss are known and acceptable.

The firm's success is attributable to the company's growing reputation and to its carefully cultivated relationships with those in the underwriting community who trust, understand, and acknowledge the expertise of the professionals at U.S. Risk. In an industry where even modest growth during the 1990s has been considered difficult, the company attained a compounded annual growth rate in excess of 25 percent from 1990 to 1996, more than 700 percent over the six-year period.

SWIFT RESPONSE IS VITAL

"We are capable of placing coverage for just about any risk our clients bring us," says U.S. Risk President and Chief Operating Officer Mac Wesson. "From designing coverage for police departments to providing product liability for aircraft parts, we have the professionals that have the expertise to get the job done. We have a broad capability, we are extremely attuned to our clients' needs, and we are highly responsive."

Responsiveness is the key to the value of service offered by U.S. Risk. The firm, which has developed a "Who *are* those guys?" mystique due to its extraordinary track record, is known within the industry for providing quotations and proof of coverage in an impressively short time frame. This rapid response time is a benefit of not being owned by a larger insurance organization that might bog down decisions with bureaucratic red tape.

As such, U.S. Risk is a highly professional, well-respected, independent company that in 1996 was responsible for $140 million in processed premiums and generated revenues of $13 million. The company has additional offices in Houston, San Antonio, Austin, Tallahassee, Nashville, San Francisco, Albuquerque, Scottsdale, and Lafayette.

"Speed is important because we're providing coverage for someone who is having difficulty finding it," Wesson explains. "Normally, when clients come to us, they've already exhausted time and effort with their standard insurance options. Very often, it's up to us to keep those clients in business."

U.S. Risk clients not only stay in business, but flourish once their risk coverage is in place. Ultimately, "what we do is provide normalcy," Wesson says. "And in the event of a loss, we provide the funds to restore normalcy. As a result of our work, U.S. Risk clients increase their productivity without fear of the prospect of debilitating loss."

"We work faster, longer, and smarter," Goss says. "The result? Our clients receive superior products and services. You can depend on it."

TRACK RECORD, A RELIABLE AND SIGNIFICANT RATE OF RETURN, and added value. These are the hallmarks of The L&B Group, a Dallas-based real estate investment firm that acquires, manages, and sells commercial real estate for an impressive roster of important institutional clients from across the nation.

The company was founded in Chicago in 1965, but as its portfolio of properties quickly grew in size and scope to take in the entire nation, the principals relocated to Dallas for the favorable business climate and the ease of travel to locations within the United States.

The L&B Group has flourished in the Texas sun. In June 1992, the company joined forces with the Boston-based United Asset Management Corporation, a major New York Stock Exchange company that has more than 6,000 clients and a $175 billion portfolio.

Operating with complete investment and management autonomy, The L&B Group has 16 regional offices around the country. Together, they manage a portfolio of $3 billion in real estate assets, representing about 100 income-producing properties. In all, the firm manages 28 million square feet of office, retail, multi-family, and industrial properties in major metropolitan areas, including Dallas.

With the goal of maximizing its clients' investments and reducing risk, the company's investment philosophy is based on client advocacy, a disciplined investment approach, active management, and consistent investment. The firm also provides asset and property management and dispositions services for its institutional investors. The result has been 30 years of achieving an excellent rate of return for the firm's clients—16.4 percent for all properties bought, managed, and sold since 1971.

The 500 employees of The L&B Group are experienced professionals working in the fields of research, acquisitions, portfolio management, asset management, property management, financial administration, and sales. More than 120 of those employees are based in the Dallas offices, which are located just north of the downtown business district, high above North Central Expressway.

A GROUP OF COMPANIES

There are four separate members of The L&B Group family of firms: L&B Realty Advisors, headed by President and Chief Executive Officer M. Thomas Lardner, and three sub-entities, including L&B Real Estate Counsel; L&B Institutional Property

CLOCKWISE FROM TOP:
THE FULLER BUILDING, a 41-story historical building managed by THE L&B group, is located in the heart of the Plaza District in midtown New York City. It includes 289,000 square feet of space that is leased to office, retail, and gallery tenants.

DALLAS office properties in the L&B portfolio include 5500 PRESTON ROAD, a 77,000-square-foot office building in the Highland Park area.

THE L&B GROUP manages the 1.8 million-square-foot FOUR OAKS PLACE office complex near HOUSTON'S GALLERIA.

erties, managing 18 million square feet of space in office buildings, shopping centers, and mixed-use facilities.

Dallas office properties in the L&B portfolio include Lakeside Centre, an office complex of 319,000 square feet; the 203,000-square-foot Executive Centre One on LBJ Freeway; and 5500 Preston Road, a 77,000-square-foot office building in Highland Park. Among L&B's other Texas properties are the three-level, enclosed Rivercenter in San Antonio; the 1.8 million-square-foot Four Oaks Place office complex near Houston's Galleria; and a host of industrial buildings throughout Dallas and Houston.

Managers, Inc.; and L&B Multi-family Advisors, Inc.

L&B Real Estate Counsel was established as a registered investment adviser to assist institutional, tax-exempt clients in the field of real estate investment. G. Andrews Smith is president of the division. L&B Real Estate Counsel's consistent performance has attracted some of the nation's largest institutional investors, including many of the 200 largest corporate and public pension funds. Among them can be counted Ford Motor and Johnson & Johnson, as well as Ohio School Employees' Retirement System and Pennsylvania Public School Employes' Retirement System.

Although the company has built its reputation on acquiring core properties on behalf of its clients, L&B's asset management and property services have kept its real estate portfolio well occupied. Headed by Daniel L. Plumlee, L&B Institutional Property Managers, Inc. is the division that adds value to the company's prop-

L&B Multifamily Advisors, Inc., led by Unit President David W. Gleeson, CRE, offers acquisition, asset management, and research services that focus on multifamily properties. More than 7,700 units in 28 apartment properties comprise L&B's multifamily portfolio. Ten of the firm's multifamily complexes are in the Dallas area.

Why has The L&B Group continued to succeed throughout the volatile real estate climate of the past decade? According to Lardner, the firm has built a successful track record that relies on a proven investment approach.

A PROVEN INVESTMENT APPROACH

"We never make an investment suddenly or without careful analysis. Each of our investments is based upon an intimate knowledge of current market conditions and well-researched projections for the future," Lardner explains. "We're not in the business of trying to guess the bottom of an investment cycle or to acquire every property that is available at a good price. Our reputation is based on our ability to successfully acquire, manage, and sell real estate on behalf of our clients."

The L&B Group's multi-faceted approach has given its clients a broad array of real estate services. "We don't exist simply to acquire properties," Lardner confirms. "In fact, asset and property management have long been our hidden strengths because we've always put capital into upgrading, expanding, retenanting, or making any other needed improvement on the properties we acquire. That's how we increase an individual property's value or improve its cash flow. It's also how we continue to keep our clients satisfied."

THE L&B GROUP HAS FLOURISHED IN THE TEXAS SUN. THE COMPANY'S DALLAS PORTFOLIO INCLUDES LAKESIDE CENTRE (TOP LEFT), AN OFFICE COMPLEX OF 319,000 SQUARE FEET, AND THE 203,000-SQUARE-FOOT EXECUTIVE CENTRE ONE ON LBJ FREEWAY (BOTTOM LEFT). OTHER TEXAS PROPERTIES INCLUDE THE THREE-LEVEL RIVERCENTER IN SAN ANTONIO (BOTTOM RIGHT), A 1 MILLION-SQUARE-FOOT SHOPPING/ENTERTAINMENT COMPLEX LOCATED ON THE RIVER WALK.

OR NEARLY 35 YEARS, RAPP COLLINS WORLDWIDE HAS PIONEERED the art of relationship marketing—a term the advertising community uses to describe the process of building positive, profitable relationships with consumers. It is the only direct marketing company in the world's top five that has its creative, information technology, production, strategic account, design, and analytic capabilities on one campus. This makes Rapp Collins attractive to clients who want a single firm to function as a full-service partner.

By developing methods to gain knowledge about its clients' customers, and then applying that knowledge in "customer-centric" marketing campaigns, Rapp Collins Worldwide has changed the way direct marketing achieves its goals. The Las Colinas-based Rapp Collins agency is considered "best in its class" at delivering personalized marketing strategies and execution based on carefully accumulated significant data about customers and prospects.

Using these measurable results, Rapp Collins increases the effectiveness and efficiency of future communications through relationship and loyalty marketing strategies. These strategies are often executed as transaction-based or frequency programs, such as those that reward purchases with air miles.

PROFILING CONSUMERS FOR INDUSTRY LEADERS

To many businesses, a customer is simply a target with a name and an address. Rapp Collins helps its clients discover additional insight about consumers. Going beyond the traditional study of demographics, the firm's analysts investigate and leverage such inventive, far-thinking marketing concepts as psychographics and synchographics.

Psychographics examines which traits make people in the same demographic behave differently. For example, which behavioral triggers compel one customer to make a purchase while another in the same demographic does not? Synchographics is the study of purchasing frequencies. These dimensions are included with the traditional methodologies to give clients a startlingly clear picture of their individual customers.

By developing relationship marketing plans that enhance the value of customers, Rapp Collins helps clients such as Sony Computer Entertainment, Hyatt Hotels Corporation, MCI Communications Corp., Loyalty Management Group of Canada, and other blue-chip companies forge lasting bonds with customers. The firm has found that when a consumer perceives added value, he or she tends to purchase more merchandise, more often.

The more than 400 Dallas-based employees are joined by some 1,200 other Rapp Collins employees working in 46 offices in 18 countries around the globe. As part of Omnicom, a multinational network of communications and advertising agencies, Rapp Collins and its clients enjoy a global synergy.

QUADRUPLING IN DALLAS

Rapp Collins was founded in New York City by innovative direct marketers Stan Rapp and Thomas L. Collins, the authors of the best-selling books *MaxiMarketing* and *Beyond MaxiMarketing*. It was their vision to develop a system of direct marketing that

DON DANIEL (LEFT) AND STEVE JUDGE ARE CO-MANAGING DIRECTORS AND RUN RAPP COLLINS' DALLAS OFFICE.

went beyond what was available in the 1970s.

Rapp Collins explored relationship marketing—building and maximizing current customer bases and acquiring new customers who best fit its clients' targeted profiles. The goal of the agency today is to continually exceed that vision.

Using frequent flyer miles and other incentives to increase brand loyalty to industry-leading firms, Rapp Collins brought the emerging science of computerized database technology into the marketing world. By leveraging this wealth of consumer knowledge, Rapp Collins could create personalized marketing brochures and mailings rather than blindly sending bulk mail to specific zip codes. Such customized methods have proved to be markedly more effective in generating sales for Rapp Collins' clients.

Rapp Collins has the capabilities to administer its projects on an expansive scale. Currently, millions of Canadians—approximately one-quarter of the country's population—are participating in a long-term brand loyalty program managed by Rapp Collins. It is the largest retail program of its kind in the world. The program provides air miles for cash and credit purchases made at thousands of locations of more than 100 partner companies.

As a measure of its success, the Dallas office of Rapp Collins has quadrupled in size in seven years. In 1996, Rapp Collins' total worldwide billings exceeded $2 billion. As a stand-alone agency, the Dallas office places in the top 10 of direct marketing advertising agencies in the country.

As a direct marketing innovator, Rapp Collins anticipates and develops marketing applications leveraging the latest advancements in technology. For instance, the firm has pioneered laser-generated, data-driven vari-

able copy; it is possible for Rapp Collins to customize 500,000 data variations, in effect making every single piece in a mailing different. This goes beyond simply personalizing a name and address, since Rapp Collins can change the message of each piece to include selected demographic, psychographic, and synchographic details about the targeted customers. By using customized delivery systems

developed by the agency—such as CD-ROMs, multimedia, and Internet sites—Rapp Collins' clients establish dialogues and relationships with individual customers.

As a true innovator in the direct marketing industry, Rapp Collins has taken the "mass" out of mass marketing, performing one-on-one marketing, millions at a time.

THE DALLAS OFFICE OF RAPP COLLINS IS THE ONLY DIRECT MARKETING COMPANY IN THE WORLD'S TOP FIVE THAT HAS ITS CREATIVE, INFORMATION TECHNOLOGY, PRODUCTION, STRATEGIC ACCOUNT, DESIGN, AND ANALYTIC CAPABILITIES ON ONE CAMPUS (TOP).

BY DEVELOPING RELATIONSHIP MARKETING PLANS THAT ENHANCE VALUE WITH CUSTOMERS, RAPP COLLINS HELPS CLIENTS SUCH AS HYATT HOTELS CORPORATION FORGE LASTING BONDS WITH CUSTOMERS (BOTTOM).

THE IDEAS THAT SHAPED KAISER PERMANENTE EMERGED FROM A series of challenges. During the Great Depression, while thousands of men sought to meet the challenge of bringing Colorado River water to Los Angeles with the 240-mile long aqueduct across the Mojave Desert, Henry J. Kaiser and Sidney R. Garfield, M.D., wrestled with how to provide quality health care to these workers. As huge numbers of workers tackled the challenge of constructing the largest dam in the history of the world, the Grand Coulee Dam, the program that would become Kaiser Permanente tackled the challenge of providing health care to these workers and their families. Today, Kaiser Permanente continues to fulfill the shared vision of Kaiser and Garfield.

Over the years, Kaiser Permanente has cared for millions of Americans and thousands of Texans. From its inception, Kaiser Permanente has been an industry leader in developing innovative approaches to health care. Many of the services Kaiser Permanente has been providing to members for years, such as the prepayment of monthly membership dues and health education classes that focus on prevention, have become accepted norms in the managed health care industry.

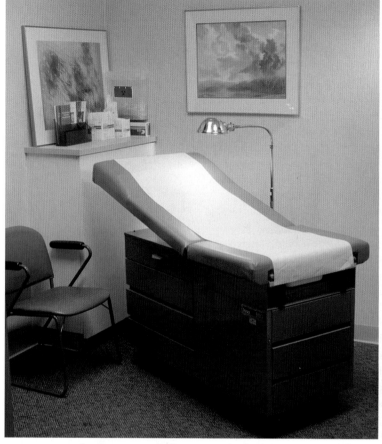

THE POWER OF KAISER PERMANENTE'S INTEGRATED HEALTH CARE DELIVERY SYSTEM LIES IN ITS POTENTIAL TO CREATE AN ENVIRONMENT THAT SUPPORTS INNOVATION AND FOCUSES ON KEEPING MEMBERS HEALTHY.

DALLAS SERVES AS THE HEADQUARTERS FOR KAISER PERMANENTE'S SOUTHWEST DIVISION, WHICH PROVIDES CARE TO MEMBERS THROUGHOUT THE DALLAS/FORT WORTH AREA AT LOCATIONS SUCH AS THE CENTRAL FORT WORTH MEDICAL OFFICE (LEFT) AND THE PLANO MEDICAL OFFICE (RIGHT).

SOUTHWEST DIVISION
Dallas serves as the headquarters for the program's Southwest Division, which provides care to members throughout the Dallas/Fort Worth area. The Southwest Division is a cooperative effort among representatives of medicine and management, sharing responsibilities for organizing, financing, and delivering quality health services to members on a prepaid basis. Kaiser Foundation Health Plan of Texas enrolls members and manages the business aspects of the health plan while the Permanente Medical Association of Texas provides medical care for health plan members. Together they serve members as Kaiser Permanente.

The power of Kaiser Permanente's integrated health care delivery system lies in its potential to create an environment that supports innovation and focuses on keeping members healthy.

The care of members is a priority for Kaiser Permanente. As one of the nation's largest group practice HMOs, the care members receive is coordinated by Kaiser Permanente providers, not an insurance company. In addition, because the health plan is not responsible to shareholders, the focus of the organization is on providing quality care, not making a profit.

In addition to the HMO plan, the Southwest Division also offers a point-of-service plan called *Added Choice*SM to employers. This plan allows members to choose between the HMO, a preferred provider organization (PPO), or traditional indemnity coverage when seeking care. Individuals may enroll in *Personal Advantage*, the division's direct pay, nongroup plan.

QUALITY CARE

Kaiser Permanente has been recognized for the quality care it provides. The Southwest Division was the first North Texas HMO to receive full accreditation from the National Committee for Quality Assurance (NCQA) the first time it was reviewed. As a result of the rigorous on-site review and grievance process, NCQA granted the Southwest Division three-year full accreditation, the highest level

of accreditation an HMO can receive. NCQA is an independent, nonprofit organization that evaluates health plans according to a predetermined set of quality standards. A team of nationally recognized doctors and experts in health care examines the credentialing process for physicians, medical records, and preventive health initiatives, to name a few, when evaluating health plans.

Kaiser Permanente seeks out physicians who are experts in their fields. A majority of the division's physicians are board certified. This means these physicians have attained a standard of excellence recognized by the national board of examiners in each of their specialties. Board certification involves additional education and rigorous training.

Kaiser Permanente has demonstrated a commitment to performance measurement by taking an active part in the initial development and refinement of the Health Plan Employer Data and Information Set (HEDIS®). As a founding member of the North Texas HEDIS Coalition, the Southwest Division, together with other

health plans, employers, and health care consultants, evaluates the care provided by the health plans and issues report cards. These report cards contain data that is used to monitor health plan performance on key indicators of quality.

SERVICES FOR MEMBERS

Kaiser Permanente, Southwest Division has medical offices throughout the Metroplex. These offices provide primary and specialty care to members. For medical services outside its medical group, Kaiser Permanente also contracts with community physicians and hospitals.

Weekend and after-hours care is also available through Kaiser Permanente's Urgent Care Centers. Medical Advice nurses are available to members to answer health-related questions. Working under the supervision of Kaiser Permanente physicians, these nurses are specially trained to answer questions from members.

Kaiser Permanente's advanced Preventive Care programs have become a staple in the managed care industry. The Southwest Division offers a wide array of health education classes to members, including smoking cessation, prenatal care, and diabetes management. The focus of the program on prevention encourages members to live healthier lives.

Since its inception, Kaiser Permanente has played a critical role in the health care of Americans. In the years ahead, members can feel confident that their social purpose to care for the communities they serve will only intensify.

KAISER PERMANENTE, SOUTHWEST DIVISION HAS MEDICAL OFFICES THROUGHOUT THE METROPLEX, INCLUDING IRVING (ABOVE) AND MESQUITE (BELOW). THESE OFFICES PROVIDE PRIMARY CARE TO MEMBERS.

ADLETA AND POSTON, REALTORS

OUNDED IN 1979, ADLETA AND POSTON, REALTORS, ONE OF Dallas' finest brokerage firms, continues to dominate the upper-end executive housing market and corporate relocation business throughout the city. Partners Lynda Adleta and Kimberly Poston have built a multibillion-dollar business by consistently providing the very best in personal service and proven results to their customers and clients.

LYNDA ADLETA AND KIMBERLY POSTON ARE PARTNERS OF ADLETA AND POSTON, REALTORS, INC.

Adleta and Poston, Realtors has assembled a team of experienced professionals who represent the city's best and brightest residential experts. Every associate has an in-depth knowledge of the Greater Dallas area and has received extensive training in the buying and selling of residential real estate and investment properties. The support staff at Adleta and Poston is also well known for their efficiency, high standards, and superior level of service.

Dedication to world-class service and a commitment to excellence has made Adleta and Poston, Realtors the real estate firm of choice for residents and newcomers alike. Chosen as the exclusive Dallas affiliate for Christies Great Estates, Adleta and Poston offers unparalleled marketing expertise and worldwide connections. For the third consecutive year, Adleta and Poston has been named the leading independent firm in the area based on closed sales volume, according to the *Dallas Business Journal*. Adleta and Poston also has been named among the Top 250 residential real estate brokerage firms in the country by *National Relocation & Real Estate* magazine and is included in *Who's Who in Luxury Homes*.

AWARD-WINNING RELOCATION

The Dallas area is a dynamic community with many options available for living, working, and recreation. Senior Vice President and Relocation Director Kitty T. Snelling, SCRP, is a nationally recognized leader in the relocation industry, and under her direction, Adleta and Poston's Relocation Division has helped hundreds of families make a smooth and enjoyable move to the Dallas area.

The firm also has been honored with many local and national awards, and has been recognized as one of the most outstanding relocation organizations in the country. Many executives of major corporations in the Dallas area have chosen Adleta and Poston to represent them in real estate transactions. Some of the leading corporations Adleta and Poston has assisted include American Airlines, JCPenney, MCI, OpTel, Quaker State, Sea Land, and Waldenbooks, just to name a few.

Above and beyond providing successful results in real estate, Adleta and Poston associates assist corporations, families, and individuals long after the transaction has closed. They make sure each customer experiences a smooth transition by coordinating every aspect of the move, including assistance with individual interests and special needs—from schools and business to civic and recreational activities.

COMMUNITY LEADERS

Adleta and Poston, Realtors has a strong commitment to the Dallas community. The company sponsors and contributes to many local and national organizations for the betterment of the city. Many of the associates and staff serve on a number of boards, chair benefits for worthwhile causes, and give back to the community in numerous ways. Some of the organizations the company is involved with are the Junior League of Dallas, Boys and Girls Clubs of Dallas, United Way, Salvation Army, Family Gateway, SPCA, March of Dimes, Genesis Women's Shelter, Southwestern Medical Center, and Dallas Museum of Art.

Clients can depend upon Adleta and Poston to provide the finest personal service, unique and exciting properties, and a solid history of proven results.

▲ DONOVAN REESE

1980-1997

1980 PRESBYTERIAN VILLAGE NORTH	1983 HALL FINANCIAL GROUP, INC.	1986 DARLING INTERNATIONAL
1980 RUSHMORE FINANCIAL GROUP	1984 AT&T	1986 TURNER CONSTRUCTION COMPANY
1982 REES ASSOCIATES, INC.	1984 UICI	1987 COLUMBIA HEALTHCARE CORPORATION, NORTH TEXAS DIVISION
1983 BRINK'S HOME SECURITY, INC.	1985 KIMBERLY-CLARK CORPORATION	
1983 CH2M HILL	1986 CORRIGAN REAL ESTATE SERVICES	1987 PARK PLACE MOTORCARS
1983 DALLAS AREA RAPID TRANSIT		1988 BYRNE JOHNSON INC.

1988 HILB, ROGAL AND HAMILTON COMPANY OF DALLAS	1991 CANMAX INC.	1992 NATIONSBANK
1989 DESIGN QUORUM	1991 CAPROCK COMMUNICATIONS CORPORATION	1993 UPTOWN REALTORS
1989 HICKS, MUSE, TATE & FURST INCORPORATED	1991 CHAMPION PARTNERS, LTD.	1994 CRESCENT REAL ESTATE EQUITIES COMPANY
1990 FAISON-STONE, INC.	1992 ABT EXECUTIVE SUITES	1996 MCKESSON CORPORATION
1990 THE REAL ESTATE COUNCIL	1992 KYNG-FM "YOUNG COUNTRY®"	1996 SUMMERFIELD SUITES HOTEL

USHMORE FINANCIAL GROUP WAS FOUNDED UPON THE FUNDA-mental principles that emerge from the heart and soul of America. True to its original vision, Rushmore Financial is a national group of integrated companies and financial professionals who have assembled their talents and resources to provide leadership and excellence in the financial services industry. Its mission is "to provide excellent, innovative financial products and services oriented to solving problems and achieving the individual objectives of our clients."

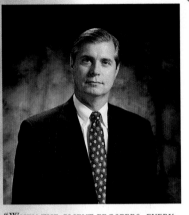

"WHEN THE CLIENT PROSPERS, EVERY-ONE PROSPERS," IS THE PHILOSOPHY OF D.M. RUSTY MOORE, PRESIDENT AND CEO OF RUSHMORE FINANCIAL GROUP.

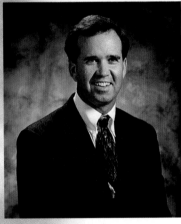

"WE WANT TO MAKE SURE THAT WHEN OUR CLIENTS ARE FINISHED WORKING FOR THEIR MONEY, THEIR MONEY WILL BE THERE TO WORK FOR THEM," EX-PLAINS JIM CLARK, PRESIDENT OF RUSHMORE SECURITIES CORPORATION.

THE RUSHMORE FINANCIAL GROUP'S NATIONAL NETWORK IS EXPANDING ACROSS THE UNITED STATES THROUGH ITS NETWORK OF BRANCH OFFICE AFFILIATES.

COMMITMENT TO QUALITY

Rushmore Financial Group is committed to conducting its business in a manner that is customer focused, quality oriented, financially disciplined, judiciously managed, and technologically innovative.

Rushmore Financial Group provides access to innovative, competitive, and, in some cases, exclusive products that offer a broad range of investment strategies. This fully diversified product portfolio includes variable and fixed annuities; variable, universal, and term life; health and disability insurance; mutual funds and money market funds; certificates of deposit; stocks and bonds; and investment advisory services.

TEAMWORK

Behind the scenes, a team of financial professionals works to provide each client with comprehensive financial products and investment advisory services. This team approach sets Rushmore Financial Group apart from other firms.

Rushmore representatives across the country are supported by various in-house, Dallas-based teams that manage customer accounts. Using this approach, Rushmore's growth has been remarkable.

The Rushmore family of companies is made up of a number of subsidiaries, with Rushmore Capital Corporation as the holding company for the Rushmore financial group of companies.

RISK MANAGEMENT

Rushmore Insurance Services, Inc., the firm's national insurance agency, seeks representatives who really care about people. "I get tremendous joy out of helping people attain their goals," says Chip Brunott, president of Rushmore Insurance Services, Inc.

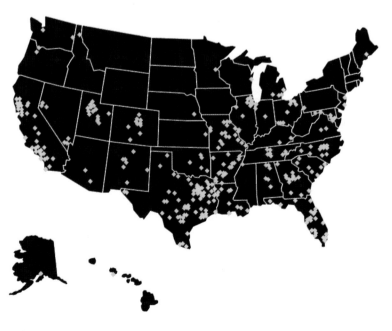

Risk management is a vital part of anyone's financial plan. Whether providing for an estate or protecting an estate, life insurance serves an essential role in reducing risk of loss. Rushmore provides the most cost-effective, strategic choices for insurance planning.

CUSTOMER FOCUSED

Rushmore Securities Corporation, a broker/dealer and a member of the NASD & SIPC, was founded in Dallas in 1980 and is involved with all aspects of investment brokerage. In this fast-paced world, only a small percentage of people retire financially independent. "We want to make sure that when our clients are finished working for their money, their money will be there to work for them," explains Jim Clark, president of Rushmore Securities Corporation. Rushmore provides solutions to clients' financial challenges.

DISCOUNT BROKERAGE

In an industry where "discount" is synonymous with being a "face in the crowd," Rushmore Discount Brokerage knows who its clients are. Brokers are always available to provide fundamental and technical information about personal investments at a discount commission on trades.

INVESTMENT ADVISORY

Rushmore Investment Advisors, Inc. offers a wide variety of fee-based portfolio management services. This advisory team offers unbiased advice on financial strategies and estate planning to maximize each client's financial success without commission charges.

Rushmore Investment Advisors' clients have unprecedented support with state-of-the-art managed programs such as IMAP™ for management of stock and bond portfolios and RushMAP™, a diversified asset allocation program, for the management of multiple mutual fund accounts. Clients gain access to in-house experts who analyze, review, research, and reposition assets, as well as generate performance reports that are simple to read and understand.

"In today's hectic life, our clients are fully occupied with the demands of their own families and careers," says Fritz Mowery, president of Rushmore Investment Advisors, Inc. "We provide the solutions to their financial challenges, with the goal of providing our clients with peace of mind and the time to enjoy the lifestyle they have built."

WHERE ASSOCIATES ARE SHARE OWNERS

Rushmore associates share in the ownership of the company by participating in a stock option plan of Rushmore Capital Corporation. They have a vested interest in the success and satisfaction of each customer.

CLOCKWISE FROM TOP RIGHT: RUSHMORE FINANCIAL GROUP PROVIDES EXCELLENT INNOVATIVE FINANCIAL PRODUCTS AND SERVICES ORIENTED TO SOLVING PROBLEMS AND ACHIEVING THE INDIVIDUAL OBJECTIVES OF ITS CLIENTS.

RUSHMORE FINANCIAL GROUP PROVIDES ACCESS TO COMPETITIVE AND, IN SOME CASES, EXCLUSIVE PRODUCTS THAT OFFER A BROAD RANGE OF INVESTMENT STRATEGIES.

TOM COLEMAN, VICE PRESIDENT, RUSHMORE SECURITIES CORPORATION, DIRECTOR OF DISCOUNT SECURITIES DIVISION

"IT GIVES ME TREMENDOUS JOY TO HELP PEOPLE ATTAIN THEIR GOALS," SAYS CHIP BRUNOTT, PRESIDENT OF RUSHMORE INSURANCE SERVICES, INC.

"WE PROVIDE THE SOLUTIONS TO THEIR FINANCIAL CHALLENGES, LEAVING OUR CLIENTS PEACE OF MIND AND THE TIME TO ENJOY THE LIFESTYLE THEY HAVE BUILT," SAYS FRITZ MOWERY, PRESIDENT OF RUSHMORE INVESTMENT ADVISORS, INC.

HALL FINANCIAL GROUP, INC.

HALL FINANCIAL GROUP, INC. (HFG) IS A DIVERSIFIED REAL ESTATE investment, management, and development company that counts among its holdings several prominent downtown Dallas structures, including Harwood Center, St. Paul Place, and The Kirby Building, one of the most historically and architecturally significant buildings in Dallas.

HFG was founded in 1968. By 1986, HFG controlled approximately $3 billion in assets and was the largest private placement company in the United States. The company practices a counter-cyclical investment approach— an against-the-trend program of upgrading distressed properties for profitable resale or purchasing assets when they are out of favor. HFG was one of the first to make a significant investment in downtown Dallas in 1994 when many thought real estate values in the area might not recover. Since that time, downtown Dallas has seen an upswing in investment interest.

Today, HFG is in a position to advance the tremendous turnaround potential in downtown Dallas. With ownership of choice properties, including parcels in and around Dallas' desirable Arts District, HFG has the capability to develop up to 5 million square feet of mixed-use facilities in the downtown area. In addition, at the nearly century-old Kirby Building, HFG is making plans to redevelop the property into residential units. HFG stands ready to be a major contributor to a revitalized downtown Dallas. In addition to a substantial presence in downtown Dallas, HFG has land holdings in Plano and Frisco. In Frisco, HFG has just announced plans for a 2 million-square-foot Stonebriar Office Park development at Highway 121 and the Dallas North Tollway. This development is expected to include office and retail—and perhaps a hotel—and is anticipated to attract strong interest in corporate build-to-suits, call centers, and office showrooms. HFG is committed to making this development the most technologically advanced, environmentally friendly, and aesthetically pleasing office park in the Metroplex.

CLOCKWISE FROM BOTTOM LEFT: THE HARWOOD CENTER IS A CLASS-A CENTRAL BUSINESS DISTRICT OFFICE TOWER ON DART'S LIGHT-RAIL LINE.

ST. PAUL PLACE IS A NEWLY REMODELED OFFICE TOWER ACROSS FROM THE DALLAS MUSEUM OF ART.

THE KIRBY RESIDENCES ON HISTORIC MAIN STREET ARE THE SITE OF FUTURE RESIDENTIAL DEVELOPMENT.

AN ARTIST'S RENDERING OF STONEBRIAR ONE DEPICTS THE FIRST PHASE OF STONEBRIAR OFFICE PARK.

F**AR FROM THE AVERAGE RETIREMENT COMMUNITY, Presbyterian** Village North (PVN) is full of surprises. Where else can one find a variety of living accommodations to suit every individual? The Village offers many of the finest independent and assisted-living

arrangements, including gracious, custom-built brick homes with two-car garages; apartments with full-sized kitchens and flowers spilling over from boxes kept on sunny balconies; soaring, 12-foot ceilings; and beautifully landscaped grounds.

Presbyterian Village North is the Metroplex's preferred retirement community, attracting discriminating seniors aged 62 and older from Dallas and around the country. As part of the renowned Presbyterian Healthcare System—which includes Presbyterian Hospital of Dallas, located just a few miles away—it is the only area retirement community directly affiliated with an acute care hospital.

A CONTINUUM OF CARE

The Village, which opened in June 1980, was developed as a special living environment that tailors its accommodations and services to the special needs of each resident. For those residents who are highly mobile and lead active lives, there is the 63-acre, landscaped Independent area, which offers executive homes, patio duplexes, and garden apartments. Residents come and go as they please, yet each room is outfitted with emergency pull cords to summon assistance.

As the resident's needs change, so does the degree of attention. In Joyce Residence Hall, residents live in their own apartments with access to 24-hour attendant care. In the Health Unit, there is full-service nursing care provided by dedicated, licensed nursing professionals.

More than 500 Village residents share such amenities as the elegant library, the various dining rooms, beauty and barber shops, and a pantry and pharmacy. The spacious Corrigan Activity Center is busy with special seminars, exercise sessions, and weekly worship services conducted by the PVN chaplain and a rotating schedule of ministers.

In 1997, the Village will add an Alzheimer's Dementia Unit and an Adult Day Care Unit, as well as additional executive homes.

LIVING IN FULFILLMENT

Dallas is a cultural and entertainment center, with museums, galleries, and concert halls. Just a few miles away from The Village, there are several large, North Dallas shopping malls. The full-time activity director regularly schedules excursions to these and other popular destinations. There is also a schedule of daily on-campus activities in which residents find recreation and friendship. Well-trained personnel in such departments as dietary, nursing, social work, engineering, and administration provide residents security, comfort, and enjoyment. These professionals are supplemented by trained volunteers from the Dallas community who contribute greatly to the quality of life Village residents experience each day.

Presbyterian Village North—a nonprofit, nondenominational community—offers its residents a place to retire without giving up their independence or lifestyle. The Village is unique in meeting individual needs at the appropriate level, with proper attention to detail for the people it serves.

RICHARD CLINTSMAN/C STUDIO

CLOCKWISE FROM TOP LEFT:
AS PART OF THE RENOWNED PRESBYTERIAN HEALTHCARE SYSTEM—WHICH INCLUDES PRESBYTERIAN HOSPITAL OF DALLAS, LOCATED JUST A FEW MILES AWAY—IT IS THE ONLY AREA RETIREMENT COMMUNITY DIRECTLY AFFILIATED WITH AN ACUTE CARE HOSPITAL.

PRESBYTERIAN VILLAGE NORTH—A NONPROFIT, NONDENOMINATIONAL COMMUNITY—OFFERS ITS RESIDENTS A PLACE TO RETIRE WITHOUT GIVING UP THEIR INDEPENDENCE OR LIFESTYLE.

PRESBYTERIAN VILLAGE NORTH IS THE METROPLEX'S PREFERRED RETIREMENT COMMUNITY, ATTRACTING DISCRIMINATING SENIORS AGED 62 AND OLDER FROM DALLAS AND AROUND THE COUNTRY.

REES ASSOCIATES, INC.

"EES ASSOCIATES, INC. HAS THE UNIQUE ABILITY TO HELP ORGANIzations determine who they really are—but, beyond that, who they would be if they were not limited by the constraints of their building," says Frank Rees Jr. "Sometimes the client's company is reborn internally concerning what they are really about after we've made our impact. We do that over and over."

Rees Associates' clients—as diverse as hospitals, assisted living centers, high-tech facilities, office buildings, correctional facilities, and television stations—have learned that Rees does more than render building designs.

Using Rees' exclusive, registered FACILITY BUSINESS PLAN® (FBP), the Rees team of professionals not only designs aesthetically pleasing, marketable, and profitable buildings, but also explores the hows and whys of what the client's employees do inside the building from day to day. A Rees plan achieves operational efficiency and reflects the desired corporate image by incorporating the spirit of the company into the plan.

"The FACILITY BUSINESS PLAN® creates a very detailed road map of where the client is today, how they function, where they will be in the future, and what kind of building they need to do what they do, but do it better," says Rees. "We help them to be more successful at what they do than ever before. The FACILITY BUSINESS PLAN® often becomes or updates the corporate mission statement. Several clients thought they were hiring us to be architects, and we ended up doing a lot of things for them that they never expected."

Businesses that have benefited from the FBP include clients in 40 states and a dozen countries around the world. Rees has designed buildings for the New York Times Company, Disney/ABC, Inc., Gannett Co. Inc, Turner Broadcasting, Texas A&M University, McGraw-Hill, NBC, Cedars-Sinai Medical Center in Los Angeles, NASA in Houston, and Methodist Hospital in Dallas. In all, Rees has worked with more than 60 of the Fortune 500 firms.

"Rees Associates is without peer in planing and designing facilities," says Frank Roberts, president of the New York Times Broadcast Group. "Two facilities they designed for the New York Times Company are the finest, and both were finished on time and within budget."

Bill Loorz, senior vice president of Tenet Healthcare Corporation, says, "We have worked on a number of projects with Rees using the FACILITY BUSINESS PLAN® approach. Rees Associates' understanding of health care and our needs makes us very satisfied with the results and our ability to achieve our targets."

"Rees involved all our people in the FACILITY BUSINESS PLAN® process," states Bob Niles, vice president and director of engineering for Disney/ABC, Inc. "They boiled down our input, identified our needs, developed the right scope to make the project realistic, and then explained it in a way that we could all understand."

When clients retain the Rees firm, "they get long-range and multiple-phase designs," Rees points out. "We design facilities

GANNETT BROADCASTING HEADQUARTERS, WASHINGTON, D.C. (TOP)

USC UNIVERSITY HOSPITAL, LOS ANGELES: WORLD'S FIRST BASE-ISOLATION EARTHQUAKE-PROOF HOSPITAL (BOTTOM)

MICHAEL FRENCH

▲ JOSEPH MILLS

to support growth and change as their organization evolves. We create a building that enhances what they're all about, now and in the future."

HOW THE FACILITY BUSINESS PLAN® WORKS

The FBP process begins with a detailed study of the site and an evaluation of existing buildings and plans—a standard first step with most architectural firms. The Rees team then may develop a strategic plan and perform a market analysis, study operational initiatives, and receive copious feed-

▲ MICHAEL FRENCH

back from employees who will be working in the building upon completion. Once the investigation phase has been completed, Rees team members meet with management and employee groups to understand the current and the future direction of the company.

"We perform two- to four-day condensed *Interactive↔WorkSessions* with the client's employees," Rees explains. "This helps the client think through their goals and future plans, and also helps align the rest of the group with the leader in the direction they want to go and, often, vice versa. But the process goes beyond listening to the client. We help get rid of their paradigms—get them out of the box so to speak—and make them think of what they can really be when they grow as an organization."

Typically, the firm conducts a series of *Interactive↔WorkSessions* later in the FBP

process, after departmental and technical requirements are established. At this stage, concepts and development options are studied, alternatives are evaluated with the full participation of the client, and budgets are produced. All information compiled throughout the entire process becomes documented in the bound volumes of the final report.

"It's a cost-effective plan to renew facilities in such a manner that helps the client reach their goals, and, quite often, learn what those goals are," says Rees. "And at a minimal fee. There have been some clients who didn't want just a new building. They wanted the FACILITY BUSINESS PLAN® to use as a prototype for a new business."

Besides having rendered architectural and engineering designs for more television facilities than any other firm in the world, Rees is ranked among the top firms in health care facility design, and is one of the top four national firms in the design of senior housing facilities, including independent living, assisted living, and long-term care.

"This firm will continue to serve companies with very unique needs," says Rees. "We don't do commodities. If you have a unique need, our unique expertise can help you."

BRINK'S HOME SECURITY, INC.

FOR DECADES, MONITORED SECURITY SYSTEMS WERE COMMONPLACE only in commercial premises and very expensive houses. However, in the mid 1980s, Brink's Home Security, Inc. pioneered the concept of mass marketing affordable security to residences. As a result, one of the most respected names in security, Brink's, quickly became the leader in this new field.

Brink's Home Security—now building a new corporate headquarters with its central monitoring center in the Dallas suburb of Irving—provides security to more than 500,000 homes and businesses in 62 markets in 39 states and Canada. For the last decade, Brink's has grown at a double-digit rate in installations and profits, and has expanded into new markets in the United States and Canada.

NOT JUST FOR MANSIONS ANYMORE

Brink's Home Security has made high-value monitored protection—which has been enjoyed for years by businesses and exclusive properties—available to average homeowners. Since unveiling this service in 1983, the company has discovered that the market continues to expand rapidly.

Each day, uniformed Brink's Home Security technicians install state-of-the-art equipment—including keypads, heat and microwave-technology motion detectors, glass-break detectors, and

DURING THE 1980S, BRINK'S HOME SECURITY WAS THE FIRST COMPANY TO MASS MARKET MONITORED HOME SECURITY SYSTEMS TO THE GENERAL PUBLIC.

magnetic contacts—in homes throughout the country. The homeowner has peace of mind in knowing that, in the event of an intrusion, fire, or medical emergency, Brink's Home Security is ready to summon help.

In the national monitoring center, Brink's Home Security employees are ready 24 hours a day to respond to electronic signals from its equipment installed in customers' homes. When an alarm is triggered, a siren sounds, and the customer's data is sent to a monitoring operator's computer screen in the monitoring center.

The monitoring center monitors more than one-half million American homes each day, and the center boasts redundancy systems and emergency backup generators, representing a substantial investment of capital and enterprise. The Brink's Home Security monitoring center and equipment is Underwriters Laboratories listed—

THE BRINK'S KEYPAD, PATENT PENDING, FEATURES OVERSIZED BUTTONS; A BACKLIT PANEL; AND POLICE, FIRE, AND MEDICAL EMERGENCY BUTTONS.

a stamp of approval for which Brink's Home Security is understandably proud.

A LONG HERITAGE OF PROTECTION

The company's high standards are simply the way Brink's has done business for more than 138 years. As a sister company to Brink's Incorporated of the Pittston Brink's Group (NYSE: PZB), Brink's Home Security continues a legacy in security popularized by the legendary Brink's armored car services. With Brink's Home Security's unrivaled experience in the security field, coupled with modern technology, the company hopes to leverage its brand into the emerging markets of the residential security industry. It is a strategy that is already working, every day, 24 hours a day.

The Brink's Home Security motto is "The right thing, the right way, right away," and it reflects the high level of integrity Brink's brings to home security services. A person's home is generally the most expensive investment he or she will make, and is certainly one of the most important. Brink's believes that protecting this investment and family members is the most important thing a family can do. This is why Brink's Home Security is investing in the infrastructure that will protect American homes, now and in the future. By underwriting the massive overhead it costs to build and

maintain a national monitoring and customer service center, Brink's has gone the extra mile in making the service affordable to those who previously could not afford such a service.

Brink's Home Security maintains a national sales force of more than 300 employees, who have been trained at "Brink's University" at the company's headquarters. Just as cable television operators experienced ardent success in the early days of cable television, Brink's is finding enthusiastic acceptance on a wide scale by homeowners in the United States and Canada who want the sophisticated Brink's technology installed in their homes so they can enjoy the protection.

The FBI calculates there is a residential break-in in America every 11 seconds. Brink's Home Security, Inc. is doing its part to keep an eye on what America values most: home and family.

CLOCKWISE FROM TOP:
THE STATE-OF-THE-ART BRINK'S MONITORING CENTER, LOCATED IN IRVING, TEXAS, KEEPS A WATCHFUL EYE ON MORE THAN 500,000 HOMES IN THE UNITED STATES AND CANADA.

BRINK'S COMMITMENT TO QUALITY AND SUPERIOR CUSTOMER SERVICE HAS MADE IT THE MOST TRUSTED NAME IN SECURITY FOR MORE THAN 135 YEARS.

TODAY, BRINK'S HOME SECURITY CARRIES ON THE TRADITION OF SUPERIOR SERVICE BY STRIVING TO PROVIDE ITS CUSTOMERS WITH THE HIGHEST LEVEL OF SERVICE IN THE INDUSTRY.

DALLAS AREA RAPID TRANSIT, KNOWN TO MILLIONS AS DART, IS the region's multimodal transportation system, serving Dallas and 12 suburban cities with a wide range of public transit services and customer facilities, each tailored to make commuters' trips fast, comfortable, and affordable.

Since its inception in August 1983—when 58 percent of voters in 14 cities and Dallas County chose to fund the agency—DART has been working to both reduce the congestion on area roads and help the region meet federal clean air standards. A one-cent sales tax took effect in January 1984 to finance the agency, which has since improved bus service, organized carpooling, assisted mobility-impaired riders, and, most significantly, constructed the Southwest's first light-rail transit system. An estimated 30 percent of all downtown Dallas workers use DART services, and with the 1996 opening of light-rail service, this number climbed to 38 percent.

ADVENT OF THE LIGHT-RAIL SYSTEM

The first yellow-and-white light-rail trains began operation in July 1996, when the debut section of the DART Rail system began transporting passengers along 11.2 miles of track to 14 stations through the heart of Dallas. Some 18,000 riders—3,000 more than originally projected—immediately began using DART Rail each workday. In January 1997, rail ridership doubled to about 30,000 passengers per day when the agency opened a six-mile extension and three new stations along Dallas' heavily congested North Central Expressway corridor. Approximately 43 percent of Dallas workers will be using the system when the service reaches the northern suburbs in the near future.

Also under construction is the Trinity Railway Express Commuter Rail, which now connects downtown Dallas with south Irving; the service will extend to Fort Worth in 1999, linking the two towns by rail for the first time since the settlement of the Wild West, and then to Dallas/Fort Worth International Airport in 2005.

In all, DART will construct and operate an integrated system of mobility modes consisting of 53 miles of light-rail transit, 37 miles of commuter rail transit, and 98 miles of high-occupancy vehicle (HOV) lanes. That's in addition to a fleet of nearly 1,000 buses transporting some 160,000 riders across a 700-square mile service area each day.

HELPING THE ENVIRONMENT, HELPING THE ECONOMY

DART helps to keep the area's environment clean by removing the equivalent of more than 60,000 car trips a day from the region's streets and highways, transporting those 160,000 daily passengers more than 60,000 miles. The agency works with the North Texas Clean Air Coalition to promote ride-sharing programs that further reduce traffic congestion by organizing carpools and vanpools. In addition, DART is purchasing 210 buses that are powered not by diesel, but by clean-burning natural gas. As a bonus, the entire electricity-powered light-rail system boasts zero emissions.

The region covered by DART is considered by the Environmental Protection Agency to be a

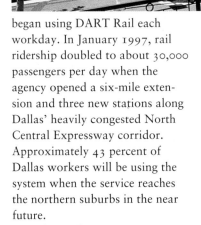

The continuing rail construction is expected to generate 21,000 jobs and pump more than $2.1 billion into the Dallas economy through 1999. Statewide, the rail project is generating some $2.8 billion.

As a fortunate by-product of DART's continually improving service, new and adaptive reuse development projects are cropping up along the path of DART's service lines. Developers are constructing and restoring retail, restaurant, and residential buildings from South Oak Cliff to the upper reaches of the North Central Expressway to serve passengers of the light-rail service. These new businesses will invigorate many areas that are in need of new shopping, banking, entertainment, and living centers, not to mention the hundreds of new jobs that will be created.

DART's integrated system of mobility projects has opened a world of opportunities and automobile alternatives to commuters and businesses. In the future, these services will certainly continue to grow with the city as DART expands to meet the changing needs of the Dallas community.

CLOCKWISE FROM TOP LEFT: THE 20-MILE LIGHT RAIL STARTER SYSTEM, COMPLETED IN MAY 1997, TRANSPORTS PASSENGERS TO 20 STATIONS THROUGH THE HEART OF DALLAS, INCLUDING THE HISTORIC WEST END ENTERTAINMENT DISTRICT.

DART's CONVENTION CENTER RAIL STATION ASSISTS IN BRINGING MAJOR CONVENTIONS TO THE AREA BY PROVIDING TRANSPORTATION FOR 250,000 VISITORS THROUGH 3,000 PRIVATE CHARTERS.

Mass Transit, A MURAL DEPICTING THE REMOVAL OF CARS OFF THE STREETS, OVERLOOKS THE WEST END TRANSFER CENTER NEAR THE WEST END RAIL STATION.

nonattainment area for ozone, volatile organic compounds, and nitrogen oxide standards, all of which are generated by increased automobile traffic. Not meeting those standards jeopardizes future federal and state funds for transportation projects.

In response, DART opened the area's first high-occupancy vehicle lane in September 1991 on a section of Interstate 30E between Jim Miller Road and the Dallas business district. The lane alleviates congestion for 15,000 carpoolers and bus riders each day. Today, DART operates 37 miles of HOV lanes on Interstates 30E, 35, and 635, the state's most congested freeway.

CLEANING UP THE FREEWAYS

DART also encourages ridership on Ozone Action days—when the

ozone level of the region is predicted to violate standards and jeopardize health—by reducing fares to just 50 cents.

DART is more than transportation; the agency and its projects impact the local economy in several ways. DART operations generate some $300 million into the Dallas-area economy, and it boosts the state economy by $496 million. DART employs 2,100 area residents, and procurement spending supports approximately 6,800 jobs across the Dallas area.

Each year DART assists in bringing major conventions to the area by providing transportation for 250,000 visitors through 3,000 private charters. Without DART's comprehensive, multimodal, totally interfaced transportation system, many of those moneymaking conventions would take place elsewhere.

"TRUST IS AN INTEGRAL PART OF REAL ESTATE," SAYS DAVID Corrigan. "Typically, real estate is an investment of significant value, and a company needs to trust the service company that handles it. One almost needs to feel like the management com-

pany is a member of the family." Corrigan should know about those things—real estate, trust, and family—intimately. He and his sister Catherine are the third generation of Corrigans to deal in Dallas real estate. As the youthful leaders of Corrigan Real Estate Services, the brother and sister operate a company that manages nearly 10 million square feet of space in the state of Texas, some 2 million of which is in Dallas.

The Corrigans' story begins with the legendary Leo F. Corrigan Sr., who took four raw acres and built a real estate and hotel empire 75 years ago; at one time, the Corrigans owned the Adolphus and Stoneleigh hotels, as well as a number of prominent buildings in Texas, the western United States, and Hong Kong. Leo Corrigan even made a run for the Empire State Building in the 1950s.

When the third generation of Corrigans came into the family business, they decided to offer their property management and leasing expertise to other real estate owners and investors. Using state-of-the-art accounting and

management software, Corrigan Real Estate Services adheres to its mission statement of "understanding our clients' needs and exceeding their expectations" so successfully that the firm offers an unconditional guarantee of services, a promise that is unique to the industry.

"We can do that because our 65 employees are very experienced and well trained," David Corrigan says. "Our senior management personnel are experienced in handling all the issues that can arise in a landlord-tenant relationship. That senior person maintains daily contact with on-site person-

SPIRIT OF FLIGHT

nel. Our senior management involvement from start to finish is something that sets Corrigan Real Estate apart from our competitors."

DALLAS-BORN, TEXAS-WIDE

Catherine Corrigan takes pride in the fact that the firm—which was founded in 1986 in a restructuring of the Corrigan development business—quickly made an impact on the local retail, office, and multifamily markets, and rapidly expanded into other Texas regions. Other offices are located in Houston, San Antonio, and McAllen.

"But, while we are a regional company and not just a city firm, we pride ourselves in giving back to the Dallas community," she says. "It's important to us to do our fair share, just like our grandfather and parents did."

The legacy of grandfather Leo, who donated the *Spirit of Flight* statue at Love Field Airport, continues as Catherine serves as president of Young Audiences of Greater Dallas, an arts in education agency, and sits on the board of trustees of the Episcopal School of Dallas. David is president of the city's Museum of Natural History and is on the board of the Lamplighter School. Other employees serve in various capacities for local nonprofit organizations.

"We're a well-rounded company, one that tries its best to provide a productive and pleasant environment in which our associates work," David Corrigan says. "And we encourage community involvement and the accomplishment of work goals all at the same time."

The policy has worked for 75 years, and it should serve the Corrigans well for the next 75.

CLOCKWISE FROM TOP: THE LEGACY OF LEO CORRIGAN, WHO DONATED THE *Spirit of Flight* STATUE AT LOVE FIELD AIRPORT, LIVES ON IN HIS GRANDCHILDREN, CATHERINE AND DAVID, WHO ARE LEADING CORRIGAN REAL ESTATE INTO THE 21ST CENTURY.

WOODLAND PLAZA SHOPPING/OFFICE COMPLEX IS LOCATED IN THE BOOMING LOVERS LANE CORRIDOR IN THE HEART OF DALLAS.

MAPLE TERRACE APARTMENTS ARE ONE OF THE MANY CLASS A MULTIFAMILY PROPERTIES THAT CORRIGAN MANAGES.

▲ STAN WOLENSKI

CH2M HILL

I N 1946, A FOUR-PERSON PARTNERSHIP IN CORVALLIS, OREGON, started a consulting engineering firm that today boasts 7,400 employees around the world. Together, these people improve the drinking water in Cairo, Egypt; make traffic easier to bear in California; develop industrial facilities in Asia; and save U.S. taxpayers money by accelerating toxic waste cleanup.

The company is CH2M HILL, which, after more than 50 years of engineering excellence, has achieved such international respect that it was chosen as the environmental adviser to the 1996 Olympic Games in Atlanta.

region function more efficiently and effectively.

Headed by Senior Vice President E. Kent Robinson, the Dallas office—one of five in Texas—has served the City of Dallas and other Metroplex municipalities, from Fort Worth to Sherman and points in between, as well as the EPA, the U.S. Air Force, and the Texas Department of Transportation. The staff of the Dallas regional office is supplemented by the company's national roster of experts. Clients frequently are pleased to learn that the engineer or scientist who assisted on their project may also have written the definitive book on the topic.

ENGINEERING EXCELLENCE

CH2M HILL is known for its innovative use—and often the invention—of cutting-edge technologies and for its understanding of existing regulations that affect its clients. The firm also provides leadership in several professional organizations, including the Water Environment Association of Texas and the Texas chapter of the American Water Works Association.

Employees of the Dallas office are involved in the local community in ways other than project delivery. Among other activities, the firm annually helps with the City of Dallas/Dallas Water Utilities' Pumphouse 5K charity run, and it donated an entire preschool playground to St. Anthony Catholic School in south Dallas.

CH2M HILL continues to grow and prosper. In 1996, it reported gross revenues of $937 million, up from $805 million in 1995. As CH2M HILL's presence in Texas grows—the company expects to double its Texas operations by the year 2000—the firm will continue to rely on the solid underpinnings established by its founders.

FROM TOP:
As a contractor to the U.S. Environmental Protection Agency, CH2M HILL provides technical assistance to ensure that site remediation efforts meet environmental standards.

CH2M HILL expanded the City of Garland's Rowlett Creek Water Recycling Center by 50 percent and provided additional treatment for all flows at a cost well below half of typical expansion costs. Partnering through the design and construction phases resulted in no claims, no accidents, early completion, and a very successful project.

Employees of the Dallas office spread wood chips donated by CH2M HILL as safety ground cover on the preschool playground at St. Anthony Catholic School.

The firm's founders—Holly Cornell, Jim Howland, Burke Hayes, and Fred Merryfield—instilled in the corporate culture a commitment to serving clients in any desired or required capacity, challenging its employees to use technology to improve communities and build a better world.

In Dallas, 60 engineers, scientists, planners, and support personnel of CH2M HILL work with municipalities, federal agencies, public utilities, and Fortune 500 companies to conceive and deliver projects that help the

AT&T

T&T HAS A LONG HISTORY IN TEXAS, BEGINNING ITS OPERATIONS in the Lone Star State in 1880, eight years before the dedication of the state capitol building in Austin. Eighteen years later, the first AT&T long-distance service was established, connecting Dallas to Houston, San Antonio, and other towns throughout the state. And the first dial switching began in three Dallas central offices in 1921.

In 1984, AT&T divested itself of the Bell-operating companies, including Southwestern Bell and, in effect, created a new AT&T in Texas. Smaller and more responsive, this new company set out to create new products and services, and it continues to do so today.

PIONEERING IN DALLAS
The Dallas division of AT&T is one of the largest of the company's centers, with 4,062 employees working at several locations throughout the Metroplex. In recent years, senior management personnel from the corporation's headquarters in New Jersey—including Rian Wren, AT&T president, Southwest region—have moved to Dallas to oversee continuing development of local services and the superior support services being provided to AT&T customers. Wren is also committed to strengthening the company's presence in the Dallas-area community through the company's many philanthropic programs.

The thousands of AT&T employees who live and work in Dallas perform a variety of functions for the company. Many of these employees are account executives, handling inside and outside sales on an individual basis to small- and large-business clients. They work with customers to develop World Wide Web sites, evaluate existing services, add new technologies, and find ways to increase the client's profitability.

AT&T PRESIDENT, SOUTHWEST REGION RIAN WREN IS COMMITTED TO STRENGTHENING THE COMPANY'S PRESENCE IN THE DALLAS-AREA COMMUNITY THROUGH THE COMPANY'S MANY PHILANTHROPIC PROGRAMS.

This value-added consultative service is the benefit of a dedicated sales force who can respond to a customer's call at any time.

The Customer Care Center near downtown Dallas, which employs 1,633 customer care associates, caters to customers' needs 24 hours a day, providing account status, service information, and clarification of billing for residential and business customers for the Southwest and beyond.

AT&T Wireless employs 600 professionals in North Dallas. This division rolled out the country's first generation of digital personal communication systems (PCSs), which are handheld devices that give cellular telephones many of the qualities of personal computers.

In a joint effort with AT&T Labs, AT&T Wireless developed a new, fixed, wireless system that can provide consumers with high-quality, secure, wireless communications to and from their homes at speeds many times faster than existing telephone lines. The new technology will initially provide each household with two phone lines and the capability for high-speed Internet access. The system also includes sophisticated encryption capability to protect privacy and prevent fraud.

The Dallas market is highly valued by AT&T, so much so that Dallas was among the first five cities to receive AT&T's DirecTV satellite entertainment service, a service that is now in high demand in virtually every market of the country.

LOCAL DIAL TONE,
LOCAL INVOLVEMENT

As a company, AT&T strives to bring people together through its dedication to community service, particularly in education, the arts, and business development. The AT&T Corporation has dedicated $150 million for the AT&T Learning Network, which will help connect America's primary and secondary schools to the Internet by the year 2000. The company has donated more than $500 million to innovative education programs since the divestiture in 1984, including funds that support the Center for Occupational Research and Development (CORD) in Waco, where schoolteachers throughout Texas are taught how to use new technologies.

Understanding that the arts are a crucial part of a well-balanced life, AT&T donates funds, resources, and manpower to the Dallas Symphony Orchestra, the African-American Museum, the Mexican Cultural Center, and other organizations that bring people together for the exchange of ideas and the building of relationships. Communication isn't just a function of technology; for AT&T, it's a function of people meeting people.

AT&T-Texas donates nearly $2.5 million to philanthropic endeavors each year. One example is a $150,000 grant over three years to support the University of Texas-Dallas President's Leadership Council, which studies ways to connect learning with business needs for profitability in today's global economy. The company also underwrites the Tate Lecture Series at Southern Methodist University, which exposes local residents to renowned business speakers. And members of the various local chambers of commerce learn from AT&T employees ways to use emerging technologies to reach more customers.

AT&T employees in Dallas enjoy the generous spirit of corporate sharing by volunteering for public service throughout the Metroplex. More than 80 percent of the firm's 4,062 Dallas employees volunteer with at least one community organization annually.

One example of AT&T employees in action is Clean Scene, a program organized by an AT&T employee in which hundreds of volunteers descend on a neglected Dallas neighborhood and rid it of debris that ranges from dozens of 55-gallon trash bags of litter to refrigerators, furniture, scrap metal, and wood.

As the "new" AT&T continues to expand its realm of com-munications services, including the introduction of local dial-tone service, the company also will continue to help people establish a common bond—across the country and in its home in Dallas.

MORE THAN 80 PERCENT OF AT&T'S 4,062 DALLAS EMPLOYEES VOLUNTEER WITH AT LEAST ONE COMMUNITY ORGANIZATION ANNUALLY (TOP).

AT&T EMPLOYEE VOLUNTEERS FEED NEEDY FAMILIES ON VALENTINE'S DAY AT DALLAS LIFE FOUNDATION (BOTTOM).

OUNDED IN DALLAS IN 1984 AS A NICHE HEALTH INSURANCE provider, *UICI* has developed into a diversified, national financial services enterprise focused on delivering value to its customers and healthy returns to its investors. While the beneficiaries of UICI's success have included its employee and agent shareholders, its market focus has been to deliver cost-effective health care solutions through niche insurance products. Increasingly, UICI has developed advanced technology and services enabling health care payers and providers to operate more cost effectively. Today, UICI provides credit services, real estate management, and automated bank transaction processing as part of an increasing array of innovative niche businesses. The company employs more than 2,500 people across the United States, with approximately 2,000 located in the Dallas/Fort Worth Metroplex.

UICI is publicly traded on the NASDAQ network as UICI and has amassed more than $1.4

billion in assets. UICI ranked first among life and health insurance companies by *Forbes* magazine in January 1997 for its five-year average return on capital of 24.6 percent. Out of 1,280 companies reviewed by *Forbes*, UICI ranked 23rd for its 719 percent increase in stock price during the previous five-year period.

UICI is a company on the move on more fronts than one. Under the leadership of Chairman of the Board and Founder Ronald L. Jensen, the entrepreneurial engine who drives the company, UICI builds its foundation on the powerhouse insurance agencies United Group Association (UGA) and Cornerstone Marketing of America (CMA). With more than 5,000 dedicated field agents, UGA and CMA generated nearly $450 million in UICI revenue in 1996. The health insurance policies sold by these groups cover more than half a million self-employed people, a very important niche market for UICI.

Through its New England-based WinterBrook subsidiaries, UICI provides a host of specialty underwriting and risk management services addressing the needs of both health care payers and providers in managing the risks they assume that require protection against potentially catastrophic losses.

UICI is the country's largest provider of health insurance to college and university students, and offers programs for students in kindergarten through 12th grade through its Student Insurance group. In total, UICI provides benefits to nearly 350,000 students at schools throughout the United States, including a number of the nation's foremost institutions of higher learning.

Health care reform initiatives, managed care plans, and market demands have changed the landscape for health care delivery in the United States. The survivors in health care will deliver the highest quality at the most competitive price. UICI is answering the call with its HealthCare

FOUNDED IN DALLAS IN 1984 AS A NICHE HEALTH INSURANCE PROVIDER, UICI HAS DEVELOPED INTO A DIVERSIFIED, NATIONAL FINANCIAL SERVICES ENTERPRISE FOCUSED ON DELIVERING VALUE TO ITS CUSTOMERS AND HEALTHY RETURNS TO ITS INVESTORS (TOP).

UICI HAS DEVELOPED ADVANCED TECHNOLOGY AND SERVICES ENABLING HEALTH CARE PAYERS AND PROVIDERS TO OPERATE MORE COST EFFECTIVELY (BOTTOM).

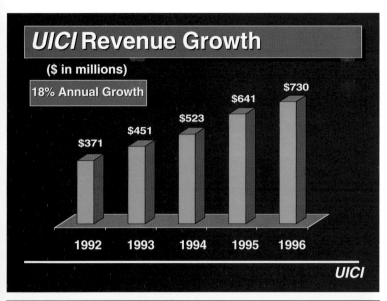

UICI Revenue Growth

($ in millions)

18% Annual Growth

$371	$451	$523	$641	$730
1992	1993	1994	1995	1996

UICI

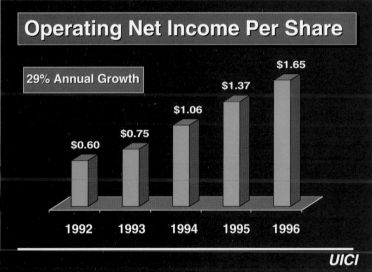

Operating Net Income Per Share

29% Annual Growth

$0.60	$0.75	$1.06	$1.37	$1.65
1992	1993	1994	1995	1996

UICI

turnkey outsourcing solutions to hospitals, physicians, and health plan administrators by providing both computer systems and functional support. Together, these firms process more than $10 billion in claim transactions per year, with expectations of future growth.

But the breadth of services doesn't stop with life and health insurance or the HealthCare Solution companies. UICI's credit services division in Denver provides education and assistance to people who want to rebuild a positive credit history. More than a quarter million individuals have applied for assistance through the program since its inception in 1993.

Chicago-based AMLI Realty Co. manages more than 1,600 acres of land and about 1 million square feet of office and industrial facilities. Through its 15 percent interest in AMLI Residential Properties Trust, a large NYSE-listed (AML) real estate investment trust, UICI owns and manages 35 apartment complexes in the southeastern, southwestern, and midwestern United States. Fifteen complexes are located in the Dallas/Fort Worth area.

UICI's Dallas-based SunTech advanced processing and switching technology allows automatic teller machines (ATMs) to process banking transactions for about one-third the cost of traditional ATM network operations. Sun's network provides the ATM service backbone for some of the nation's leading financial institutions.

These are exciting times for the UICI family of companies as it looks to capture an even greater share of the core insurance markets it serves. UICI is working to expand its future with high-technology developments to lower overall health care costs and to build a greater marketplace for its credit services, real estate, and ATM network technology operations.

UICI RANKED FIRST AMONG LIFE AND HEALTH INSURANCE COMPANIES BY *Forbes* MAGAZINE IN JANUARY 1997 FOR ITS FIVE-YEAR AVERAGE RETURN ON CAPITAL OF 24.6 PERCENT.

Solution group of companies. Through the development and integration of unique paperless claims systems, electronic capture and transmission of dental X rays, digital-image-enabled work-flow solutions, and outsourcing services for health care payers and providers, UICI enables its clients to work more efficiently and more profitably. For example, UICI turns paper claim forms into an electronic format for rapid data entry and easy storage, at one-third of the cost of traditional methods.

But that's not the end of UICI's technological endeavors. Take for instance New Jersey-based PCI. PCI's advanced processing system allows physicians to directly verify benefit eligibility and fully settle health claims on-line with insurers. A transaction process that would traditionally take 30 days at a relatively high cost can now be accomplished with PCI for significantly less while the patient is still in the physician's office. Insurance companies, Blue Cross plans, and managed care organizations around the country are installing PCI's system in physicians' offices to lower operating expenses and improve overall service to plan members.

Other UICI HealthCare Solution companies, specifically IPN Network in Nashville, Tennessee, and Insurdata in Irving, Texas, deliver advanced technology and

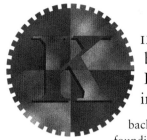

IMBERLY-CLARK MAKES PRODUCTS THAT MAKE PEOPLE'S LIVES better. Products such as Kleenex facial tissue, Huggies diapers, Kotex feminine care products, and Scott paper towels have immediate name recognition in households worldwide. Dating back to its founding in 1872 in Neenah, Wisconsin, the company has a rich history of quality, service, and fair dealing wherever it does business. Today, this global company's products are sold in more than 150 countries, and Dallas is one of its hometowns.

THE MOVE TO DALLAS

After 113 years of prosperous growth in Wisconsin, the company's then-chairman and chief executive officer, Darwin E. Smith, sought to give the young managers of the company's various business units more autonomy. He concluded that the global company would be even more successful if its 110-person corporate staff was located somewhere other than the manufacturing and operations centers. As a result, Smith conducted a one-man search for the city that would be the new home of the world headquarters.

Alone and unannounced, Smith visited various cities to get a feel for their true rhythm and spirit. In Dallas, he found a town with a high quality of life and a burgeoning pro-business climate. But there was something else that made Dallas more attractive than the other cities: the positive, enthusiastic attitude of the people.

The move to the Dallas area in 1985 proved successful, as Kimberly-Clark continued its international expansion. In 1995, the company completed the largest transaction in its history when it merged with Scott Paper, creating a larger, more competitive company with greater operating efficiencies and more opportunities for market expansion. Now, when consumers purchase one of the many popular Scott products such as Scott bathroom tissue and Viva paper towels, they are purchasing a Kimberly-Clark product.

Today, with 55,000 employees worldwide, Kimberly-Clark is a leading manufacturer of personal care, consumer tissue, and away-from-home products. It is first in market share in virtually all of its U.S. consumer product lines, including disposable diapers, baby wipes, feminine care products, and facial tissue. The company is also a major producer of professional health care products and premium business, correspondence, and technical papers.

Naturally, any company with $13 billion in annual sales will find itself in the Fortune 500. Kimberly-Clark goes one better—it has been named by *Fortune*

KIMBERLY-CLARK'S DISPOSABLE DIAPERS, TRAINING PANTS, ADULT INCONTINENCE, AND FEMININE CARE PRODUCTS FULFILL IMPORTANT CONSUMER NEEDS AROUND THE WORLD EVERY DAY.

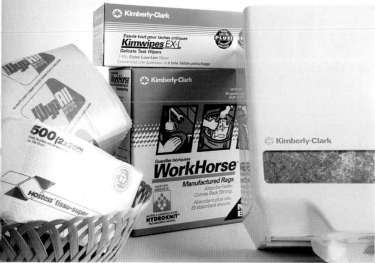

dollars to numerous organizations, including the Dallas Opera, Dallas Museum of Art, Boys & Girls Clubs, Dallas Can! Academy, Southwestern Medical Center, and Paul Quinn College. The company recently made a donation of $1 million to the Dallas Zoo's capital campaign.

Wayne R. Sanders, Kimberly-Clark's chairman and CEO since 1992, notes, "We gladly support charitable organizations in Dallas and are proud to be part of an active business community that has both a can-do attitude and a genuine interest in the area."

The caring attitude of Kimberly-Clark is evidenced by the actions of its employees. Thousands of Kimberly-Clarkers volunteer their time and talents each year to support community organizations such as literacy councils, schools, hospitals, volunteer fire departments, and youth programs. Kimberly-Clark proudly recognizes its employees' efforts annually through $500 grants to the organizations at which they volunteer.

CULTURE OF TRUST AND RESPECT

Since the company's founding, the men and women of Kimberly-Clark have thrived in a corporate culture that values people as much as profits. The company fosters a culture that is based on trust and respect. As a result, Kimberly-Clarkers work together on a first-name basis and do not stand on rank. They focus their individual strengths on common goals. Although they take their jobs seriously, Kimberly-Clark employees try not to take themselves too seriously.

Manufacturing the best possible products, caring about employees and their hometowns, and generating outstanding returns to shareholders all contribute to making Kimberly-Clark one of the recognized best companies not only in Dallas, but in the world.

IN THE KITCHEN, BATHROOM, AND ALL AROUND THE HOUSE, KIMBERLY-CLARK TISSUE PRODUCTS MAKE DAILY LIFE A LITTLE BETTER IN 1,001 WAYS. THE COMPANY IS THE LARGEST TISSUE MANUFACTURER IN THE WORLD (TOP).

INDUSTRIAL, HOTEL, AND INSTITUTIONAL CUSTOMERS AROUND THE WORLD USE KIMBERLY-CLARK HAND TOWELS, SOAPS, AND WIPERS IN WASHROOMS AND AT WORKSTATIONS (BOTTOM).

magazine as a Most Admired Corporation each year since 1983.

COMMUNITY INVOLVEMENT

Kimberly-Clark wants its employees and their families to live and work in vibrant communities that encourage education, health, and social welfare, and that value cultural and civic programs. For that reason, the company supports

charitable organizations and programs that are important to its employees. Recipients of the company's support range from the Nature Conservancy to medical research programs, from colleges and universities to minority scholarship funds, from symphony orchestras to city zoos, and from homeless shelters to disaster relief.

In the Dallas area, Kimberly-Clark has pledged its charitable

TURNER CONSTRUCTION COMPANY

HE New York-based Turner Construction Company has been recognized as an industry leader, and with 44 branch offices and nearly $3.5 billion in annual revenues, who can argue? Founded by Henry C. Turner in 1902, the company has become the builder of choice for the nation's commercial high-rise buildings; airports; sports, retail, education, and health care facilities; hotels; multifamily housing developments; and civic and judicial centers.

Of Turner's 44 branches, the Dallas-based office has emerged as an industry leader itself. Using the annual top 400 contractors from the trade publication *Engineering News Record* as a comparison, Turner's Southwest Business Unit does enough business each year to rank among the top 200 construction companies in the country. With more than 100 employees, the unit completed more than $130 million in volume in 1995, with projects ranging from $50,000 interior renovations to $40 million new construction.

TEXAS: AN EARLY DESTINATION

Turner's first project in Texas was for the Humble Oil Company in 1919. Today, a half-dozen of the tallest buildings in the skyline of Houston are Turner-built buildings, including the award-winning Republic Bank Center (now NationsBank) and the Texas Commerce Tower. Other award-winning Texas sites include the landmark Texas A&M Bell Tower at College Station and First City Center in Austin.

But the management and employees of Turner's Dallas office are not content with simply providing the buildings where people live and work. They also want to make the Dallas community more livable, and they do that through volunteering.

"Most people think of us as a big company, and we are, but we make it part of our operating procedure to understand and get involved in local concerns," says Steven T. Whitcraft, manager of Turner's Dallas office.

As participants in Youth Force 2000, Turner's professionals in Dallas adopted Rusk Middle School, providing mentors, construction assistance, tours of construction sites, and classroom visits in an effort to encourage students to explore all facets of the industry. Turner employees also give construction management seminars to educate women and minorities who wish to open businesses in the industry. The Dallas branch recently awarded 35 percent of the $30 million Townview Magnet School project to firms owned by women and minorities.

Turner employees participate in the Hearts & Hammers Community Day festival, the People Helping People/City of Dallas Housing Authority Community Day, the Adopt-a-Family outreach program, and the Dallas Independent School District mentoring program. The firm also sponsors squads in local Little League sports programs.

As Turner's Dallas office continues to build the future of north Texas, its commitment to the community continues as well. "We will always be involved in the Dallas community and will encourage our employees and subcontractors to participate and celebrate our success and growth through increased volunteer efforts," says Robert Kimmig, Turner's general manager for the Southwest Region. "As we grow, we intend to grow better and stronger. Our goal is to be the best builder in the Metroplex, and we are committed to remaining a banner office and a leader in contributing to the company."

CLOCKWISE FROM TOP: THE DALLAS BRANCH OF TURNER CONSTRUCTION COMPANY RECENTLY AWARDED 35 PERCENT OF THE $30 MILLION TOWNVIEW MAGNET SCHOOL PROJECT TO FIRMS OWNED BY WOMEN AND MINORITIES.

AN EXAMPLE OF TURNER'S EXPERTISE IN BUILDING HEALTH CARE FACILITIES CAN BE FOUND IN ALL SAINTS EPISCOPAL HOSPITAL CITYVIEW IN FORT WORTH.

AMONG THE NUMEROUS EDUCATION FACILITIES BUILT BY TURNER IS ROCKWALL HIGH SCHOOL.

N 1882, A CHICAGO FAMILY NAMED DARLING JOINED FORCES with the meatpacking firm of Swift & Co. to find markets for waste fat, bones, and other by-products. Three years later, the Darlings separated from the meatpacking part of the business to

concentrate on rendering and expanding the company, building and purchasing rendering plants throughout the United States. Today, Darling International—the largest independent food waste recycler in the country—is one of the Dallas area's premier corporations. It is one of the top five exporting companies in Dallas and the only company in its industry that is publicly traded. In addition, Darling boasts the second-largest fleet of railcars in its industry.

Darling operates more than 40 plants across the United States, including 33 rendering plants where animal and food waste products are turned into useful commerical goods, including tallow, protein meals, and yellow grease. These materials turn up as ingredients in everyday products ranging from fuels and lubricants to tires and crayons. The company also contributes to the balance of trade by exporting approximately 40 percent of what it produces.

This "invisible industry" contributes $22 billion per year to the U.S. gross national product, and Darling is proud to be the industry leader. "Ours is an essential industry," says Darling Chairman and Chief Executive Officer Dennis B. Longmire from his office at Darling's corporate headquarters in downtown Las Colinas. "Without the function we perform, our society would have major prob-

lems. We take a waste product nobody wants and turn it into a product that is used as a raw material for the production of meat, milk, and eggs."

THE "GREEN" RECYCLER
"We recycle at the most basic level for the public, and we do it in a 'green' way. This year we will spend about one-third of our profits on environmental protection systems," says Longmire. "It is our major single capital expenditure. Not too many companies can say that."

Longmire says one of the firm's proudest moments came when it was notified by the International Organization for Standardization (ISO) of its approval for ISO 9002 certification, a coveted award that recognizes the most effective means of producing continuous improvements in quality, reducing errors, and increasing customer satisfaction. Darling is the only U.S. independent renderer to win ISO approval.

In 1996, Darling was also the top independent company in processing bakery goods by-products. This position was helped by the firm's acquisition of International Processing Company (IPC), an industry-leading bakery waste recycler.

The company continues to expand in its scope. A new research and development division is moving Darling away from the commodity-only status to one that provides value-added products, creating new markets. The company's innovative CleanStar-2000 system of recycling waste grease with on-site collections from restaurants is finding a voracious market in the nation's quick service establishments.

Darling—which has nearly 2,000 employees, 100 of whom are in Dallas—is active in the local community as well as in its international industry. Members can be found working at a number of nonprofit organizations, including the Buckner Children's Home, the North Hills Charter School, and the Dallas Chamber of Commerce.

Longmire says Darling is committed to steady, sustained growth while improving both the volume and the quality of the material it recycles. Darling is well positioned to be the most visible player in the "invisible" industry.

FROM LEFT:
DARLING'S INNOVATIVE CLEANSTAR-2000 SYSTEM OF RECYCLING WASTE GREASE WITH ON-SITE COLLECTIONS FROM RESTAURANTS IS FINDING A VORACIOUS MARKET IN THE NATION'S QUICK SERVICE ESTABLISHMENTS.

JOHN PALAZZO IS QUALITY MANAGER FOR THE ISO 9002 PROGRAM FOR THE COMPANY, AND GORDON LEE IS LEAD INTERNAL AUDITOR FOR SAN FRANCISCO'S ISO QUALITY PROGRAM.

THE COMPANY HAS MORE THAN 600 RAILCARS SERVICING THE UNITED STATES AND MEXICO. LAX RAO IS QUALITY SYSTEMS MANAGER FOR THE COLDWATER, MICHIGAN, PLANT.

COLUMBIA HEALTHCARE CORPORATION, NORTH TEXAS DIVISION

OLUMBIA HEALTHCARE CORPORATION, NORTH TEXAS DIVISION is the largest health care system locally, with more than 11,000 employees at 17 hospitals, nine ambulatory surgery centers, several senior health centers, rural health and convenient care clinics, and home health agencies in 25 locations in a 12-county region. Columbia's aim is to be not only the largest, but also the most integrated health care delivery system for patients, employers, and third-party payers through its convenience, quality, services, and price.

In 1996, more than 95,000 patients were admitted to Columbia's North Texas Division hospitals. In addition, more than 365,000 outpatient visits, 515,000 home health visits, and 95,000 surgeries were completed.

Columbia has "branded" all facilities and programs, including hospitals, home health agencies, and surgery centers, under the Columbia name to effectively position all its health providers under one common identity. The branding campaign goal is to increase awareness of Columbia

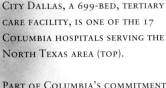

COLUMBIA HOSPITAL AT MEDICAL CITY DALLAS, A 699-BED, TERTIARY CARE FACILITY, IS ONE OF THE 17 COLUMBIA HOSPITALS SERVING THE NORTH TEXAS AREA (TOP).

PART OF COLUMBIA'S COMMITMENT TO DELIVERING QUALITY CARE INCLUDES SHARING IN SPECIAL FAMILY MOMENTS (BOTTOM).

Healthcare Corporation throughout the nation. In addition, a free physician referral service and information line is being implemented nationwide, and Columbia has a site on the Internet at http://www.columbia.net.

Outside their walls, Columbia hospitals are recognized as being leaders in their local communities, providing a continuum of health, education, and wellness programs, as well as collaborative programs with community agencies.

WORLD-CLASS HEALTH CARE FOR NORTH TEXANS

Columbia Healthcare, North Texas Division takes pride in its excellence and the full range of services offered to the people of Dallas, Tarrant, Collin, Grayson, Denton, Navarro, and surrounding counties. Every program in the network is testament to the ongoing commitment to exceptional medical and genuine human care.

Columbia Healthcare Corporation comprises more than 343 hospitals, 150 surgery centers, and more than 500 home health loca-

tions in 38 states, England, Switzerland, and Spain. Columbia is building comprehensive networks of health care services, including home health, rehabilitation, and skilled nursing units in local markets around the country.

Columbia Healthcare Corporation is the largest provider of health care services in the United States and is the nation's leading provider of cancer, cardiovascular, and orthopedic services. Columbia facilities provided more than 40 million patient visits in 1996, and more than 200,000 babies were delivered at Columbia hospitals.

Columbia's commitment to the community is evident through charity care, reinvesting in improving hospital facilities, the recent pledge to immunize 1 million youths, and thousands of health screenings and health fairs held annually. In fact, in 1996, Columbia had a tremendous impact on local communities by providing $1.4 billion in uncompensated care; purchasing $2 billion in supplies; and paying nearly $2 billion in local, state, and federal taxes.

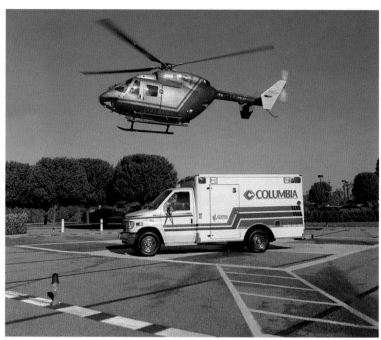

SETTING A NEW STANDARD

Richard Scott, president and chief executive officer, gives the credit for the company's impressive growth to the hard work of its 285,000 employees and 75,000 associated physicians. *Fortune* magazine recently named Columbia as the country's most respected health care organization. The Advisory Board, a health care research organization, noted that Columbia has set the new competitive standard in the industry. The Advisory Board points to Columbia's quality, admissions, growth, and strong operating principles.

The Columbia hospital system is committed to being known as the top provider of consumer health care information. Its Web site had more that 1 million hits in January 1997, and a *USA Today/IntelliQuest* survey termed its page the most informative health care site on the World Wide Web.

Columbia continues to receive high marks for quality. In December 1996, a Benchmarks for Success survey conducted by Mercer/HCA found that Columbia owned 17 of the top 100 hospitals in the United States, which is impressive because the system operates only 7 percent of all hospitals nationwide. During 1996, another 57 of Columbia's facilities earned Joint Commission Accreditation with Commendation, bringing its total to 124, or 36 percent of Columbia's facilities. This far exceeds the industry standard of 10 percent.

Perhaps no division in the nationwide Columbia network offers a better glimpse of how an integrated health care delivery system can operate than the North Texas Division, which serves a 12-county area. Comprehensive acute care services are provided throughout North Texas with tertiary care facilities in Dallas and Fort Worth: Columbia Hospital and Columbia Children's Hospital at Medical City Dallas, and Columbia Plaza Medical Center of Fort Worth. Other hospitals in the system include Columbia Medical Centers of Lewisville, Sherman, Dallas Southwest, Plano, Lancaster, Terrell, Denton, Arlington, and McKinney. Additional facilities include Columbia North Hills, Columbia Medical Arts, Columbia Navarro Regional, Columbia HEB, and Columbia Specialty Hospitals. This comprehensive and diverse group of health care facilities is networked together through state-of-the-art computer systems, and air and ground patient transportation systems. Leading the way into the next century will be Columbia Medical Center of Las Colinas, scheduled to open in August 1997, and Columbia East Regional Medical Center, opening in December 1998.

In addition to the communities served by the system, Columbia's North Texas Division is also the official health care provider for the World Champion Dallas Cowboys NFL football team, the Texas Rangers baseball team, and the Texas Motor Speedway.

Columbia One IS THE NEWEST CRITICAL CARE TRANSPORT HELICOPTER SERVING NORTH TEXAS. THE HELICOPTER, AN AMERICAN EUROCOPTER BK-117, IS CONFIGURED TO MEET THE NEEDS OF THE MOST CRITICAL ADULT, PEDIATRIC, AND NEONATAL PATIENTS. THE COLUMBIA AMBULANCES COMPLEMENT THE SYSTEM WITH SEVERAL SUCH VEHICLES IN THE NORTH TEXAS DIVISION (TOP).

GROWING TO MEET THE NEEDS OF THE DALLAS/FORT WORTH AREA, COLUMBIA HOSPITAL AT MEDICAL CITY DALLAS RECENTLY EXPANDED. SHOWN IS BUILDING D, WHICH HOUSES THE COLUMBIA CHILDREN'S HOSPITAL, THE HEART AND LUNG CENTER, THE CANCER CENTER, AND WOMEN'S SERVICES (BOTTOM).

SINCE 1987, PARK PLACE MOTORCARS HAS BEEN THE PREMIER dealer in Dallas of fine, luxury automobiles. Customers from throughout the Southwest visit Park Place to select from the dealership's extensive inventory of Mercedes-Benz, Lexus, Porsche, and Audi brands. It isn't just the large selection and significant values that have made Park Place the largest and most respected dealership in the region: The knowledgeable staff, conscientious customer service, and high quality of care offered by each of the dealership's showrooms are in a class by themselves.

For 10 years, the Park Place name has been synonymous with unparalleled quality and service. Owned and operated by Ken Schnitzer, a fourth-generation Texan, the dealership has been recognized year after year for its outstanding performance in these two areas.

PARK PLACE MOTORCARS IS THE LARGEST AUDI DEALER IN THE DALLAS/ FORT WORTH REGION.

THE RIGHT PLACE

Schnitzer opened his first Mercedes-Benz dealership in 1987, bringing the brand's successful history, existing commitment to customer service, and solid growth potential to the heart of the exclusive Park Cities community near downtown Dallas. The area provided the perfect setting for Mercedes-Benz, and Mercedes-Benz was perfect for the neighborhood.

Schnitzer named the four-showroom, 11,000-square-foot dealership Park Place Motorcars, and focused every facet of the dealership's services on one mission: to treat each customer with personalized superior service, every time. This dedication to customer service crosses all levels of the dealership's operations, from the way each customer is greeted at the door to the way each car is serviced by factory-trained technicians. White-glove treatment, such as free rental cars, pickup and delivery service, and donuts and bagels in the plush service waiting lounge are just a few of the small touches that represent an overall

MICHAEL BODYCOMB

PARK PLACE LEXUS HAS CAPTURED THE NATIONAL ELITE OF LEXUS AWARD FIVE TIMES. THE AWARD IS GIVEN EACH YEAR TO THE LEXUS DEALERSHIP THAT DEMONSTRATES OUTSTANDING SALES, CUSTOMER SERVICE, AND COMMITMENT TO EXCELLENCE.

dedication to making the customer feel welcome.

Clearly, the first decade of operation has been a success. The company accounts for a significant portion of all new car sales for Mercedes-Benz, Audi, and Porsche in the Dallas/Fort Worth region. As a significant measure of success, the majority of those sales are made to repeat or referral customers of Park Place Motorcars.

SUCCESS FUELS EXPANSION

The dealerships' growth in the last 10 years has presented new opportunities for the Park Place family. After his first four years in the luxury automobile business, Schnitzer expanded his operations to the burgeoning suburbs of Plano, north of Dallas, and opened Park Place Lexus. The dealership was successful from the day its doors opened in 1991. In its first year of eligibility, Park Place Lexus captured the National Elite of Lexus award, given each year to the Lexus dealership that demonstrates outstanding sales, customer service, and commitment to excellence. Since then, Park Place Lexus has received the Elite award four other times, most recently in 1996.

The Park Place family expanded again in 1993 when the firm added two more dealerships and an off-site body repair shop. The first dealership was Audi, followed a few months later by Porsche; the showrooms of the Park Place Porsche/Audi dealerships are adjacent to the Mercedes-Benz dealership. Park Place Porsche is the only Porsche dealership in the state of Texas to win the distinguished Premier Dealer award, one of the highest honors bestowed by Porsche Cars of North America. And in just four years of business, Park Place Audi has become the number one volume dealer in its trading region.

The off-site, 35,000-square-foot, full-service paint and body shop, called Bodywerks, handles body work for more than 2,300 Mercedes-Benz, Lexus, Porsche, and Audi cars each year.

In 1995, Schnitzer added a second Mercedes-Benz dealership in his hometown of Houston. Also called Park Place Motorcars, the dealership quickly became the number one retailer of Mercedes-Benz in the city.

Each of Park Place Motorcars' dealerships is represented in the "virtual dealership" the firm maintains on the World Wide Web. This site can be found at http://www.parkplacetexas.com. In addition to scheduling appointments for maintenance work and test drives, customers can also peruse the dealerships' inventory, all with the click of a mouse.

PEOPLE ON A MISSION

Schnitzer credits each of the 400 employees of the firm for their contributions to Park Place's success in the last decade, and he's looking ahead toward additional growth in the next one. It's the competency of those employees that separates Park Place from the competition, and the firm doesn't hesitate to invest in their education and training. The turnover rate for the company's employees is extremely low in an industry where it is traditionally very high, an indication that the management's efforts to create an environment that is mutually rewarding is working.

As Park Place Motorcars prepares for the future, the combined dealerships and the employees will continue to focus on the original mission of the firm to treat each customer with personalized, superior service, every time.

MICHAEL BODYCOMB

MICHAEL BODYCOMB

FROM TOP:
JORDAN CASE IS THE GENERAL MANAGER FOR PARK PLACE LEXUS, WHICH OPENED ITS DOORS IN 1991.

PARK PLACE MOTORCARS SELLS A MAJORITY OF ALL PORSCHES DRIVEN BY MOTORISTS IN THE METROPLEX, MANY OF WHICH ARE TO REPEAT OR REFERRAL CUSTOMERS.

KEN SCHNITZER, FOUNDER OF PARK PLACE MOTORCARS, OPENED HIS FIRST MERCEDES-BENZ DEALERSHIP IN 1987, BRINGING THE BRAND'S SUCCESSFUL HISTORY, EXISTING COMMITMENT TO CUSTOMER SERVICE, AND SOLID GROWTH POTENTIAL TO THE HEART OF THE EXCLUSIVE PARK CITIES COMMUNITY NEAR DOWNTOWN DALLAS.

MICHAEL BODYCOMB

"E EFFECTIVELY BRIDGE THE GAP BETWEEN HIGHLY CREATIVE APproaches and real-life applications," says Richard J. Johnson. "You can have incredibly creative ideas, but what good are they if they don't produce results?" Kathleen Byrne Johnson adds, "We measure success by the results we get for our clients. We gauge our work or counsel by whether we helped increase the client's revenue or market share."

Richard, chief executive officer, and Kathleen, chief operating officer, are co-presidents of Byrne Johnson Inc., an advertising/design/public relations firm they formed in 1988. The agency was named Small Business of the Year in 1994 by the North Dallas Chamber of Commerce and was first cited in 1996 by the *Dallas Business Journal* as one of the top 25 public relations firms.

While many other communications firms specialize in a single industry, Byrne Johnson boasts a diverse client base that, according to Richard, gives the firm a degree of stability not typically found among those that are devoted to only one industry. "We get equally excited working with a client on a campaign about commercial mortgage-backed securities as we do on a campaign for a dude ranch," he says.

The key difference with Byrne Johnson Inc. is the firm's eclectic mixture of experience. "Ours is a company of highly practical business people who also are very creative and have an intuition for making that creativity perform for the client," says Kathleen. "In addition to their inherent talents, most of our employees have either been on the client side or operated their own businesses. This perspective enables us to understand a client's business and produce targeted results."

CASE HISTORIES
TELL THE STORY

Through public relations, marketing, and advertising initiatives, Byrne Johnson's contributions to the success of its clients are documented through testimonials. For example, in securing a two-page feature story in the *Dallas Morning News*, Byrne Johnson Inc. helped one of its clients acquire a $20 million contract from an international Fortune 100 company.

Byrne Johnson Inc. also created the logo, name, and packaging for a new product for a regional automotive parts remanufacturer. Since the debut, major retail chains have signed contracts

CLOCKWISE FROM TOP: BEING AT THE FOREFRONT OF TECHNOLOGY IS PARAMOUNT AT BYRNE JOHNSON, WHERE COMPUTERS HAVE REPLACED DRAWING BOARDS. CREATIVE DIRECTOR STEVE JAMES HEADS BYRNE JOHNSON'S DESIGN STUDIO, WHERE HE AND HIS TEAM OF ART DIRECTORS CREATE LOGOS, BROCHURES, PACKAGING, DIRECT MAIL, WEB SITES, AND MORE.

DURADRIVE INDUSTRIES, AN AUTOMOTIVE PARTS REMANUFACTURER, CREDITS BYRNE JOHNSON'S PACKAGING DESIGN AND BRANDING STRATEGY WITH TRIGGERING A 50 PERCENT INCREASE IN UNITS SHIPPED OVER SIX MONTHS.

BYRNE JOHNSON EASILY ADAPTS TO AN ARRAY OF STYLES FOR A VARIETY OF CLIENTS AND INDUSTRIES; THE COMMON DENOMINATOR IS HIGH-END GRAPHICS.

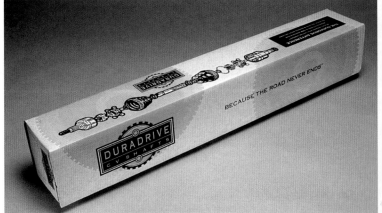

to sell the product, and the client was able to build a six-figure monthly revenue base in a whole new market.

Additionally, a major health maintenance organization credited Byrne Johnson's recommended direct marketing program with

yielding sales far above the company's goal for four straight years.

These are just a few of the many success stories attributed to Byrne Johnson Inc. since its founding in 1988 by clients as dissimilar as GE Capital, Rosewood Corporation, City of Mesquite, Mapsco,

Woodmont Property Management Company, Mobil Oil Corporation, manufacturers, professional service firms, hospitals, technology companies, and others.

"We feel it's our role to be the catalyst for making things happen," says Richard. "We like to have a proactive role in the relationship we develop with our clients. We're business people first and foremost, and creatives second. That's not such a bad mix."

Richard and Kathleen are committed to investing in the continued growth of their firm. They are prepared for increased demand as new businesses come to Byrne Johnson, and for expansion nationally and internationally. Already, the company is beginning to link U.S. companies with those in Mexico, and vice versa, as they attempt to market to each other. "We'll continue to be a quiet but big player in the market," says Richard.

"I would hope any company in any industry would realize they can have a meaningful dialogue with us," says Kathleen. "We know business, we know marketing, and we hit the ground running regardless of the industry. And then we revel in our clients' success."

CLOCKWISE FROM TOP LEFT: PUBLIC RELATIONS INITIATIVES BY BYRNE JOHNSON PLAY A SIGNIFICANT ROLE IN CARVING OUT MARKET SHARE FOR A VARIETY OF CLIENTS. TWO STAND-OUT EXAMPLES OF THIS INCLUDE A RETAIL CLIENT'S 11 PERCENT INCREASE IN SALES THE DAY AFTER A TELEVISION FEATURE AIRED, AND AN ARCHITECTURAL FIRM'S $20 MILLION CONTRACT THAT RESULTED FROM A NEWS ARTICLE SECURED BY THE FIRM.

DIRECT MAIL CAMPAIGNS FROM BYRNE JOHNSON CAN PERFORM FOR SEVERAL YEARS, YIELDING SALES, IN KAISER PERMANENTE'S CASE, OF 134 PERCENT OF GOAL.

RICHARD J. JOHNSON SERVES AS THE FIRM'S PRESIDENT/CEO, AND KATHLEEN BYRNE JOHNSON IS PRESIDENT/COO.

HERE IS A POINT WHERE ELEGANCE AND UTILITY MEET, WHERE practicality joins the creative, and where fun and function converge. This is the point the dynamic staff at Design Quorum strives to reach with each project, whether it's in a hospital, a courtroom, or a corporate suite.

"We're a progressive space-planning and interiors firm that pushes the envelope," says Design Quorum President Kathryn Kelley. "One sentence that's not in our vocabulary is 'It's just not done that way.' If it works functionally and is appropriate for that application, we will try to approach the client by asking, 'Have you thought about it this way?' We can give a corporation something conservative, but with a slightly different approach," Kelley continues. "I like to integrate the element of surprise: When people turn a corner, I want them to see something a little unexpected. I believe we can give this to a client, while providing them with efficient and effective space planning and design solutions."

FLUID CONCEPTS, INSIDE AND OUT

The approach has worked: Design Quorum has grown rapidly, while providing personal attention to each client. "We work closely with architects and end users," Kelley says. "We specify all the finishes—the carpets, the walls, all the applications on the interiors—for continuity from the exterior to the interior. We are able to provide the entire package, down to custom-designed furniture." Floor plans and furniture ideas cover large worktables as designers refine their ideas at nearby computer terminals. Design Quorum maintains an extensive library including product information; hundreds of samples of paint, wall coverings, fabrics, and flooring options; and furniture catalogs.

"SOFA, SO GOOD"

While understandably proud of her firm's rapid rise, solid reputation, and considerable achievements, there is one accomplishment that Kelley holds most special: a sofa.

It's the sofa that adorns the toddler waiting room of the Pediatric Oncology Center at Medical City Dallas. The oversized sofa looks like something inspired by the pages of a Dr. Seuss book: There are three padded steps built into the sofa's platform, taking the kids who climb it five and a half feet above the matching ottomans intended for their parents. A swirling gold and orange mural painted on the wall behind the sofa displays a mischievous cat; a whimsical, cockeyed landscape; and a pair of dancing lampposts that appear to hold up the lamps at either side of the sofa (actually the lamp shades are built into the wall). The sofa epitomizes Design Quorum's creativity. "I knew the room was for the children. I wanted them to have a unique area that they would look forward to visiting during such a difficult time. The moment I saw how the children responded to the room, I felt it was a success," Kelley says.

Design Quorum clients include corporate facilities, justice centers, health care facilities, and even an aquatic park. Kelley says the firm would like to branch into other areas of design in the future, both near and far. "We've worked with clients in Texas from Dallas to Brownsville to El Paso. We're anxious to take our innovative and creative approach across the nation."

CLOCKWISE FROM TOP:
IN ALL ITS DESIGNS, DESIGN QUORUM STRIVES TO REACH A POINT WHERE ELEGANCE AND UTILITY MEET, WHERE PRACTICALITY JOINS THE CREATIVE, AND WHERE FUN AND FUNCTION CONVERGE.

DESIGN QUORUM HAS DONE EXTENSIVE HEALTH CARE WORK THROUGHOUT TEXAS, FROM DALLAS TO BROWNSVILLE TO EL PASO.

THE SOFA THAT ADORNS THE TODDLER WAITING ROOM OF THE PEDIATRIC ONCOLOGY CENTER AT MEDICAL CITY DALLAS IS A SHINING EXAMPLE OF DESIGN QUORUM'S CREATIVITY.

Hilb, Rogal and Hamilton Company of Dallas

IT IS A STAND-ALONE FIRM THAT HAS THE LOCAL AUTONOMY TO develop close relationships with business and personal clients while having the sophistication and authority that comes from being part of a $158 million revenue multinational company, with

69 insurance agencies in both the United States and Canada.

Hilb, Rogal and Hamilton Company of Dallas (HRH) serves as an intermediary between its core clients—medium-sized commercial and industrial accounts—and some 30 insurance companies that underwrite the client's risks. "We've been in Dallas and in the insurance industry long enough to have established a track record of stability, a record of strong earnings, and a reputation of providing our clients with unparalleled service," says Patrick J. Bonds, president of HRH of Dallas.

Based in Richmond, Virginia, HRH is a publicly traded company that ranks as the largest brokerage firm in the midsize market, the ninth largest in the United States, and the 16th largest in the world. It represents more than 100 insurance carriers, including United States Fidelity & Guaranty, Crum & Forster, St. Paul, Hartford, Fireman's Fund, Travelers/ Aetna, CNA, Chubb, and American International Group. "We have virtually unlimited access to the country's insurance companies. That's the advantage of being a national brokerage," Bonds explains.

The Dallas office draws from those nationwide relationships when it comes to finding coverage for Texas clients in need of risk management, life and health, personal lines, property, general liability, workers' compensation, nonsubscriber, and marine insurance. HRH of Dallas has the authority to make underwriting decisions, develop and maintain client relationships, and select insurance carriers and areas of specialization, while the Richmond headquarters provides rock-solid

centralized administrative and accounting controls.

INTERNATIONAL IN SCOPE, LOCAL IN FOCUS

"Our clients have expectations of the firm representing them in solving their problems at a competitive price, and we frequently exceed those expectations," Bonds says. Besides working with more than 30 companies at the Dallas office alone, HRH has a variety of other value-added services, including an in-house safety engineer for rapid response in risk insurance coverage.

"You can't get the services and diversity that we offer directly from the local agent," Bonds says. "And that reflects in the diversity of our accounts."

By targeting its services to companies with 50 to 1,500 employees and working with so many carriers, HRH is capable of customizing insurance products that fit the bill on a case-by-case basis. And the company is constantly developing a wider range of services and streamlining delivery processes—in other words, working to do more than simply transfer risk. The firm is committed to developing services that

improve loss control and claims administration.

"This company has come a long way in a few short years because of an outstanding entrepreneurial spirit," says Bonds. "It's in that spirit that we will continue doing business at Hilb, Rogal and Hamilton Company of Dallas."

F YOU HAVE WORN A STETSON HAT; ENJOYED A GHIRARDELLI chocolate; watched television supplied by Marcus Cable; pushed a child on an outdoor swing; used a gas log, space heater, or electric chain saw; or slept in a bed filled with fiber and foam,

chances are it was made by a company owned by Hicks, Muse, Tate & Furst Incorporated. From its headquarters at the Crescent in downtown Dallas, the principals of Hicks Muse carefully review the capabilities of potential acquisitions and devise strategies that enhance earnings, improve operations and management, grow business, and pay down debt. Drawing on pools of committed capital, Hicks Muse acquires controlling interests in leading businesses that occupy well-defined niches, focusing only on companies that are poised for substantial growth.

Hicks Muse accomplishes its acquisitions by cultivating its extensive, 20-year-old network of professional relationships with operating managers and intermediaries within the financial community, as well as through active, in-house origination of transactions. Hicks Muse's investment philosophy is to invest with management in support of the long-term growth of the business. And the firm is well known for making synergistic add-on acquisitions to its core portfolio companies as a means of creating value for investors.

ENTREPRENEURIAL SPIRIT GUIDED BY EXPERIENCE

The firm was founded in 1989 by longtime Dallasites Thomas O. Hicks, chairman and chief executive officer, and John R. Muse. They were later joined by Jack D. Furst, a former colleague of Hicks' at a predecessor firm; Charles W. Tate, former managing director of Morgan Stanley & Co. in New York; Lawrence D. Stuart Jr., a leading legal strategist for leveraged acquisitions; Michael J. Levitt, former managing director at Smith Barney; and Alan B. Menkes, a former vice president at Hicks Muse.

These men have more than 100 years of combined experience in advising, financing, originating, monitoring, and exiting leveraged acquisitions, and have worked together in various capacities for more than 10 years. Their astonishing track record at Hicks Muse,

LEFT: HICKS, MUSE, TATE & FURST INC.'S PRINCIPALS INCLUDE (STANDING FROM LEFT) ALAN B. MENKES, CHARLES W. TATE, JACK O. FURST, JOHN R. MUSE, LAWRENCE D. STUART, JR., MICHAEL J. LEVITT, AND (SEATED) THOMAS O. HICKS.

RIGHT: CRAIN INDUSTRIES—A COMPANY CONTROLLED BY HICKS, MUSE, TATE & FURST INC.—MAKES POLYURETHANE FOAM AND FIBER FOR FURNITURE AND BEDDING.

as well as its predecessor firm of Hicks & Haas Incorporated, speaks for itself.

Since its formation in 1989, Hicks Muse has invested equity capital in more than 70 platform portfolio investments, with combined transaction values exceeding $19 billion. The equity capital invested by the firm represents funds managed on behalf of the firm's limited partners as well as the principals' own capital. Hicks Muse Fund I was capitalized at $255 million in 1989, and Fund II reached $800 million in 1993. Fund III, established in 1997, has successfully raised in excess of $2.2 billion.

This investor confidence in the firm stems from the 25 to 30 percent or more return on investment Hicks Muse traditionally generates.

Among the companies Hicks Muse has acquired, several are based in Dallas. However, the firm—which has branch offices in New York City, St. Louis, and Mexico City—is likely to acquire companies anywhere. Hat Brands Inc. of Garland is the largest manufacturer of head wear in the United States, trading under the brand names of Stetson, Resistol, Knox, Churchill, and others. The Morningstar Group of Dallas makes branded and private label

specialty dairy food products, including Lactaid, International Delight, and Second Nature. Marcus Cable Company, L.P. provides cable television to the Park Cities and Fort Worth, as well as to 1.1 million other subscribers in 18 other states.

Among others holdings, there is Berg Electronics, Inc., one of the world's largest makers of electronic connectors and related products; Ghirardelli Chocolate Company, one of the best-known makers of premium chocolate; Capstar Broadcasting Partners, which is the largest operator of radio stations in the country, with more than 100 stations; Crain Industries, which makes polyurethane foam and fiber for furniture and bedding; and International Home Foods, a $1 billion company that makes

Chef Boyardee, Gulden's mustard, Ranch Style beans, and Jiffy Pop popcorn.

EXECUTIVE LEADERSHIP GOES BEYOND THE OFFICE

Hicks Muse encourages its partners and employees to explore volunteer activities in and around Dallas, and in this spirit of volunteerism, the principals lead by example. Hicks is a member of the board of regents for the University of Texas Systems, is a director of the Dallas Symphony Association, and sits on the board of trustees of the Dallas Museum of Art. In addition, he is also chairman of the board and owner of the Dallas Stars, a professional hockey club. Muse serves on the boards of directors of the Edwin L. Cox School of Business at Southern Methodist University (SMU), St. Philip's School and Community Center, University of Texas at Tyler Health Center, Dallas Summer Musicals, and Goodwill Industries.

And Furst is a director of the Boy Scouts of America-Circle Ten Council and serves as a council member of the College of Business Administration and the MBA Investment Fund at the University of Texas in Austin. He also serves on the board of advisers of SMU's Center for the Study of Financial Institutions and Markets.

Since its formation, Hicks Muse has been one of the most active, yet disciplined, private investment firms in the country. In the future, the firm will look beyond U.S. boundaries and continue exploring opportunities in other countries.

I N 1990, A GROUP OF EXECUTIVES WHO HAD EXPERIENCED THE real estate bust of the 1980s believed that the industry's recovery should be driven by job growth and issues affecting the quality of life throughout the Greater Dallas area. These volunteers founded

The Real Estate Council (TREC) with a commitment to making a difference for the entire community.

Today, the real estate business has indeed recovered; but the mission of The Real Estate Council is still based on the core belief that the success of the commercial real estate industry—and industry in general—is dependent on a healthy, vibrant Dallas. As a nonprofit organization, the council represents 1,200 volunteer members who work together on initiatives designed to make Dallas a better place to live, work, and raise families.

EMPHASIS ON COMMUNITY ISSUES, NOT SELF-INTEREST

This broad-based group of brokers, architects, engineers, builders, attorneys, accountants, bankers, and other real estate-related professionals is far from being a self-interest group. The focus is, in fact, community interest. Competitors become partners as members work together to promote job growth and enhance the area's quality of life.

To achieve its objectives, the board of directors meets annually to evaluate prospective initiatives, then mobilizes volunteer manpower and resources, and, as a team, develops ways to make an impact on issues they have identified. Past and present initiatives include a downtown campaign, environmental concerns, economic development issues, education, regional transportation, affordable housing, corporate relocations, and governmental policy.

Programs created by The Real Estate Council include the Associate Leadership Council, which provides training and mentoring each year to a group of young real estate professionals. In the political arena, the Community Leadership Committee supports leaders for public office who are committed to similar goals of long-term job growth and enhanced quality of life.

Two years ago, The Real Estate Council participated in the drafting of the Dallas Plan, a city-wide, long-range master plan that outlines priorities for public expenditures and social services over the next 30 years. Members are now participating in its implementation, and the council is recognized as the only nonprofit organization in a long list of major Dallas corporations that have made a significant five-year commitment to the plan's funding.

HOPE FOR DALLAS NEIGHBORHOODS

In 1993, the board identified as the single most urgent crisis facing Dallas the rising tide of poverty, crime, and despair that grips many inner-city neighborhoods. The Community Development Assistance Corporation (CDAC) was created as a separate charitable organization to focus solely on neighborhood revitalization. Pooling the vast professional talents of Real Estate Council volunteers, CDAC assists in creating a total program to restore a neighborhood's businesses and homes, reduce its crime, and reclaim its streets.

CDAC works *through* the neighborhood citizens, not *for* them; it is an active partnership. CDAC challenges neighborhood

citizens to remake their neighborhoods, then helps them do it.
CDAC's volunteer professionals
deliver a wide range of expert
services, without cost—including
real estate expertise, legal assistance, land planning, and architectural and construction help—to
meet each neighborhood's most
critical concerns.

CDAC's work is financially
supported with proceeds of The
Real Estate Council's annual
black-tie fund-raiser, Dallas Fight-
Night, which has generated more
than $1.3 million for CDAC since
1994. Dallas FightNight has become recognized nationwide as the
real estate networking event of the
year. In addition, funds raised at
FightNight are used to attract additional money from private foun-
dations and government sources
interested in CDAC's neighborhood work.

EVENTS MAKE THE HARD WORK REWARDING AND FUN

An Evening Honoring Dreamers,
Doers, and Unsung Heroes, a fall
gala, rewards individuals for their
unsung work in the community.
Each awardee receives $1,000
to be donated to his or her de-
signated charity. A night of
celebration and entertainment,
the annual gala has featured such
celebrities as George Plimpton,
Tom Wolfe, Dionne Warwick,
and the Temptations.

DOZENS OF COMMUNITY DEVELOP-
MENT ASSISTANCE CORPORATION
(CDAC) VOLUNTEERS ASSISTED IN
BUILDING HOMES IN THE LA CALLE
DIEZ NEIGHBORHOOD IN NORTH OAK
CLIFF (TOP LEFT AND RIGHT).

AS A RESULT OF CDAC'S DEDICATION
TO NEIGHBORHOOD IMPROVEMENT,
A SINGLE MOTHER AND HER DAUGH-
TER WERE MOVED INTO THEIR FIRST
HOME, WHICH WAS BUILT BY TREC
VOLUNTEERS AND NEIGHBORHOOD
RESIDENTS.

The Real Estate Council's
ability to weld the professional
world of real estate with the
entire community is its greatest
strength, say its members. The
membership is further benefited
through bimonthly breakfast
meetings with nationally and
locally recognized speakers dis-
cussing current trends affecting the
real estate industry and the community. "Fireside chats," more
informal question-and-answer sessions with speakers, are held peri-
odically as a special privilege for
full and sustaining members.

The Real Estate Council's
core mission has remained the
same since its founding in 1990.
As a result of its efforts to promote job growth and an enhanced
quality of life, the real estate
industry, the general business
community, and many individual
citizens and neighborhoods continue to benefit.

THREE HUNDRED NEIGHBORHOOD
RESIDENTS AND TREC VOLUNTEERS
PARTICIPATED IN A SATURDAY MORN-
ING CLEANUP OF THE LA CALLE DIEZ
NEIGHBORHOOD, ONE OF THREE COM-
MUNITIES TARGETED FOR REVITALIZA-
TION BY THE REAL ESTATE COUNCIL.

CANMAX INC.

THERE ARE 200,000 CONVENIENCE STORE AND PETROLEUM RETAILER outlets in the United States and 500,000 around the world. Fewer than 20 percent of these have automated point-of-sale equipment, but Canmax Inc. is hoping to change that. Canmax is a publicly traded software development company that has engineered point-of-sale solutions for some of the largest convenience store and gas station operators in the world. Some 5,000 of The Southland Corporation's 7-Eleven stores have equipment operating with Canmax software. With this solid foundation, the growth-oriented firm continues to develop its unique technology for all its customers and has built unprecedented strength in the marketplace.

C-SERVE: A PATHWAY TO SUCCESSFUL STORE AUTOMATION

Ninety percent of Canmax's 110 employees are skilled developers and customer support personnel, providing the best products and services on the market today. While Canmax markets a variety of software, services, and hardware, the principal product of the company is an application for convenience stores and gas stations called C-Serve. When introduced in 1988, it was an industry first. The second generation of C-Serve, introduced in 1997, includes new features to enhance decision support, merchandising, labor scheduling, and forecasting, and it operates in both Windows NT or Unix/ Motif systems.

C-Serve controls and monitors automated operations in retail outlets and provides an information link to corporate headquarters, where a range of detailed data can be examined throughout the day for up-to-the-minute decisions. Canmax systems help retailers manage customer convenience, peripheral integration, government regulations, inventory, promotional pricing, customer loyalties, and reporting of sales. Automation of these processes by Canmax systems leads to increased profitability and a more competitive position in the marketplace.

But Canmax is more than a supplier. Through a process Canmax calls Pathmation, the company becomes a partner with its clients—analyzing their needs and assessing the options, and then using the best resources available to build a path that leads customers to their ultimate goals. The key steps of Pathmation include consultation, which helps both parties understand the business needs of the client; development, which determines what technology is required; installation, which implements business processes and technology; training, which ensures the processes are understood; and support, which includes account management, professional services, and a 24-hour help desk.

Canmax professionals analyze each customer's business to determine precisely what is needed from a retail system, thus determining which service areas provided by the software and equipment have the most value and relevance. Canmax applies its experience and expertise to eliminate any difficulties and to streamline its customers' businesses in order to enhance their profitability.

Having established its position in the marketplace as an innovator of computer systems, Canmax will continue to lead the way to technological improvements that enhance the operations of all its customers.

CANMAX MAINTAINS A WORLD-CLASS DEVELOPMENT FACILITY, WHICH, COUPLED WITH ITS 24-HOUR HELP DESK SERVICES, ENSURES THAT CUSTOMERS MAXIMIZE THE BENEFITS TO THEIR ORGANIZATIONS.

FAISON-STONE, INC.

TWENTY-FIVE YEARS AGO, IT WAS A SPRAWLING RANCH WHERE cattle grazed under spiky mesquite trees and jackrabbits darted under dense brush. Today, this rolling land is the master-planned community of Las Colinas—Spanish for "the hills." It is home to

one of the highest concentrations of Fortune 500 companies in the nation. Since its inception in the 1970s, Las Colinas' 12,000 acres have become one of the most prestigious business locations in the country.

Yet it is not a jumble of industrial parks. Indeed, the community is easily navigated by wide roadways, the buildings are contemporary with regional accents, and garish signage is nonexistent. This pleasant atmosphere is attributed to the fact that one-third of the 12,000 acres is dedicated to open space, greenbelts, and waterways—not to mention the four golf courses located in the area.

This visionary development is managed by Faison-Stone, Inc., led by President Dary Stone, who looks out from his 11th-story corner office of the elegant Williams Square and sees a business and residential community that has few equals.

"Las Colinas is the benchmark for master-planned communities worldwide," says Stone, whose company has been involved in some of the area's largest relocations while working closely with local economic development groups, city councils, and chambers of commerce. "It is virtually impossible to build another development of its size and quality in the United States. Never again will a tract of raw land, situated in the heart of a major metropolitan area—adjacent to one of the world's busiest airports—be developed with the visionary master plan, massive infrastructure, and commitment of capital that created Las Colinas."

Strategically located in Irving at the apex of growth between Dallas and Fort Worth, Las Colinas offers unparalleled accessibility to major business, medical, shopping, entertainment, recreational, cultural, and educational centers. Only minutes from DFW International Airport, a Las Colinas address places you less than three hours from every major U.S. market and only a few hours from international destinations. For those living in the residential villages of Las Colinas or in nearby communities, some of the area's best schools are located within a 10-mile radius.

THE WORD IS OUT, LAS COLINAS IS IN
In the last 10 years, a large percent of Fortune 500 relocations have been to Las Colinas. "The

quality of the business atmosphere is equal to New York or Los Angeles. The businesspeople are as sophisticated and well connected as any you will find in the country," says Stone. "Yet, they can get home for their children's 6 p.m. soccer games and really enjoy the community without a difficult commute. That, in turn, makes business more productive."

Kimberly Clark, GTE Telephone Operations, Exxon, Quaker State Corp., and even Boy Scouts of America make their homes in Las Colinas. Why? "Options," says Stone. "You have an urban environment the size of Charlotte, North Carolina, but the aesthetics and the safety of a suburban environment."

Faison-Stone's mission is to "oversee the completion of the Las Colinas vision," says Stone, "which will involve implementing innovative ideas and maintaining quality for long-term value. Las Colinas will be the most organized combination of urban facilities and suburban amenities in the world, creating a synergistic environment in which to live, work, and play."

CLOCKWISE FROM TOP:
THE FOUR SEASONS RESORT AND CLUB SPANS 400 ACRES OF ROLLING HILLS IN LAS COLINAS.

THE AREA PERSONAL TRANSIT (APT) PROVIDES TRANSPORTATION WITHIN THE LAS COLINAS URBAN CENTER.

THE MASTER PLAN FOR LAS COLINAS INCORPORATES A BALANCE OF COMMERCIAL, RESIDENTIAL, AND ENVIRONMENTAL LAND USES.

N 1991, A BUSINESS THEN KNOWN AS SYNERGY TELEMANAGEMENT was started by three young men who have remained friends since their high school days in Dallas. Tim Terrell, Tim Rogers, and Scott Roberts drew on their combined 25 years of telecommuni-

cations experience and started the company to compete in the emerging field of long-distance services.

In 1992, they had two employees, and revenues were a respectable $102,000. But by 1996, the company had been renamed CapRock Communications Corporation and boasted more than 45 employees, and revenues of $24 million. So great and so fast was the company's rise that the Dallas 100 survey dubbed CapRock the number one fastest-growing privately held company in the Metroplex.

Relying on its solid reputation as a dependable, high-quality provider of long-distance services in the wholesale market, CapRock expanded in 1995 into commercial sales and began offering international products. In 1997, the company made the dramatic leap into the realm of local dial-tone service, opening its market to virtually every residence and business that has a telephone line.

"We are the only Dallas-based company providing local and long-distance services," Roberts points out. "And we're Dallas' fastest-

growing company in one of the most competitive cities in the telecommunications field, which says something about our character."

Terrell says of the firm's success, "I think what appeals to our customers is our can-do attitude. Every one of our customers has come to us from a larger competitor. They came to us and stayed because ours is a relationship based on customer service."

INVESTMENT IN TECHNOLOGY

In an effort to reduce its dependence on a single vendor, CapRock acquired in 1994 a Digital Switch Corporation DEX 600, which is a

massive piece of switching equipment that assured CapRock its independence. The switching equipment, coupled with the firm's existing high-quality digital fiber-optic network, creates the ideal framework for the transmission of long-distance calls with immediate, clear connections. The switch allows CapRock to provide its customers sophisticated calling products and more competitively priced long-distance service.

With rates already lower than those of the telecommunications Big Three, and with the acquisition of its switching equipment, CapRock is in a unique position to focus on the all-important customer service

DUBBED THE NUMBER ONE FAST-EST-GROWING PRIVATELY HELD COMPANY IN THE METROPLEX, CAPROCK COMMUNICATIONS ENJOYS A SOLID REPUTATION AS A DEPENDABLE, HIGH-QUALITY PROVIDER OF LONG-DISTANCE SERVICES TO THE WHOLESALE AND COMMERCIAL TELECOMMUNICATIONS MARKET (TOP).

CAPROCK'S DIGITAL SWITCH CORPORATION DEX 600, COUPLED WITH THE FIRM'S EXISTING HIGH-QUALITY DIGITAL FIBER-OPTIC NETWORK, CREATES THE IDEAL FRAMEWORK FOR THE TRANSMISSION OF LONG-DISTANCE CALLS WITH IMMEDIATE, CLEAR CONNECTIONS (BOTTOM).

The expansion into the commercial end of the telecommunications industry, after establishing a foundation in the wholesale side, is the opposite of the way the business usually works. But, with an increase in revenues of 2,500 percent in five years, CapRock is headed in the right direction.

"We shifted into commercial to heighten our brand awareness," says Rogers. "On the wholesale side, everyone knows who we are, and the opportunities in commercial are huge."

Jere W. Thompson Jr., president of CapRock Communications Corporation, also notes, "This is a $100 billion business, and we hope to capture an increasing portion of it, but our focus is on the Southwest and managing our growth. We want to stay focused on what we're doing while expanding throughout Texas and the surrounding states." Thompson is no stranger to Dallas business. The Dallas native is the chairman of the Texas Turnpike Authority, originally appointed to the position by Governor Bill Clements in 1989 and then reappointed to the board in 1995 by Governor George Bush. He has served since 1985 on the board of Cistercian Preparatory School and has cochaired three of its capital campaigns.

Other company principals are also active in Dallas-area civic and charitable organizations: Rogers and Terrell are participants in the Chip Moody's Children's Cancer Fund, as is Roberts, who also has participated in the Make-A-Wish Foundation as a wish grantor.

CapRock is committed to providing innovative, cost-effective solutions to its customers, as well as to taking an active part in the Dallas community.

that has been a guiding value since the inception of the firm. Largely due to its responsiveness to client needs and a continuing tradition of introducing new and more flexible products and programs, the company has garnered high praise from customers across the board, from small family businesses to medium-sized corporations.

CapRock offers simple flat-rate billing programs that clear up any confusion about how much a company's monthly telecommunications costs will be. Among the services offered by CapRock are dedicated access, international calling plans, calling cards, conference calling, voice mail, toll-free 800 and 888 service, accounting codes, detailed billing, and 24-hour customer service. CapRock is a facility-based carrier that offers an affordable total telecommunications package, which is ideal for the small- to medium-sized businesses in the Dallas area that depend on the company. CapRock's services and rates are particularly attractive to companies that want to outsource their telecommunications departments.

CUSTOMER SERVICE HAS BEEN A GUIDING VALUE SINCE THE INCEPTION OF CAPROCK. LARGELY DUE TO ITS RESPONSIVENESS TO CLIENT NEEDS AND A CONTINUING TRADITION OF INTRODUCING NEW AND MORE FLEXIBLE PRODUCTS AND PROGRAMS, THE COMPANY HAS GARNERED HIGH PRAISE FROM CUSTOMERS ACROSS THE BOARD.

TODAY, THE FOUR PRINCIPALS AT CAPROCK COMMUNICATIONS— (SEATED FROM LEFT) TIM ROGERS, TIM TERRELL, (STANDING FROM LEFT) JERE W. THOMPSON JR., AND SCOTT ROBERTS—REMAIN ACTIVE NOT ONLY IN THE LIFE OF THEIR COMPANY, BUT ALSO IN DALLAS-AREA CIVIC AND CHARITABLE ORGANIZATIONS.

SINCE ITS INCEPTION, CHAMPION PARTNERS, LTD. HAS EXCELLED AS a commercial real estate company. Now the firm is taking the next step: "To be known as an extraordinary real estate company," says Founder and Managing Partner Jeffrey L. Swope.

In its first five years, the dynamic firm has been involved with the development and/or acquisition of more than 11 million square feet of office and industrial space—valued at some $425 million—in regions around the country. Swope and company are renowned for putting together leading-edge corporations that need specialized space with real estate capital investors interested in accomplishing successful solutions.

"We blend our skill and expertise within both the property and capital markets to create opportunities and enhance value for ourselves and our partners," says Swope. "It seems simple on the surface; however, it's pretty complicated unless you have the processes, systems, and experience to successfully strategize and implement. We do."

Champion has completed or is currently at work acquiring or developing office or distribution facilities for clients as diverse as American Airlines, Hunt-Wesson, Perrier, General Electric, and Duracell, among others. Over

the needs of future clients by building facilities in Dallas, Memphis, Atlanta, and New Jersey. More than 2 million square feet of building space is currently under construction, including

the 91-acre Regency Business Park in Grand Prairie just west of Dallas. The 470,000-square-foot General Electric distribution center and a 405,780-square-foot warehouse have already been constructed in the park. When the project is completed, Champion will have created nearly 2 million square feet in six separate facilities.

Swope also channels Champion's resources into speculative office construction, with Dallas Landmark Center—a two-building, 260,000-square-foot project on 20 acres near the North Tollway—and a 72-acre office park called Sierra at Las Colinas in Irving, where a 170,000-square-foot project is under construction.

"We view Dallas as a tremendous home base for us to do our nationwide activities," says Swope, a Dallas native who is active in numerous civic endeavors. "We know Dallas is one of the best places in the country to do business now and for at least the next 10 years. Corporations in any type of industry can locate here and find the labor they need to get up and running, and we know we can provide them with the appropriate type of space."

OVER THE PAST 20 YEARS, CHAMPION'S DALLAS-BASED PRINCIPALS HAVE COMPLETED NUMEROUS LARGE-SCALE PROJECTS, INCLUDING NEARLY 1 MILLION SQUARE FEET OF DISTRIBUTION SPACE FOR MATSUSHITA ELECTRIC COMPANY IN ELGIN, ILLINOIS (TOP), AND 5.5 MILLION SQUARE FEET IN SEVEN REGIONAL DISTRIBUTION CENTERS FOR NESTLÉ, INCLUDING DE KALB, ILLINOIS (LEFT), AND LATHROP, CALIFORNIA (BOTTOM).

the past 20 years, Champion's Dallas-based principals have completed numerous large-scale projects, including a 1 million-square-foot campus in Dallas for Texas Instruments; 600,000 square feet of office and nearly 1 million square feet of distribution space for Matsushita Electric Company; and 5.5 million square feet in seven regional distribution centers for Nestlé.

BUILDING THE FUTURE

Champion is currently forging headlong into the world of real estate development. Secure in the knowledge afforded by experience, Champion is anticipating

WHILE MANY METROPLEX REALTORS EXPEND THEIR ENERGIES ON THE cluster developments rapidly rising in the outer suburbs, there is one firm that sees the established neighborhoods of inner Dallas as viable, vital territory. Uptown Realtors has always focused on the

hidden enclaves and the little-known, quaint communities that give Dallas its unique culture and preserve its domestic history.

"What people are finding out is that the inner city is a great place to live," says Uptown President Mike Grossman, but then, Grossman has always known that. As the *Dallas Morning News* pointed out in a recent profile, ". . . the veteran residential broker has created a major real estate firm from scratch by focusing on the unconventional and the under-represented."

It's not only what and where Uptown sells, but also to whom it sells that makes the firm a community leader. "We serve and reflect the diversity of Dallas," Grossman says. "We're proud of the fact that we handle a diverse clientele and many first-time home buyers."

That focus—and a meaningful merger with an existing firm just two weeks after Uptown started in 1993—has put Uptown in the top 10 of Dallas' largest real estate companies. There are 55 agents in the 65-associate firm, working out of three branch offices, including the company headquarters in

a restored 1910 estate near Turtle Creek. Other offices are located in a restored historic home in Oak Cliff, and at Cedar Creek Lake, about 65 miles south of Dallas.

Uptown Realtors also houses two in-house mortgage companies and a title company. "It's very important to have those support services on the premises," Grossman says. "We do quite a bit of work with home buyers with specific needs—for example, those with domestic partners—and sometimes those buyers have difficulties that we can overcome."

Not content to simply serve the diverse community of Dallas with home sales and mortgages, Grossman, his partners George

Amerson and Jeff Updike, and members of the staff take the lead in performing volunteer work for like-minded groups and agencies.

The AIDS Food Pantry, the AIDS LifeWalk, the Children's Medical Center of Dallas, the American Heart Association, the Turtle Creek Chorale, and public television station KERA (Channel 13) have benefited from Uptown's participation on their boards, in their coffers, or in the field. Also, Grossman, who is past director of state and local Realtor® boards, and his associates serve on and work with the city's minority chambers of commerce.

"We consider ourselves an old-fashioned real estate company that just happens to use state-of-the-art technology, probably more so than any Realtor® in the state of Texas," Grossman says. While listings, presentations, contracts, and virtually all other aspects of the business are on networked computers, Grossman points out that the firm's name dangles on humble shingles in the yards of the branch offices, a throwback to earlier times.

The shingle is symbolic of how and where Uptown Realtors does business. "The inner city is a great place to live," Grossman says, "and it's the diversity of people there that makes it so."

"WE CONSIDER OURSELVES AN OLD-FASHIONED REAL ESTATE COMPANY THAT JUST HAPPENS TO USE STATE-OF-THE-ART TECHNOLOGY," SAYS UPTOWN PRESIDENT MIKE GROSSMAN (FAR RIGHT), PICTURED HERE WITH (FROM LEFT) PARTNERS GEORGE AMERSON AND JEFF UPDIKE.

THIS WATERCOLOR RENDERING DEPICTS UPTOWN REALTORS' HEADQUARTERS NEAR TURTLE CREEK.

"**G**IVING BACK TO THE COMMUNITY IS PART OF OUR programming," says Scott D. Savage, vice president and general manager of KYNG-FM (105.3), better known to country music fans in north Texas as Young Country. "The station goes beyond the ordinary," he continues. "We provide entertainment values unique to the marketplace, but that isn't enough: We want to use our airwaves do good things for the community."

This dedicated commitment to the community is the way Young Country has operated since it burst onto the airwaves in 1992. While the music that launched the 100,000-watt station was provided by such international recording artists as Garth Brooks, Reba McEntire, George Strait, and Clint Black, KYNG-FM's local personnel began their unceasing efforts to raise money for local and national charities with a focus on organizations that benefit women, children, the environment, and animals.

The list of events sponsored by the charity-minded station is long and includes the Road Trip for Charity, the Leukemia Society Chili Cook Off, the Turkey Bowl, Santa's Helpers, Hero on the Job, Boo at the Zoo, and the Salvation Army Fan Drive. Station personalities devote time and creativity to these and other events, some-times making 40 to 50 public appearances per month.

Since its inception, the station has won national and local recognition for its charitable efforts, including awards from the National Leukemia Society of America for its donation of more than $1 million in airtime and financial contributions during a four-year relationship. In 1995, Young Country was one of 44 finalists for the National Association of Broadcasters' Crystal Award, which recognizes philanthropic efforts and community involvement. And the Salvation Army presented the station with its Partner Award, in tribute to the man-power KYNG-FM has provided over the years.

"Our signature event—the Young Country Christmas Fireworks to Music—is one of the most anticipated events in the area," says Savage, referring to the free annual event that simulcasts holiday music on the airwaves with fireworks exploding over Las Colinas. "Approximately 100,000 spectators attend the show, which features choirs, dancers—including the Young Country troupe—and a concert by a nationally known act after the fireworks."

The elaborate event certainly raises the station's profile, but it would be meaningless to KYNG-

CLOCKWISE FROM TOP:
A.W. PANTOJA SPICES UP THE AFTER-NOON DRIVE WITH HIS ANTICS, BUT HE ALWAYS HAS TIME TO LEND A HAND TO COMMUNITY FUND-RAISING EVENTS.

PROVIDING A FUN AND FESTIVE PLAY-GROUND FOR KIDS AND THEIR FAMI-LIES, YOUNG COUNTRY HOSTS ONE OF THE MOST POPULAR FREE EASTER-TIME EVENTS.

YOUNG COUNTRY HELPS TO ROUND UP SOME STAR-SPANGLED FUN IN THE ARLINGTON 4TH OF JULY PARADE.

FM if it didn't benefit a charity. As it happens, thousands of dollars in proceeds generated by one-of-a-kind commemorative T-shirt sales are donated to Ronald McDonald House Charities each year.

Just as the aggressive charity drives were incorporated as part of the station's master plan, so was its intention to become known as a station that interacts with its listeners and provides useful information from the community throughout the day. "We address issues on the air that we know are of interest to our listeners," says Savage.

"Young Country radio is first and foremost personality driven," Savage continues. "If you regard the music as the stage, then our air talent are the performers on that stage. We provide entertainment and information, and we count on a lot of listener interaction. It's like having a morning show all day long."

PERSONALITIES WITH PERSONALITY

Young Country's mandate calls for bright, lively, and interesting on-air personalities. In an industry that is infamous for frequent personnel changes, it is significant to note that five of KYNG-FM's original six core hosts have remained at the station since its in-

ception in 1992. Johnnie Stone and Martha Martinez plug listeners into the world each morning; Katie Pruett's midday show promises to "make your workday go faster"; A.W. Pantoja and Jimbo have made the afternoon drive show one of the most listened to and talked about shows in the Metroplex; Stubie Doak's evening show is a fun-filled shift that comes off a different wall each day; and overnight personality Cody McCoy keeps listeners awake with country's hottest music.

"The longer the talent stays and becomes familiar to the audience, the more equity they build for themselves and the station," explains Savage. "No other station can have an A.W. Pantoja or a Katie Pruett except us, and we intend to build our ratings and growth on that fact."

The Young Country concept is working. In fact, it's exceeding even Savage's wildest expectations. Savage was thrilled to see Young Country become a Top 10 station in Dallas within its first six months on the air. "Currently, we are consistently in the Top 5 in all the major demographics," Savage says. The station also is one of the top five revenue generators in the Dallas/Fort Worth radio industry, which is the fifth-largest radio market in the country.

Sometimes the station doesn't realize its own popularity: The day after the 1996 presidential elections, the station offered 25 cents for each political road sign brought to a collection site. The civic promotion attracted thousands of participants and collected some 12,000 signs in two hours, exceeding the event's budget, which Savage accepted as a cost of helping clean up the community. Clearly, the personalities and the charity efforts are attracting both listeners and business.

"As a station that is only five years old, we're still brand new," Savage says. "We're only beginning, but just wait . . . there's still a lot more to come!"

ATIONSBANK IS BUILDING DALLAS. FROM WITHIN AND WITHOUT, NationsBank plays a vital role in the continuing development of the city, from revitalizing low- and moderate-income neighborhoods to helping new and established businesses sharpen their competitive edges.

Although NationsBank has been in Dallas since 1992, the company actually traces its roots through predecessor banks to 1968, beginning as First National Bank and Republic National Bank, two competitors that merged in 1987 to form First RepublicBank Corp. Today, NationsBank has established a strong presence throughout the Metroplex.

Capitalizing on the vast resources provided by Charlotte-based NationsBank Corporation, the Dallas franchise, with nearly 7,000 employees, has more than 60 banking centers in the city, 17 of them in low- and moderate-income areas. There are more than 150 automatic teller machines (ATMs), including many in Albertsons supermarkets, giving NationsBank consumers easy and immediate access to their accounts. In Texas, NationsBank has more than 330 banking centers and 1,041 ATMs, ensuring customers that in any corner of the state they may go, NationsBank will be there for them.

ABOVE ALL ELSE, CUSTOMER SERVICE

Comprehensive customer service is the key to the NationsBank philosophy. Since the company is part of the fourth-largest banking company in the United States, with $227 billion in assets and $2.4 billion in earnings, NationsBank is quick to invest in technology that makes it easier for customers to access their accounts, from ATMs and banking centers to telephone, PC, and Internet access.

As a leader in banking technology, NationsBank spends more than $500 million per year on technology to improve sales, enhance product delivery, and speed up customer service in banking centers throughout its franchise. Much of that money has gone toward computers in order to stay abreast of technological developments that affect the company's core consumers: American households.

This expansion of banking technology brings NationsBank ever closer to its goal of making its services available however, whenever, and wherever the customer wants.

A PRESENCE FELT AND SEEN

The NationsBank presence in Dallas is distinguished by the 71-story NationsBank building that stands taller than any other in the downtown Dallas skyline. The building, 40 percent of which is occupied by NationsBank offices, serves—with its distinctive emerald green argon illumination—as the centerpiece of the Dallas nighttime skyline. In photographs seen in publications around the world, the NationsBank building helps give Dallas an image that is readily identified.

The tower's pivotal position in the city is symbolic of how the corporation fits into the Dallas landscape at large. Of all the institutions, corporations, and firms that contribute time, talent, and resources to help develop, manage, and build the Dallas community, few top the commitment of NationsBank. The United Way, the Dallas Symphony Orchestra, the South Dallas Cultural Center, the Dallas Children's Advocacy Center, and the 1996 Sun and Star celebration of Japanese art and culture have all benefited from relationships with NationsBank.

Those high-profile activities are complemented by many other charitable and not-for-profit programs supported by the Dallas division of NationsBank. NationsBank in Dallas contributes nearly $300,000 each year to predominantly minority organizations, and its support of Paul Quinn College, with a $1.1 million commitment, is the largest of any Dallas financial institution. As for the Dallas County United Way, the bank and its associates contribute nearly $1.5 million per year, making it one of the United Way's top supporters.

Bank associates donate time to represent NationsBank at mi-

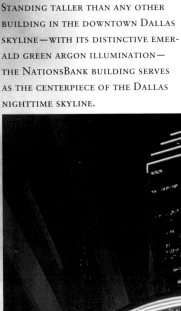

STANDING TALLER THAN ANY OTHER BUILDING IN THE DOWNTOWN DALLAS SKYLINE—WITH ITS DISTINCTIVE EMERALD GREEN ARGON ILLUMINATION—THE NATIONSBANK BUILDING SERVES AS THE CENTERPIECE OF THE DALLAS NIGHTTIME SKYLINE.

nority business development fairs and educational seminars. These employees also serve on various committees as chairpersons, cochairpersons, and members who promote the work of the D/FW Minority Business Development Council, the Greater Dallas Chamber of Commerce, the Greater Dallas Hispanic Chamber of Commerce, the Dallas Black Chamber of Commerce, the American Indian Chamber of Commerce, the Dallas Asian American Chamber of Commerce, and the North Texas Commission.

INVESTING IN THE COMMUNITY

In 1991, NationsBank Corporation pledged to lend $10 billion over 10 years to residents and businesses in low- and moderate-income neighborhoods throughout the communities it serves. By 1995, this lending had already topped $13 billion in just four years. Unquestionably, the $10 billion was not a ceiling, but a foundation.

During the past four years in Dallas, NationsBank has made more than $1 billion in community development loans, including $11.3 million loaned in a partnership with Dallas City Homes. The funding enabled the purchase and rehabilitation of The Parks at Wynnewood, a multifamily housing development in Oak Cliff,

which now provides 408 units of affordable housing. A second partnership with a developer financed the $7.1 million acquisition and rehabilitation of 269 units in Carlton Court I and II in Dallas.

NationsBank has committed $40 million in lending and equity investments in a five-year plan to revitalize the South Dallas/Fair Park area, which will, among other things, create 100 single-family residences, 300 multifamily housing units, and two day care

facilities. It's no wonder that NationsBank has been rated outstanding, the highest rating possible by federal regulators who measure performance and compliance with the Community Reinvestment Act by financial institutions.

Clearly, as the record shows, NationsBank is committed to making significant contributions to the overall economic development of Dallas, both from within and without.

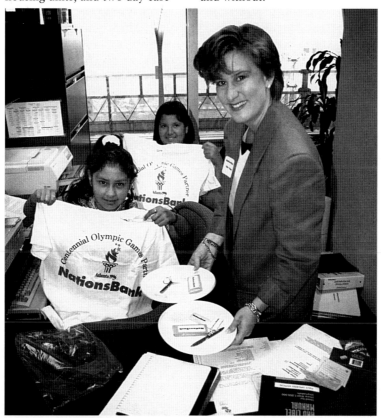

NATIONSBANK IN DALLAS IS PROUD TO PARTICIPATE IN TAKE OUR DAUGHTERS TO WORK DAY (TOP).

NATIONSBANK FUNDING ENABLED THE PURCHASE AND REHABILITATION OF THE PARKS AT WYNNEWOOD, A MULTIFAMILY HOUSING DEVELOPMENT IN OAK CLIFF, WHICH NOW PROVIDES 408 UNITS OF AFFORDABLE HOUSING (BOTTOM).

ABT EXECUTIVE SUITES

STABLISHING A COST-EFFECTIVE, YET PRESTIGIOUS CORPORATE presence in Dallas can be a challenge, particularly for start-up companies, independent professionals, and emerging entrepreneurs. Even established, bottom-line-oriented Fortune 500 and multinational companies facing the economic realities of doing business in the 1990s are adopting leaner and more streamlined corporate profiles.

ABT Executive Suites provides companies—large and small—with immediate access to convenient, flexible turnkey office space and prestigious addresses all around the Dallas Metroplex. A wide range of amenities and support services is available, including fully furnished private offices, conference rooms, concierge services, and a support staff of receptionists, telephone operators, administrative assistants, and word processing and desktop publishing professionals. Additional staff services can be provided on a moment's notice and are competitively priced on a pay-per-use basis.

WHAT ABT MEANS
Founding president Bret Chapman began ABT Executive Suites with his partner and brother Patton Chapman in 1992 with just one suite. "It was our Dallas Parkway

location, and it was just 12,000 square feet," Bret Chapman recalls today. "But I knew then that in a very short time, we were going to be the biggest and the best in the Metroplex."

True to his word, by 1996 ABT was the largest executive suite company in Dallas, with some 150,000 square feet of space in eight different sites, including downtown Dallas, Oak Lawn, and others in north Dallas, Preston Center, Lake Highlands, and Valley Ranch. "We've grown 100 percent a year since 1992," says Bret Chapman.

While the "ABT" in the corporate name stands for Advanced Business Technology—a description of the accommodations and fixtures the firm makes available to clients—Bret Chapman suggests ABT means much more than that in a figurative sense. "We strive so hard and give such extra effort in service that, in all of our years in business, we've lost exactly one tenant to a competing executive suite company," he says proudly. "We consistently exceed expectations."

ABT Executive Suites has provided creative solutions for affordable first-class office space in premier locations for national computer software companies, the Money Store, and Hollywood's MTM Entertainment, to name a few. But lawyers and accountants are something of a specialty and account for some 40 percent of ABT's tenants. "That's because we have large legal and tax libraries," Bret Chapman says. "Law partners, attorneys, accountants—they find that we really make life easy for them."

THE "VIRTUAL OFFICE"
More than a real estate or office broker, ABT provides superior

business environments without significant investment or long-term obligation. As an industry leader, ABT Executive Suites capitalizes on the decentralized office environment made possible by the proliferation of accessible and affordable communications and business technology, such as cellular phones, modems, faxes, personal computers, and computer networks.

Among the ABT program advantages is the availability of part-time virtual offices, which offer the same professional support staff and facilities that full-time clients enjoy, with use of private office space for as few as four hours per month. This option has proved particularly effective for new businesses seeking to limit investment risk and start-up costs, and for home-based companies that need an occasional in-town presence.

The innate flexibility of the facilities and the affirmative attitude of ABT's staff of 24 employees make it a practical solution for companies looking to establish a cost-effective presence in Dallas.

CLOCKWISE FROM TOP:
ABT EXECUTIVE SUITES PROVIDES AFFORDABLE FIRST-CLASS OFFICE SPACE IN PREMIER LOCATIONS FOR NUMEROUS BUSINESS AND PROFESSIONAL CLIENTS.

BY 1996, ABT WAS THE LARGEST EXECUTIVE SUITE COMPANY IN DALLAS, WITH SOME 150,000 SQUARE FEET OF SPACE IN EIGHT DIFFERENT SITES.

TENANTS AT ABT EXECUTIVE SUITES HAVE ACCESS TO A SUPPORT STAFF OF RECEPTIONISTS, TELEPHONE OPERATORS, AND ADMINISTRATIVE ASSISTANTS.

s North America's largest health care supply management company, McKesson Corp., a Fortune 100 firm, provides pharmaceutical, medical-surgical, and health care products and services to independent and chain pharmacies; hospitals; alternate site facilities,

including physicians and clinics; long-term care and home care sites; and integrated health networks. The San Francisco-based company expanded its presence in the Texas market after acquiring the distribution business of Carrollton-based FoxMeyer Drug Company in 1996. In early 1997, McKesson acquired General Medical, Inc., one of the nation's leading all-market distributors of medical-surgical supplies. As a result, McKesson will have annualized sales of approximately $17 billion in health care products and services.

REMODELING PHARMACEUTICAL DISTRIBUTION

Operating from a campus near the Stemmons Freeway, McKesson's Carrollton Operations facility employs 700 professionals working as partners with retail pharmacies, hospitals, integrated health networks, alternate sites, and others to distribute products in a timely and efficient manner throughout the United States.

In response to a rapidly changing industry, McKesson provides marketing services that help pharmaceutical and biotech manufacturers in their efforts to develop new products to improve health care quality. Regulatory, managed care, and competitive issues constantly complicate the development and marketing of new drugs, and McKesson provides a crucial link in health care supply management.

Pharmaceuticals, health care, and beauty care products distributed by McKesson reach retail pharmacies, hospitals, and alternate-site locations efficiently, safely, and in a timely manner. McKesson leverages the company's scale and technological sophistication to improve the quality of pharmaceutical care and to reduce costs. McKesson offers a broad range of comprehensive pharmaceutical products and services, including the OmniLink℠ software application; OmniLink Financial Services; SupplyNET℠ advanced supply-chain product utilization management system; BidLink℠ on-line real-time system for managing contracts; and RxOBOT™, a completely automated medication-retrieval and physical inventory management system, produced by a subsidiary, Automated Healthcare, Inc.

McKesson measures its success in several ways: by building its shareholders' value and by helping its customers maintain quality patient care while managing their businesses more efficiently and cost effectively. By continuing the path that has made the firm a leader in its industry, McKesson will continue providing its customers and suppliers with the broadest range of products and innovative services well into the next century.

McKESSON'S ACUMAX® PLUS WAREHOUSE MANAGEMENT COMPUTER (LEFT)

McKESSON'S TECHNOLOGY CENTER, CARROLLTON, TEXAS (RIGHT)

▶ SELECT STUDIO

HE CRESCENT®. ALL OF DALLAS KNOWS THIS DISTINCTIVE LAND-mark building as the address for some of the premier businesses in Texas. With its old-world mansard roof and limestone facing, the majestic, mixed-use complex sets the standard in refined

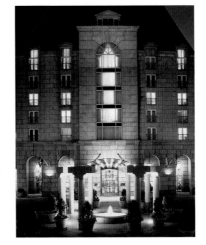

elegance for rental property.

Indeed, everyone knows The Crescent®. But not everyone knows about Crescent Real Estate Equities Company, the real estate investment trust (REIT) and its affiliates that own the 1.4 million-square-foot signature office building and retail center. Besides The Crescent® complex, Crescent owns dominant, high-quality office properties in such growth markets as Austin, Houston, Denver, Phoenix, Colorado Springs, Albuquerque, San Francisco, and San Diego.

In all, the firm owns and operates some 21.5 million square feet of office, retail, and residential space, most of it consisting of Class A properties and all of it situated in prime locations. And, like The Crescent Office Towers, which is 99 percent leased, those buildings enjoy an average occupancy rate of nearly 85 percent.

THE HOTEL CRESCENT COURT IS PART OF THE CRESCENT® PROJECT, LOCATED ADJACENT TO THE HOTEL. THE LUXURY HOTEL OFFERS (CLOCKWISE FROM TOP LEFT) SPLENDID VIEWS FROM ITS COURTYARD, NEARBY ACCESS TO THE CRESCENT OFFICE TOWERS, PANORAMIC VIEWS OF THE DALLAS SKYLINE, FINE DINING AT THE BEAU NASH, A GRAND WELCOME IN THE GREAT HALL, AND PREMIER MEETING FACILITIES IN THE GARDEN ROOM.

CAREFUL MANAGEMENT AND ACQUISITION STRATEGIES

The Fort Worth-based Crescent Real Estate Equities began in 1994 with the acquisitions of Dallas-area properties; in May 1994, the firm made its initial public offering, and since then has completed more than $2.1 billion of real estate investments. These include $206 million invested in full-service hotels and $25 million in residential land developments in strategic regions.

In March 1997, Crescent announced plans to acquire $383 million in assets of Carter-Crowley Properties, Inc. This portfolio includes 14 office properties in seven suburban Dallas areas totaling 3.5 million square feet. In a separate transaction, Crescent also plans to acquire 1,221 acres of commercially zoned, undeveloped land in the Dallas Metroplex, as well as inter-

ests in the National Basketball Association's local franchise, the Dallas Mavericks.

"As major investors in the Dallas/Fort Worth metropolitan area, and most recently in downtown Dallas," says Gerald Haddock, Crescent's president and CEO, "we will be pleased to participate in support of the majority owners of the Dallas Mavericks with regards to the future location and development of a new arena complex now being discussed by the City of Dallas and the basketball team."

Crescent's other Dallas properties include the highly visible Trammell Crow Center, a 1.2 million-square-foot building in downtown Dallas; 3333 Lee Parkway, a 234,000-square-foot glass building in Oaklawn; The Aberdeen, PepsiCo. Inc.'s headquarters in North Dallas; the 100 percent-leased Liberty Plaza I and II; Stanford Corporate Centre, home of TENET Healthcare, Inc.; and 12404 Park Central, future home of Perot Systems. In 1997, the firm acquired Greenway I, IA, and II in Richardson's Telecom Corridor, with all 147,000 square feet leased to Northern Telecom.

Beyond the Dallas area, Crescent's impressive portfolio of real estate assets includes 55 office

properties and six retail locations, six full-service hotels totaling 1,471 rooms, two destination health and fitness resorts, and economic interests in six single-family residential land developments.

Those buildings are located in 19 metropolitan submarkets that Crescent's principals have identified as having historically experienced above-average office employment growth. Crescent's studies verify that the growth is driven by both internal job growth, the migration of people and companies attracted by a better quality of life, favorable corporate and individual tax structures, affordable housing, and an available skilled workforce.

CREATING A SENSE OF PLACE

Crescent's operating philosophy goes beyond simply making acquisitions; once a property becomes a Crescent property, it is put into the able hands of the firm's experienced managers and building operators who work to make an immediate impact. A strategic plan is developed for needed improvements, such as increased parking garage lighting, upgrades to lobbies and corridors, and walk-off mats that feature the building's name and the Crescent logo. Crescent's management philosophy provides for empowering its managers to make decisions at the property level rather than only the corporate level in situations affecting tenants' day-to-day utilization and enjoyment of the property.

Crescent provides a working atmosphere that is conducive to the highest profitability of the tenant, and strives to create a sense of place for those who work in, live in, and visit the property. But Crescent is careful to communicate with tenants to assure them of the positive changes they will be enjoying. In fact, Crescent's long-term devotion to its acquisitions often creates unprecedented relationships with tenants that

lead to other business opportunities. It's not surprising that Crescent has been retained by tenants to find suitable office space to accommodate their expansion in other regions. Crescent regards its tenants as its customers, and the relationship is based on understanding both short- and long-term needs.

COMMUNITY INVOLVEMENT

The 250 employees of Crescent Real Estate Equities Company are encouraged by Haddock to become involved in charitable activities in their regions. In Dallas, Crescent is represented in trade and civic organizations, associations, and various chambers of commerce, and has on occasion donated space for meetings to area nonprofit organizations.

Most significantly, Crescent Real Estate Equities, in collaboration with the Rainwater Charitable Foundation, began a partnership with a Fort Worth day care and learning center called SAVE OUR CHILDREN (SOC). The mission of the partnership was, and still is, to support the success of the children by integrating the school community with corporate partners for the enhancement of a successful learning environment.

Besides providing facility needs for SOC and other needs of equipment, supplies, and friendship, Crescent has established the FACES of Change project. FACES of Change is a three-year partnership between Crescent office properties and elementary schools. This is a tenant-driven project through which the office community and the school community work together for the success of children. Through the events conducted as a part of the pilot program with SOC at Continental Plaza, there were many touching moments between the tenants and the children. The tenants came to know the children, and the results were so successful that additional, simi-

lar programs are being brought to each area where there is a Crescent property.

It says a lot about a company when such a long-term commitment is made to the community by its administrators. With the integration of the FACES of Change project in the Crescent culture, it is clear that Crescent intends to make an impact on and give something back to the communities where it does business.

THE LOBBY OF THE MIDDLE TOWER OF THE CRESCENT OFFICE TOWERS PROVIDES CONVENIENT ACCESS TO THE MANY BUSINESSES LOCATED IN THE COMPLEX (TOP).

THE SPA AT THE HOTEL CRESCENT COURT OFFERS AN OASIS FOR THE HEALTH AND FITNESS NEEDS OF ALL GUESTS (BOTTOM).

SUMMERFIELD SUITES HOTEL

SUMMERFIELD SUITES HOTEL IS A GROWING CHAIN OF ALL-SUITES hotels that provide business travelers and families with accommodations that surpass those of standard—or even luxury—hotels. The rooms and grounds of Summerfield Suites were developed with a campus layout identical to that of many modern garden apartment complexes. In addition to the Addison location, Summerfield Suites has a second Dallas hotel in Las Colinas; both opened in February 1996.

CLOCKWISE FROM TOP:
A DISTINGUISHING FACTOR OF SUMMERFIELD SUITES HOTEL IS THE TWO-BEDROOM/TWO-BATH SUITE, WHICH IS COMPRISED OF TWO BEDROOMS ADJOINED BY A LIVING ROOM AND A FULLY EQUIPPED KITCHEN.

SUMMERFIELD SUITES HOTEL IS A GROWING CHAIN OF ALL-SUITES HOTELS THAT PROVIDE BUSINESS TRAVELERS AND FAMILIES WITH ACCOMMODATIONS THAT SURPASS THOSE OF STANDARD—OR EVEN LUXURY—HOTELS.

FROM OUTSTANDING GUEST SERVICE TO AMENITIES THAT REALLY MATTER, SUMMERFIELD SUITES HOTELS ARE DESIGNED TO FIT THE WAY GUESTS LIVE.

UNIQUE CONCEPT

The Summerfield concept is the brainchild of Rolf Ruhfus, who in the 1980s was a founder of the popular Residence Inn chain. Ruhfus sold the business to Marriott in 1987 and began building the Summerfield Hotel Corporation. Today, the Wichita, Kansas-based company boasts 28 suites-only hotels in 21 cities around the country, with several more hotels scheduled to open in 1998.

A distinguishing factor of Summerfield Suites Hotel is the two-bedroom/two-bath suite, which is comprised of two bedrooms adjoined by a living room and a fully equipped kitchen. This floor plan is extremely functional and cost effective because it allows more people per suite with about the same amount of privacy as two separate rooms.

COMFORTS OF HOME

The sandy-stucco and teal-trimmed two-story buildings contain 132 suites. In the two-bedroom/two-bathroom suites, each bedroom has its own private bath, television, and phone line. The living room is equipped with a television and videocassette player, and the fully equipped kitchen includes a refrigerator, coffeemaker, microwave, and dishwasher. For those needing a little less room, one-bedroom suites are also available; the only difference is the absence of the second bedroom.

Summerfield Suites Hotel makes the guests feel even more at home by providing necessities—a guest laundry room is available, as well as a free grocery shopping service.

There is also room to relax and plenty to do outside the suites themselves. The central courtyard contains a multipurpose SportCourt®; a swimming pool with heated whirlpool; and a large, covered gazebo just off the pool area, where barbecue grills are available for use. In addition, Summerfield Suites has a 24-hour fitness center and a 24-hour convenience store called the Guest Stop®, which offers snacks and sundry items.

EXCEPTIONAL SERVICE

Regardless of the purpose of a guest's visit, a team of service professionals is on hand to exceed his or her expectations. This team is committed to making guests want to come back to Summerfield Suites Hotel and is determined to provide the highest level of service.

TAKING CARE OF BUSINESS

Because it was founded by business travelers, Summerfield Suites Hotel is conscious about meeting the needs of those who work away from home. In each suite, there are separate phone lines for phone use and modem hookup. In addition, the hotel offers a complimentary breakfast buffet every morning in the Guesthouse®, a sunlit area off the main lobby. Monday through Thursday evenings, the hotel hosts a complimentary social hour there as well, serving light appetizers and beverages. Summerfield Suites also has three meeting rooms, all with natural light and state-of-the-art audio-visual equipment.

Whatever the reason for the visit, Summerfield Suites Hotel guests can be assured of accommodations and service unmatched by any other hotel.

PHOTOGRAPHERS

JAMES BLAND is a lifelong Dallasite who studied at the University of Texas at Arlington. A self-employed photographer, he specializes in entertainment, editorial, and corporate images for such clients as Mercury, Island, TVT, Capitol, and Columbia recording studios, and the Hard Rock Cafe. Bland's pictures have been featured in *Guitar World*, *Guitar Player*, *Spin*, *Rolling Stone*, *Time*, and *People* magazines.

EMANUEL BOROK is originally from Russia. A graduate of the Gnessin Institute of Music, he moved to Dallas in 1985. Specializing in architectural and people photography, Borok has had solo exhibitions of his work in Dallas and New Mexico, and has been represented by Afterimage Gallery and Photographic Archives & Lab Gallery—both in Dallas. His favorite photographic subjects are old towns, buildings, and architectural detail.

STEWART CHARLES COHEN, a native of Montreal, established his own studio in Dallas in 1985. A graduate of the University of Texas at Austin, Cohen has traveled on assignment to more than 30 countries, building an international reputation in the advertising industry for creating moving and beautiful images. The winner of more than 50 industry awards, Cohen has had his work published in numerous advertising and photography publications, and 14 of his images have been selected for inclusion in the *Communication Arts Photography Annual*.

LOUIS DELUCA, who hails from Huntsville, Alabama, is a sports photographer and photojournalist for the *Dallas Morning News*. A graduate of Stephen F. Austin State University, he has been named Regional Photographer of the Year four times by the National Press Photographers Association. DeLuca's work has been published in *Life*, *Sports Illustrated*, *Time*, *Newsweek*, and *The Sporting News*, and is on display at the National Baseball Hall of Fame and Pro Football Hall of Fame.

CHARLENE FARIS, a native of Fleming County, Kentucky, is the owner and operator of Charlene Faris Photos and the director of an exhibition group called Photography: A Diverse Focus. Specializing in travel, historic, and inspirational photography, Faris has won numerous awards during her career, including several honors from the National League of American Pen Women art shows. She was a 1994 Pulitzer Prize nominee for wedding photos of Lyle Lovett and Julia Roberts, which have now been published in 25 nations. Faris' images have appeared in several Towery publications, including *Louisville: A River Serenade*, *The Towery Report on Northern Kentucky*, and *Indianapolis: Crossroads of the American Dream*.

PAUL GREENBERG is a self-employed people and landscape photographer who hails from Kansas City, Missouri. His work is included in the permanent collections of Fort Worth's Amon Carter Museum, Houston's Museum of Fine Arts, and the Dallas Museum of Art, where his images have also been exhibited in a one-person show. A graduate of the University of Missouri, Greenberg moved to Dallas in 1961.

ANDY HANSON, the events photographer for the *Dallas Times Herald* from 1960 to 1990, was the last photographer in the darkroom when the paper closed its doors in December 1990. A solitary box labeled "The Final Rolls of the *Dallas Times Herald*," which contains approximately 60 rolls of Hanson's uncut, unprinted film, serves as a testimony to his prolific and tireless career as a photojournalist. He is represented by Photographic Archives Lab & Gallery in Dallas.

JAN WILSON JOROLAN, formerly of Dallas, is a nature and international travel photographer who lives in Hot Springs, Arkansas. She is a member of the Photographic Society of America, Nikon Professional Services, and International Network of Publishing Photographers. Her work has appeared in various travel publications, as well as another Towery photojournal, *Little Rock: One from the Heart*, and has won regional, state, and international honors.

B'LAN APRIL KAO is a freelance photographer specializing in portraiture and black-and-white documentary photography. She attended the Fu-Shin Art Institute in her native Taipei, Taiwan, as well as taking photography classes at Richland College, Collin County Community College, and Texas Woman's University in Dallas. Kao has won numerous awards in the course of her career.

LAYNE MURDOCH, a native of Dallas, established his own photography studio in 1980. Specializing in sports and corporate photography, as well as personality portraits, Murdoch is a former staff photographer for the *Dallas Times Herald* and United Press International. A single father raising three children, Murdoch is currently under contract with the NBA as the team photographer for the Dallas Mavericks.

DONOVAN REESE hails from Minnesota and moved to Dallas in 1967. A student of photojournalism at the University of North Texas, he specializes in corporate, travel, and stock photography. Reese has worked with Texas Tourism, GTE, RSR Manufacturing, Tandy Corporation, Lone Star Gas, American Airlines, and Apple Computers.

ANDY REISBERG, a native Dallasite, started his own custom darkroom business called Flying Horse Photography in 1981. Originally conceived as a copy and restoration service, today the business, known as Photographic Archives Lab & Gallery, offers such services as preservation, conservation framing, and retail archival supplies. Its clientele includes libraries, historical societies, photographers, collectors, and genealogists.

ROBIN SACHS is a third-generation Dallasite who specializes in corporate and industrial photography. An adjunct professor at Collin County Community College and membership chairman for the local chapter of the American Society of Media Photographers, Sachs is the author/photographer of *I Am a Teacher*, a collection of photographs of and interview excerpts from teachers in a variety of classrooms, from inner cities to one-room schoolhouses, throughout the United States.

RICK YEATTS is a self-taught freelance photographer whose pictures of such sporting events as the Dallas Freeze professional hockey team and the World Cup soccer matches have appeared in *USA Today*, the *New York Times*, and *Olympian*. Yeatts, who also specializes in high-fashion photography, has been a professional hairdresser for more than 20 years, styling such celebrities as Leeza Gibbons.

Other photographers and organizations that have contributed to *Dallas: World-Class Texas* include the Dallas Public Library, Douglas Newby, Moses Olmos, Chris Regas, Joan Sheahan, and Southwestern Medical Center.

INDEX OF PROFILES